HOLY GROUND

HOLY GROUND

THE NATIONAL BLACK THEATRE FESTIVAL ANTHOLOGY

Edited by Michael D. Dinwiddie

THEATRE COMMUNICATIONS GROUP   NEW YORK   2022

The publication of *Holy Ground: The National Black Theatre Festival Anthology*, by North Carolina Black Repertory Company/National Black Theatre Festival, through TCG Books, is made possible with support by Mellon Foundation.

Special thanks to the Thomas S. Kenan Institute for the Arts, established at the University of North Carolina School of the Arts, for their support of this publication.

UNIVERSITY OF NORTH CAROLINA
SCHOOL
OF THE
ARTS

TCG books are exclusively distributed to the book trade by Consortium Book Sales and Distribution.

ISBN 978-1-63670-003-8 (paperback) / ISBN 978-1-63670-004-5 (ebook)
A catalog record for this book is available from the Library of Congress.

Book design and composition by Lisa Govan
Cover design by Monet Cogbill
Cover image by Owens Daniels
Cover logo by LaVon Van Williams

First Edition, July 2022

MANIFESTO

By Dr. Maya Angelou

On August 14, 1989, Dr. Maya Angelou,
first National Chairperson of the National Black Theatre Festival,
delivered this manifesto to attendees of the first-ever
National Black Theatre Festival.

From Boston to Birmingham, from Los Angeles to Louisiana, the threads of the Afro-American cultural tapestry display themselves with certainties and subtleties.

We have lifted praise songs in cemeteries and shouted field hollers in the Black Delta loam of Georgia.

Our singers, from Black Patti, Todd Duncan, and Big Bill Broonzy to Stevie Wonder, Roberta Flack, and Michael Jackson have sung spirituals, blues, European classical music, and jazz, defining our presence in what was a strange land and describing our staying power in this still-resistant country which we have forged into the shape of home.

Our dancers, from Asadata Dafora, Bill Robinson, and Katherine Dunham to Judith Jameson, Mel Tomlinson, and

Gregory Hines, have told and are telling our histories *en pointe*, on barefoot, in Capezios, and with tap shoes.

Our writers, from Frederick Douglass to Nikki Giovanni, from Charles Chesnut to Alice Childress, from Countee Cullen to Alice Walker, inspect and explain our values to us ourselves and to a larger society which needs to know that we are no more nor less exotic than our fellow human beings from China to Czechoslovakia.

Now, on August 14, 1989, Black dramatists, actors, and set, costume, and lighting designers from around the country are coming to Winston-Salem, North Carolina. They intend to celebrate at once their formidable talent and simultaneously the survival of that talent despite hard times, mean times, and in-between times. This dramatic, theatrical heritage was in place long before Ira Aldridge performed Shakespearean roles in Britain during the 1800s. It was in evidence long before Black actors signed on to perform under the aegis of the Toby (nickname for the Theatre Owners Booking Association, or "Tough on Black Actors") circuit in rickety, segregated halls, and before the Black Bert Williams donned blackface to imitate white actors who had donned blackface in order to do degrading imitations of Black folks who were living out lives beyond imitation.

This Festival, as the daring dream of Larry Leon Hamlin and the North Carolina Black Repertory Company, is equal only to the effort, the energy, and creative talents of the nationally known dramatists and the as yet little-known performers from Black regional theaters who are in attendance.

This is a time of great joy, a time when we can show each other the new projects we are daring to dream, and a time to dream even greater dreams.

All the world might not be a stage after all, but the National Black Theatre Festival hopes this week to provide a stage upon which all the Black theatrical personages can reveal the worlds they know, and even those they dare to hope for.

Winston-Salem, North Carolina
1989

CONTENTS

FOREWORD

By Dr. Tommie (Tonea) Stewart

I first met Larry Leon Hamlin in the late 1970s at a convening of The Southern Arts Federation, an organization funded by the National Endowment for the Arts. Its avowed mission was to assist arts organizations in our southern region of the country. Each year an additional minority representative was cautiously added to the committee. Larry Leon Hamlin and I emerged the same year. He was quite original in his purple garb and with his positive, friendly energy. Everyone took note of him right away.

The Federation met in Atlanta, Georgia, to discuss and report on our successes, strategize, and plan. Larry and I soon realized that our needs were being ignored. The insensitive notions and criteria which guided the dispensation of funding for our programs were less than subtle and literally unfair. We soon realized that the guidelines established were often too restrictive for minority organizations to satisfy. In brief, tradition-bound thinkers refused to be sensitive to minority organizations and required such groups to follow models that could not succeed because of the lack of financial resources in the minority community.

After attending a few years of meetings, Larry and I understood that plans were being concocted to create a national theater festival in Atlanta. To our surprise, small theaters in the South were not being considered. These successful theaters included Louisiana's Free Southern Theatre; Larry's respected North Carolina Black Repertory Company; and the acclaimed Carpetbag Theatre in Knoxville, Tennessee; as well as the versatile theater company I founded, the Repertory Theatre of Mississippi, in Jackson, Mississippi. These companies were producing works by Ossie Davis, James Baldwin, Ntozake Shange, and others, yet they were ignored, deemed unqualified, not recognized, and excluded from plans for the festival. Larry and I questioned the validity of the Federation's criteria and reminded them of the great work being done by minority organizations in our region.

We soon realized that our arguments were falling on deaf ears. During one memorable session, Larry threw up his hands and declared, "I will show all of you. There will be a theater festival, a national Black theater festival, and it will not be in Atlanta. It will showcase talent from all over the United States. Watch me!"

He stormed out of the meeting, and I followed close behind. I believed him, and that moment felt GOOD. We stopped in the hallway, shared ideas, exchanged numbers, decided that it could be done, and *Holy Ground* was born.

What a visionary, what a leader, what a giant of a man. He refused to accept the notion that we as a people were unprepared and lacking in ability to create our own institutions. He not only talked, Larry Leon Hamlin walked the walk. He saw his vision through to fruition. I am a witness! No other theater festival in this country serves to embrace our African American culture, validate the beauty of our spirit, or ignite our passionate pride.

To this end, let's continue to raise our heads, our hands, and our talents in tribute to Larry Leon Hamlin and the National Black Theatre Festival, a place where we feel whole, complete, unapologetic, and on "Holy Ground."

Montgomery, Alabama
May 2022

PREFACE

By Jackie Alexander

In 1988, at a theater conference in Atlanta, Larry Leon Hamlin, founder of the North Carolina Black Repertory Company, heard a discussion on the dire straits of African American theater companies across the country and decided to take on a new challenge; one with the goal of uniting these companies to ensure the survival of Black theater into the next millennium. His answer to the problem, his dream, was an event where companies would be able to perform before the general public, troubleshoot challenges faced by all, share resources, and raise awareness of the quality and importance of their work: a national Black theater festival.

To start the process, Mr. Hamlin approached Dr. Maya Angelou, who happened to be a Winston-Salem resident and professor at Wake Forest University, asking for her assistance. Dr. Angelou agreed and became the chairperson of the first festival, inviting celebrity guests—television talk-show host Oprah Winfrey; and the cast of the Off-Broadway production of *The Blacks*, a play in which Dr. Angelou had starred, and which included theater legends: James Earl Jones; Roscoe Lee Brown;

Louis Gossett, Jr.; Cicely Tyson; Godfrey Cambridge; Helen Martin; and Charles Gordone.

The inaugural National Black Theatre Festival (NBTF), was held August 14–20, 1989, and its theme was "A Celebration and Reunion of Spirit." The Festival offered thirty performances by seventeen of America's best professional Black theater companies. It attracted national and international media coverage, with the *New York Times* calling it: "One of the most historic cultural events in the history of Black theater and American theater in general." Mr. Hamlin's dream was now a reality, one that, as of today, has generated more than 240 million dollars to the economy of Winston-Salem.

Funny thing is, I'm told that when Mr. Hamlin started NBTF in 1989, a large portion of the Winston-Salem community was concerned with what could be a very large number of Black people descending on the city all at one time—wouldn't there be fights, crime, drugs?

Thirty years later, it seems that every resident of Winston-Salem I encounter, regardless of race, speaks of the Festival with an infectious pride. Why? Because NBTF so beautifully redefined a false narrative. You see, people, communities, and even nations fear what they don't know or understand. And the arts can be an incredibly powerful tool in erasing those fears. It can remove the fear of the unknown, instill the desire to learn, remind us of the shared struggles we face, and introduce us to people and places we may never encounter in our daily lives. And in a world that is seemingly becoming more intolerant by the day, a lesson that we must all learn is that engaging in the arts is not only crucial to our community, but to the world at large.

John Henrik Clarke once said that "slavery ended and left its false images of Black people intact." I grew up on a steady diet of those false images on televisions, theater stages, and movie screens, so I decided to focus my career on creating work that honestly examined the African American experience. Which is one of the reasons I'm so proud to be Artistic Director of the North Carolina Black Repertory Company, producers of the NBTF, a biennial celebration and reunion of spirit that has cemented Winston-Salem as Black Theater Holy Ground on a global scale.

There are many people to thank for my good fortune and the good fortune of countless other actors, writers, directors, designers, and everyday theater lovers who have been blessed to experience a week on Holy Ground. There's the Black theater legends and celebrities who have championed the festival since its inception; the unwavering support of a purple-and-black army of volunteers; the city of Winston-Salem, which lives up to its moniker, "The city of arts and innovation," by leaving no stone unturned each Festival to ensure NBTF is a success; a committed staff and board of directors; the dedication and sacrifice of NBTF Executive Producer Sylvia Sprinkle-Hamlin (1945–2022); and of course the brilliance, audacity, and vision of our founder, Larry Leon Hamlin (1948–2007).

Holy Ground celebrates the stories, characters, and images that define the National Black Theatre Festival. Highlighted by three new plays that eschew cookie-cutter representations of African American life in favor of complex storytelling that examines universal themes, this anthology shines a light on qualities that have sustained Black theater: family, love, humor, intellect, resilience, and strength.

My hope is that after turning the last page, you will join countless other theater lovers who make the biennial pilgrimage to Black Theater Holy Ground—and in that case, please remember all roads lead to Winston-Salem, and we are saving a seat at the theater just for you.

Winston-Salem, North Carolina
May 2022

INTRODUCTION

By Michael D. Dinwiddie

In 1821, the African Grove Theatre became the first playhouse in America founded by a Black producer. William Alexander Brown, a retired West Indian ship steward who erected his theater in New York's Greenwich Village, produced original works that dealt with slave rebellions, musicales, pantomime ballets, and such Shakespeare staples as *Richard III* and *Othello*. Even though Mr. Brown's theater was a financial and artistic success, he could not contend with the hostility of mobs, which—at the instigation of white producers and local authorities—ransacked the African Grove Theatre and attacked its company of actors, musicians, and designers.

Through his founding in 1989 of the National Black Theatre Festival (NBTF), Larry Leon Hamlin actualized what pioneers like Mr. Brown could only dream of accomplishing. He created a safe space where African American theater in all its forms and permutations could thrive. It is this legacy that is celebrated in *Holy Ground: The National Black Theatre Festival Anthology*. This volume offers a cornucopia of treasures for those who wish to know more about the African Diaspora as it is reflected in American theater. The eminent scholar Errol Hill, in the article "Black Black Theatre in Form and Style," poses a question that continues to resonate:

> To determine what elements of Black theater should be preserved for posterity presupposes a clear notion among scholars and practitioners of what Black theater is. Decades ago W. E. B. Du Bois defined it as a theater *about us, by us, for us, and near us,* meaning in that last requirement that the theater should be located in the Black community.[1]

It was the return to his community that led Larry Leon Hamlin to become a theater impresario. He had been busily pursuing a career as an actor in New York City and Washington, DC, when family circumstances brought him back to his home state. When Hamlin realized that there was no local, professional Black theater where he could hone his craft, he set about creating one. In 1979, the North Carolina Black Repertory Company (NC Black Rep) was born.

Ten years later, Hamlin issued invitations to Black theaters across the nation to participate in a festival to be held in Winston-Salem. The catch was, there was no formal organization and no model for what he set out to do. But he understood that for Black theaters to survive into the twenty-first century, they would have to come together and support each other. They would have to share ideas and resources, and build upon their collective strengths in order to reach a national audience.

Dr. Maya Angelou's manifesto sent forth a clarion call for artists. A key supporter from the beginning, she was instrumental in bringing Jean Genet's absurdist classic *The Blacks* to the inaugural Festival, with such luminaries as Roscoe Lee Browne, Moses Gunn, and Helen Martin reviving roles they had premiered in New York.

1. Errol Hill, "Black Black Theatre in Form and Style," *The Black Scholar*, July/August 1979, Vol. 10, No. 10: "Black Theatre," pp. 29–31, Taylor & Francis, Ltd.

Since that time, the NBTF has grown into a cultural phenomenon whose semi-annual gatherings bring together tens of thousands of patrons from around the world. Its audiences experience canon-defining—and defying—theatrical happenings. The NBTF has honored Black celebrities with its opening night galas and attracted scholars, practitioners, students, and educators with the International Colloquium, as well as filmmakers and entrepreneurs with its African Marketplace.

But always at the center of the juggernaut is the role of Black theater in community-building. *Holy Ground* pays homage to all the plays, spoken-word presentations, and musical performances that merit serious consideration in the pantheon of African American theater. The works that have been chosen are representative of the various theater traditions and performance styles that have grown up over the past three decades. Monologues and scenes from each year of the Festival are featured, as well as three full-length plays published for the first time: *Maid's Door* by Cheryl L. Davis, *Berta, Berta* by Angelica Chéri, and *Looking for Leroy* by Larry Muhammad.

Holy Ground includes monologues from such works as Endesha Ida Mae Holland's three-character ode to joy, *From the Mississippi Delta*; a decades-long love affair in Dr. John Shévin Foster's *Plenty of Time*; Ifa Bayeza's heart-rending *The Ballad of Emmett Till*; and the searing *Chain*, which Pearl Cleage links to a person overcoming addiction. Religious hypocrisy is what animates Roger Furman's *Monsieur Baptiste, the Con Man*, which is adapted from Molière's *Tartuffe*. And Rhodessa Jones fearlessly takes us into a prison where *Big Butt Girls, Hard-Headed Women* hold forth. *Washington's Boy* by Ted Lange is historical, while Javon Johnson's *Breathe* bespeaks a more modern world where freedom can be a burden to survive.

On June 6, 2007, surrounded by close friends and family, Larry Leon Hamlin died at his home in Pfafftown, North Carolina. The next morning, the NBTF went ahead with its planned press conference to announce the lineup of thirty-plus plays, musical revues, a staged reading series, and presentations by scholars and practitioners in the International Colloquium. The trio of Gerry Patton, Mabel Robinson, and Sylvia Sprinkle-

Hamlin not only oversaw the Festival and the NC Black Rep, but made sure that Larry's dream would continue to thrive in the following years. And the cadre of the NBTF volunteers—hundreds of women and men who make everyone feel welcome; who do their best to manage visitors of all ages, races, and theatrical persuasions through sometimes difficult moments—has become an intergenerational tribute to the community that Larry Leon Hamlin envisioned.

In 2020, at its annual gala in New York City, Theatre Communications Group (TCG) honored the NBTF. Teresa Eyring, Executive Director of TCG, exclaimed that: "Every other year, I join tens of thousands of theater lovers in Winston-Salem, North Carolina, for the joyous community and expansive artistry provided by the National Black Theatre Festival. We are excited to honor the impact of the Festival and Black theater and our broader culture."

Jackie Alexander, who was named Artistic Director of the NC Black Rep in 2016 and Artistic Producer of the NBTF, praised TCG's recognition as "an honor and testament to the importance and vibrancy of Black theater."

Then, at a convening of the International Black Theatre Summit, Dr. Monica White Ndounou (Associate Professor of Theater at Dartmouth College and Founding Executive Director of the CRAFT Institute), suggested that a partnership between TCG and the NBTF could be memorialized with a publication. *Holy Ground* is the result of Monica's conversation.

To celebrate the first thirty years of the NBTF, TCG, which oversees the largest independent publisher of dramatic literature in North America with more than sixteen hundred titles and two hundred and thirty-five plays, including nineteen winners of the Pulitzer Prize for Drama, one Nobel Prize for Literature, as well as numerous Tony Awards, Drama Desk Awards, and Obie Awards, entered into the collaboration that has led to the publication of *Holy Ground: The National Black Theatre Festival Anthology.*

Legendary producer Woodie King, Jr., in the article "A Marvtastic Life," borrows a word invented by Larry ("marvelous + fantastic") to describe the unique mission that shaped

Hamlin's life: "He likened Black theater artists to a lost tribe scattered throughout the African Diaspora—constantly creating but rarely communicating. He saw all this and called us together. He said, 'Let's celebrate and have a reunion—a reunion of spirit! Let's have a festival as we've had and continue to have in Dakar, in Ghana, and in Nigeria! Let's celebrate Black theater—on Holy Ground!'"

King praises Hamlin as "a force in Black theater in America. But what is a force? A force by its own sheer energy moves seemingly fixed and stationary things.

"Larry forced old ideas out of his path. His vision was to bring all who work and struggle in Black theater together, in spirit. Larry Leon Hamlin, through his uncompromising will, created the NBTF; it was in the wind, an idea whose time was upon us."[2]

New York City
May 2022

2. Woodie King, Jr., "A Marvtastic Life," *Black Masks*, January/February 2008, Vol. 18, No. 3, p. 7, Black Masks Publication.

PART 1
MONOLOGUES/SCENES

FROM THE MISSISSIPPI DELTA

Endesha Ida Mae Holland

1989

A dramatic biography in eleven scenes for three women. Each actor plays multiple roles: young/old, male/female, and Black/white. Language is a key factor in this drama and must be spoken exactly as written. The time spans the early 1940s to the mid-1980s.

SECOND DOCTOR LADY

Lights up on Woman Three (as Aint Baby) and Woman One (as Phelia, Girl in Her Early Teens) on the porch. Woman Three is fanning herself and swatting at flies. Woman One is obviously bored.

WOMAN THREE: Here, gal, now ya pay 'taintion. Now ya see dis here?

WOMAN ONE: Yas'm, Aint Baby.

WOMAN THREE: Dis here's de old thread; grab hit like dis . . .

WOMAN ONE: Yas'm . . . yas'm . . . I see now, Aint Baby.

WOMAN THREE: Loop hit like dis . . .

WOMAN ONE *(To audience)*: Yas'm. Aint Baby and me was setting on the porch together. She was taking the hem outa my choir robe, and I was sitting there watching—'cause I was learning how to sew. I rather been at the Walthall picture show watching Shirley Temple and keeping cool in the air-condition theater. We set on the side nearest Miss Sug's house to escape the hot glare of "Old Hannah," as Aint Baby called the sun. "Old Hannah" was some kinda terrible; she was bearing down so hard you could see the heat waves. It was so hot that the flies wouldn't even now fly. Since Aint Baby didn't have no 'lectric fan, we set on the porch trying to catch any breeze blowing. We didn't talk much; 'cause talking just made us hotter.

WOMAN TWO (*As Man Son, who is a young boy, offstage*): Aint Baby, uh Aint Baby—Sweetney call you!

WOMAN THREE: Who is dat, Phelia, making all dat racket?

WOMAN ONE (*To Aint Baby*): Sounds like Man Son Matthews, running to beat the band in Dixie Lane Alley.

WOMAN TWO (*As Man Son, offstage*): Uh, Aint Baby! Aint Baby!

WOMAN THREE: Whoa. What's de matter, boy? Come mere and let me git some of dis dust off'n ya. Git hold of yaself, chile.

WOMAN ONE (*To audience*): Man Son musta come through the sand pile out by Mr. Will Huggins' house; that's the quickest way to our house from the Buckeye where Man Son lived with his six brothers and susters and his mama, Sweetney.

WOMAN TWO (*As Man Son, entering*): Oh, Aint Baby, Sweetney needs you real quick. She's crying! Her stomach hurt real bad!

WOMAN ONE: Aint Baby opened her arms to catch the stumbling chile. Man Son laid his cucker-burr head in Aint Baby's bosum and cried and cried, tears meeting under his chin.

WOMAN THREE: Whoa here, boy. Hold it for a minute. Come on in, chile, come on in. Phelia, ya git in yonder and git dis here boy a drank of water . . . and one of dem teacakes; and, boy, ya set rat here on dis garry and take holt of yaself . . . Hurry up, Phelia, and quit slow-poking round. Set down, son, set down rat here, everthangs all right now.

WOMAN TWO (*As Man Son*): But, Aint Baby, we better git on back to de house, 'cause Sweetney is some sick. She told me to come rat on back—soon is I tell you to "come mere."

WOMAN THREE: Hush up now, Man Son; here, blow ya snotty nose . . .

WOMAN ONE: I came back on the porch with Man Son's glass of

water and teacake. The boy drained the glass and started nibbling on his teacake. He had delivered his important message and now he was satisfied that help was coming. I knew Aint Baby was going to see 'bout Miss Sweetney, although I had heard her tell Miss Nollie Bee, Miss Dossie Ree, Miss Susie Brooks, and Miss Willie Lee—that she wasn't gone wait on Miss Sweetney Matthews no moe—'cause Miss Sweetney hadn't paid her granny bill from the last baby. I knew Aint Baby's steady voice would soon put Miss Sweetney at ease; her strong arms would encircle her body, her quick fangers would gently pull and push, while her iron eyes would plead with Miss Sweetney to "bear down."

WOMAN THREE: Ya run on back now, boy—and tell ya mama dat I'll be dere in a hour or so. She be all right till I git dere. Tell her: I'll be dere as soon as I ketch up wit Buddy Boy. Tell dat I got to stop 'long de way to see 'bout Lily Mae—'cause she kinda sick too. Run on now, boy.

WOMAN ONE: I just knew she was going, she always did. Somehow, she always managed to catch up with Buddy Boy, the cab driver. When nobody else could find Buddy Boy—Aint Baby could. Buddy Boy would waddle outa his old Chrysler, he weighted near 'bout four hundred pounds, and catch Aint Baby uner one arm, take her "doctor bag" in the other hand, and lead her to his trap, and off they'd go; anybody seeing them riding together would know that Aint Baby was on another case.

Aint Baby delivered many of the Black babies in our county. She was even called in to the county horsepital to "assist" the white doctors with the white womens—when they couldn't birth their babies. Ever since the time that Miss Sweet Chile Brown died trying to have her baby, Aint Baby hadn't wanted to go to the county horsepital to wait on the white womens no moe. Miss Sweet Chile Brown died a few years ago. She bled to death down in Goodson Alley 'cause the white folks sent her back home from the county horsepital 'cause they "didn't have no beds left." She died in Mr. Sonny Love ammulance, 'fore they could get her back into the house. When Aint Baby heard 'bout Miss

Sweet Chile, silent tears rolled down Aint Baby's cheeks till the front of her smock was soaking wet.

WOMAN THREE: F'n Dr. Feinberg hada been at de horsepital dey da tooken pore ole Sweet Chile in, 'stead'a sending her back home.

WOMAN ONE: Aint Baby had a lot of confidence in this Dr. Feinberg. He had talked Aint Baby into becoming a midwife. A few years ago, Dr. Feinberg and the other folks in the Delta stopped calling Aint Baby a midwife and started saying she was a "Second Doctor Lady." She could reach inside a woman's body and do all sorts of thangs with her hands— thangs even Dr. Feinberg couldn't do. I remember one time that Aint Baby hada case way out in Duck Hill, and she took me with her. She told me to stay in the yard with the rest of the chullins; I tried to, honest—but my curiosity got the best of me; so I led the line of peeping chullins to the window—and that's how I got the chance to see Aint Baby do her "Second Doctor Lady" work. Miss Magnolia Johnson had thirteen chullins already. Dr. Feinberg told Miss Mag that if she had some moe babies—she was going to die. But Miss Mag didn't pay him no mind. Her and Mr. Johnson said that when the Lawd got ready for her—she'd go and not before. So they kept rat on, till Miss Mag got in the family way again. And that's why Aint Baby and me was there; I guess they really didn't want Miss Mag to die— 'cause they sent for the best—Aint Baby.

(Aint Baby goes about her duty: checking her bag for supplies, examining the patient, drinking from her RC Cola, and soothing the patient.)

Well, anyhow, we chullins was peeking through the window when Miss Mag started whimpering and almost jumped outa the bed. Aint Baby didn't say nothing. She just moved her chair and RC Cola closer to the bed; then she made clicking sounds deep down in her throat and her iron eyes closed for a minute or two. Miss Mag started screaming real loud and the bed was fulla blood and doo-doo. *(Aint*

*Baby's mournful chant intensifies as Magnolia's labor pains
quicken)* The more Aint Baby cleaned, the more Miss Mag
doo-dooed. I was some kinda scared. Mr. Johnson heard
Miss Mag hollering way down at the oil mill, so he quit
work and come home. When Mr. Johnson walked in the
front door, Aint Baby made him take off his pances; she
laid them on Miss Mag's bed, to ease the pain. Frankly,
I couldn't see how Mr. Johnson's ole greasy, smelly pances
could do any good. But I guess Aint Baby knew what she
was doing. Mr. Johnson was so sad; he was holding Miss
Mag's hand and crying over and over again . . .

WOMAN TWO *(As Mr. Johnson)*: Hit's all right, Maggie; de Lawd'll
make a way.

WOMAN ONE: Aint Baby's strong arms picked Miss Mag up and
turned her head northbound and slid the ironing board
underneath her. Miss Mag was moaning now and white
stuff was coming outa her mouth. You could see rat then
that Mr. Johnson was scared; so was we chullins peeking
through the window.

WOMAN TWO *(As Magnolia)*: Lawdy, Lawdy, Lawdy, help me
Savior—Ya know I need Ya, Lawd! Ooooooh, Sweet Jesus,
help me!

WOMAN ONE: Woohwe! I saw a tiny foot pop outa Miss Mag's
bloody slit. Mr. Johnson's eyes was as big as a saucer. But
Aint Baby acted like she was in a trance, 'cause she just set
there and turned her ageless brown face to the tar-paper
ceiling. Miss Mag was hollering some kinda pitiful. She
kept trying to git up. Aint Baby took her by the shoulders
and gently laid her back on the pillow. Then Aint Baby's
iron eyes started to glow, and the muscle right over her left
eye started to jumping real fast. And then, her eyes flowed
into her as she knelt twixt Miss Mag's open legs. I saw Aint
Baby take the tiny black foot and gently push. She pushed
till the small foot was back into Miss Mag's stomach.

WOMAN TWO *(As Phelia)*: And then, she took both her hands
and folded them like she do when she's praying; then,
she put her hands way up into Miss Mag. Miss Magnolia
moaned so sad the walls was shaking and I thought that

two-room house would fall down. Then Miss Mag passed out. By this time all the chullins was hollering and crying.

(As child) Ole Baby Brother looked like he was gone faint; big ole Jesse Lee's shirt was full of thoe-up; but I refused to take my eyes from the window. Aint Baby had both of her arms into Miss Mag; she was twisting and prodding and talking in a low, strong voice; but thangs didn't look no better. Miss Mag was hardly breathing now and Mr. Johnson wasn't no good at all. He'd pulled the other chair up to the foot of the bed and he had his hands over his face. I could hear his tears hitting the newspaper 'longside the bed. Aint Baby nodded her head to Mr. Johnson; he got up and stood by the door with just his shorts on—'cause his pances was still on Miss Mag's bed. Then Aint Baby took her hands outa Miss Mag's stomach; they was some kinda bloody. The front of her white smock was soaked with blood. She backed into the corner near the crack in the wall—and let me tell you: she started speaking a language I had never heard before. I was scared then. I just knew Miss Mag was dead.

WOMAN ONE: Now the thang that happened next is what really scared me. Aint Baby walked slowly back to the bed and without touching Miss Mag at all, she began to talk in this strange talk again. This talk that sounded like the clicking of the tongue. I thought Aint Baby had gone crazy . . . Lawd, have mercy! A black ball appeared twixt Miss Mag's open legs; the slit was now round. Aint Baby kept on making these sounds and moving her arms like Mr. Monroe the choir director. Miss Mag was still passed out and Mr. Johnson just stood and looked like he couldn't believe what was happening . . . The round ball slid out a little—I could see it was the head of the baby . . . Aint Baby done turnted that baby round! Mr. Johnson sprang to life. He ran to the bed and fell on his knees and turnted his head towards the tarpaper ceiling. He looked at Aint Baby a long time with tears rolling freely over his worn face. Aint Baby slapped the baby's bloody black bootie, and her cry filled the two-room shack . . . Aint Baby then, she spit in Miss Mag's navel, and added something outa the nature sack she wore round her neck . . . And then, she took her dog fanger and stirred in Miss Mag's navel . . . I swear, Miss Mag opened her eyes and reached for her baby. She was sitting up in bed—even smiling.

WOMAN TWO: All of us chullins was crowded round the bed—trying to git a look at Baby Brother and Jesse Lee's little suster . . . And shortly after that, Dr. Feinberg and the other folks started calling Aint Baby the "Second Doctor Lady."

WOMAN ONE: Aint Baby would come outa the front door wearing her white uniform, stockings, shoes, and cap. She would have her black doctor's bag in one hand—and her RC Cola in the other. She would stop and tuck her RC under her arm, then she would feel round her neck for the strang that her nature sack hung on. And then she would start smiling . . .

WOMAN TWO: Buddy Boy's old car would slide up to the curb; he would git out and come up our steps—and escort Aint Baby to the car. He would help her in, then waddle back to the driver's side and take off amid much horn-blowing and grinning.

WOMAN ONE: Aint Baby was going to see 'bout Miss Lily Mae—then on to brang Miss Sweetney's little baby into the world . . . When—I have a baby, I'm not gone send for nobody—but the "Second Doctor Lady."

ABOUT THE PLAY

From the Mississippi Delta was produced at the National Black Theatre Festival by the Negro Ensemble Company. There have been numerous national and international productions for this Pulitzer Prize–nominated play.

From the Mississippi Delta is copyright © 1987, renewed 2005, by Dr. Endesha Ida Mae Holland. For further information contact: Amy Langton, Dramatic Publishing, 800-448-7469, customerservice@dpcplays.com.

ABOUT THE PLAYWRIGHT

Dr. Endesha Ida Mae Holland (1944–2006) earned her BA, MA and PhD from the University of Minnesota in American Studies, with a concentration in Theater Arts (Playwriting). While at Minnesota, Holland was honored with the Theater Arts department's first Student Playwriting Award and the American College Theatre Festival's Region 5 Student Playwriting Award. She then went on to receive the 1981 Lorraine Hansberry Playwriting Award from the American College Theatre Festival for her one-act plays *Second Doctor Lady* (1980) and *The Reconstruction of Dossie Ree Hemphill* (1980). In 2003 she retired as a professor emerita from the University of Southern California, where she taught in the School of Theatre and the program of the Study of Men and Women in Society for twenty years. The documentary *Freedom on My Mind*, which features Holland, received an Academy Award nomination. Her memoir *From the Mississippi Delta* was published by Simon & Schuster in 1997.

Dr. Holland's honors include: 1993 Finalist for the Susan Smith Blackburn Prize for *Parader without a Permit*; the Western New York Region Martin Luther King, Jr. Commission-Life Achievement Award; the 1992 Oni Award from the International Black Women's Congress, the Black Women's Forum, Inc., Award for outstanding academic and creative achievement, sponsored by United States Congresswoman Maxine Waters, 29th District, Los Angeles; and the *Buffalo News*'s forty-third Annual Citizens of the Year Award.

BIG BUTT GIRLS, HARD-HEADED WOMEN

Idris Ackamoor and Rhodessa Jones

1991

When presented with the prestigious New York Dance and Performance Bessie Award, Big Butt Girls, Hard-Headed Women was described as "a provocative, compelling docudrama of the lives, desires, and inner strength of incarcerated women—a door thrown open upon those who refuse to be the forgotten among us, in a unique collaboration of creator-performer and director Rhodessa Jones." The following monologues give us a view of two such women, Mama Pearl and Regina Brown.

MAMA PEARL

Baby, that's why they made me the trustee. I take pride in my appearance. They know they can send me all over this place. Yeah, I can come and go instead of sitting in that day room with all that noise and these bitches smoking. Somebody always cussin', clownin', or fightin'. But I'm glad you're here, and if you don't do nothing else, teach them how to have enough self-respect to wash they funky asses. Here my hand to God, some of them so young they don't know how to use a Tampax. I've been in and out of the joint since 1965 and I ain't never seen it as bad as it is now. The young women coming and going in this day and time don't have no sense of theyself. I got three daughters. My older daughter was born deaf and dumb. She's the reason I went to jail in the first place.

(She pauses and looks around, before continuing in a more secretive tone:)

You see, I embezzled some money from the company that I was working at so my daughter could get special training, so that she could take care of herself, despite her handicap.

These girls need somebody to help them understand that you ain't got to be in and out of jail to feel important. They got to find a reason to let go of that crack and cut loose these men that pimp them for drugs, money, cars, even a leather coat. Look at them. Most of them not even twenty-five yet and have the nerve to be pregnant up in here. Like I told you, I got three daughters and I'd rather see these bitches flush these babies down the toilet than grunt them into the world and treat them the way they do. How? The way they will sell them, lease them to the dope man for some rock. They're flesh and blood, honey. Then the dope man, he gon get busted, and then the baby is lost to child protective services. And these bitches want to cry about they babies. This ain't something I heard; I seen this with my own eyes. You know what I tell 'em? "Take that whining and complaining some place else 'cause when you was out there fucking and sucking, high out of your mind, I did not get one nut. I did not experience one thrill behind your bullshit. So take all that drama somewhere else."

(She pauses and addresses the audience:)

Here my hand to God, please, I know that it's a hard line, but in this life I've learned you better come with something if you wanna get something.

REGINA BROWN

Public Enemy's "Terminator" is heard. As the music plays the Artist portrays glimpses of many different women. As the music crescendos, Artist assumes the character of Regina Brown, who is having sex with two other women. Regina is an African American woman of about thirty. She is strong and aggressive and appears taller than she is.

Fuck a bitch. Hit me! Bigger and better bitches than you have hit me. Just because I let you smell my pussy don't make it your pussy. It's still my pussy. Everybody and anybody will use you so you best get to using first. I learned early, a man or a woman ain't nothin' but a plaything. I tell them all, "It's like the lotto, baby. You got to be in it to win it." Later for all that "Ooh, baby" this and "Ooh, baby" that. I believe in action, so you best get on with the A-team. Like Tyrone, he's in love with me, always has been, and I can understand that. But I told him, "I was born a full-grown woman, and it ain't about 'my woman this' and 'my woman that.' I'm my own woman." But, like a lot of men, he don't want to listen. Wanted to control me . . . Thought he was my daddy. My daddy is dead, baby. And my mama raised me to be strong and on my own. He got all mad, 'cause he wasn't ready for the real deal. Brought some other girl, some Lily Lunchmeat–lookin' bitch I don't know, home! I told him, "Hey, if sister girl can hang, it's all in the family." Thought he was gonna work my nerves with that shit. And now who's crying? Tyrone. Because I'm carrying another man's baby. And that man ain't even important. The reality check has to do with me, my baby, and my baby's staying with Gerber's. I am a prostitute, straight up. I decided a long time ago, wasn't no man gonna tell me what to do. I'm a full-grown woman, straight up and down. Or my name ain't Regina Brown. WORD! Hit me bitch . . .

ABOUT THE PLAY

Cultural Odyssey's production of *Big Butt Girls, Hard-Headed Women* is based on the lives and times of real women who are incarcerated. The performance utilizes theater, movement, and song to anchor words born out of the silence that is so particular to women who are waiting: women waiting for bail, for mail, for the latest word concerning her child, money from her man, the next visit from her sister, her mother, or the word from her lawyer. The theatrics are based on the question: "Is there a way to retrieve the lives of our sisters and their families?" Performed by Rhodessa Jones and directed by Idris Ackamoor, who also performed the original score live onstage.

For further information about *Big Butt Girls, Hard-Headed Women* contact: Cultural Odyssey, info@culturalodyssey.org.

ABOUT THE PLAYWRIGHTS

After traveling in Africa, Idris Ackamoor observed the close connection between African artists and their communities. He was inspired to found an organization responsive to the needs of San Francisco's Black community, and in 1979 Cultural Odyssey was created with Idris as Executive Director. He is a saxophonist, actor, administrator, and Black theater visionary. Cultural Odyssey is one of the oldest Black performing arts organizations in the Bay Area.

Rhodessa Jones is an activist/actress, teaching artist, director, writer, and social scientist who serves as Co-Director of the company. She is Founder/Artistic Director of the award-winning *Medea Project: Theater for Incarcerated Women* and *HIV Circle*, a performance workshop designed to achieve personal and social transformation with incarcerated women and women living with HIV. Ms. Jones performed as the voice of Lulu in the Disney/Pixar animated film *Soul*, which won the 2021 Academy Award for Best Animated Feature Film. In 2019, Idris Ackamoor and Rhodessa Jones received a Special Recognition Award for their service to Black theater, which was presented at the National Black Theatre Festival's Awards Gala.

OLIVIA'S OPUS

Nora Cole

1993

Olivia's Opus *is a collection of remembrances of Olivia Bradford Long. It's the mid-sixties somewhere near the Mason-Dixon Line. Olivia reflects on the excitement and trauma, the fun and the trials, and the history-making events of the time that weave in and around her life. Some touch her deeply, some barely brush her existence, and growing up is hard to do. This is a multimedia performance piece created to portray the commonalities and peculiarities of Black life through the eyes of an adolescent.*

NEGROES ON TV

Every Sunday afternoon we'd watch, "It's the Ted Mack Original Amateur Hour!" And every Sunday there'd be an accordion player, a tall skinny white boy with acne and a smile stamped on since birth tap dancing at the speed of light and always, always, always there was somebody singing, *(Sings familiar bars of "Queen of the Night," an aria from* The Magic Flute*).* And I'd think, well I can do that. So I'd put on a whole lot of makeup like I was gettin' ready to do *Aida* or somethin' and I'd stack my hair on top of my head in some outrageous hairstyle. See, with all the grease, I mean oil, I mean hairdressing, from when I got it fried, I mean pressed, I mean straightened. I could stack it higher than a Clara Ward wig. Remember Clara Ward on *Shindig!*? *(Sings a few bars of "Move on Up a Little Higher")* And I'd go through the house singing *(Repeats "Queen of the Night" bars).* Drove my daddy nuts! But then, "Mer-Lue! Mer . . ." (that's Black for Mary Lue) "Mer-Lue come look!" And we'd all run and gather round to see a "Negro" on our TV!

Yeah, sure Mitch Miller had had that little Black girl on all the time, and we'd seen Bill Robinson and Hattie McDaniel in those old-time movies with Shirley Temple, and there was even this girl from our neighborhood who'd been crowned queen on the local-talent television show. But now we were showing up on prime time. We were on the *ED SULLIVAN SHOW*! And look, there's a whole Black family on the *Twilight Zone,* and then there was my idol, Diana Sands on that episode of *Dr. Kildare.* "What do you know, Dr. Kildare? You don't know me. And you don't know anything about what it's like to be me."

We'd stare, we'd watch, mouths hanging open and humongous smiles in our hearts. It was a message. It was an unconscious message that destroyed and obliterated two hundred years of systematic brainwashing. It was a secret signal to every cell in your body and your brain to take action and dispel the myth of what we were not supposed to be. And inferior? Who's inferior? We would swell with so much pride and get chills like you do every time you hear one of those Martin Luther King speeches. Then after the initial excitement, "Look at that dress. Is that her hair?" "Now you know that's not her hair. That's a wig." And, "He sure has a pretty set of teeth."

But wait. Even before that. "Mer-Lue! Mer-Lue! Mer-Lue come look!" They had unleashed the Colored bands on America's football fields for the halftime shows. Remember when they used to show the halftime shows on TV? *(Marching)* Lord have mercy those children they marched, they stepped, they strutted, and the one to really watch was the drum major. He personified all the pride of the race. "I'm here and I'm hot and I'm on nation-wide TV. You cain't tell me nothin'! I know what I'm doin' and I'm doin' it better than you will ever see anybody do what I'm doin'." And those children couldn't help marching the way they did. White people hadn't never seen marching like this before. They were used to—

(Hums off-key, a familiar John Philip Sousa march, and imitates a white majorette twirling a baton. She throws it so far up in the air that it takes a long while before it comes down, and she is able to catch it behind her back.)

But the Colored bands had this real fast step *(Imitates fast-moving, quickstep of Black marching bands)* and they'd stop, and step, and dip, and sway. And they had majorettes too. For the first time, nationwide TV confirmed the fact that Negro girls had legs, serious thighs, and that the Hottentot ancestral trait was well represented and made manifest in sisters' butts. They had be-hinds. They had pos-ter-riers. And they knew before the proclamation "Black is Beautiful" had even been thought of, that they were just that and more. Yeah, Negroes on TV.

ABOUT THE PLAY

Herman LeVern Jones Theatre Consultant Agency, Inc. co-produced *Olivia's Opus*, directed by Mr. Jones, at the 1993 National Black Theatre Festival. Written and performed by Nora Cole, the multimedia production featured actress Anastasia Baron, with lighting by Ina Mayhew, and Jesse Wooten as stage manager. *Olivia's Opus* was first read at Second Stage. It was co-produced at Castillo in New York for the AUDELCO Black Arts Festival in 1992 and opened Castillo's 1993–1994 season. Later productions included Primary Stages, The Negro Ensemble Company and the M Ensemble, Hartford Stage Company, and the Richard Allen Center for Culture and Art (RACCA).

For further information about *Olivia's Opus* contact: NC Black Rep, info@ncblackrep.org, www.ncblackrep.org.

ABOUT THE PLAYWRIGHT

Nora Cole's solo shows include *Olivia's Opus*, an autobiographical ode to adolescence; *Voices of the Spirits in My Soul* (NBTF 2007 and 2009), which is partially based on her Kentucky family slave history; and *Katherine's Colored Lieutenant*. A veteran performing artist, Cole's credits include *Jelly's Last Jam* opposite Gregory Hines and Maurice Hines; Rinde Eckert's Obie Award–winning, two-character chamber opera *And God Created Whales* (AUDELCO nomination); Vinnette Carroll's *Your Arms Too Short to Box with God* with Patti LaBelle; and at the Royal National Theatre: *Fences, Intimate Apparel, To Kill a Mockingbird, Doubt, Guess Who's Coming to Dinner, On Golden Pond*, and *Caroline or Change*. Ms. Cole is a graduate of the Goodman School of Drama at the Art Institute of Chicago. She has served as an adjunct professor and director at Eastern Connecticut State University. Other recognitions include the TCG/Fox Foundation Resident Actor Fellowship for Distinguished Achievement, Black Theatre Torch Bearer, the Actors Theatre of Louisville Women in Music Award, and a Cherashore Fund Individual Artist Grant.

SHANGO DE IMA:
A YORUBA MYSTERY PLAY

Pepe Carril

1995

Shango de Ima *is a series of legends or histories edited, abridged, and linked together to illustrate one aspect of the orisha Shango. Shango typifies Man and his struggles to gain mastery of himself.*

Shango marries Obba, a mysterious female orisha related to the interaction of Man in trade and commerce. He incurs the wrath of Ogun, the orisha related to power in Nature and in Man, and engages him in battle. Finally, Shango is brought to Olofi for trial, presumably for his mistreatment of the female orishas.

Shango de Ima *is a mystery play in the traditional sense. Shango is tried and sentenced symbolically as a representative of mankind. He is sentenced to the recurring cycles of birth and death, to the never-ending struggle to understand himself by understanding the natural and social world. He must, as in the beginning of the play, search for his true father, and struggle, as must all mankind, to seek out and comprehend his true origins.*[1]

In this scene, Agayu Sola, Shango's father—ferryman of all the rivers, the one who cares for the waters—has left Shango to die. Iku—the spirit of death—prevents the news of this murder from traveling.

---

1. Excerpted from Edward James's introduction to *Shango de Ima: A Yoruba Mystery Play* by Pepe Carril, translated by Susan Sherman, Doubleday & Company, 1970.

THE DEATH OF SHANGO

Agayu Sola leaves Shango to burn in the bonfire.

Iku frightens away Cana, the sacred bird, so that he cannot carry the news of what has happened to Olofi, the supreme father.

Two children: Oya—queen of the cemetery, lightning, and the whirlwind—and Oshun—orisha of love, the sweet waters, and coquetry—witness the funeral ceremony of Iku before the bonfire and promptly go to Olofi—the supreme father/the sun—for aid.

VOICE, CHORUS, AND DRUMS:
> Chon, chon, chon . . .
> como la lame fami chobode . . .
> chon, chon, chon,
> como la lame fami chobode . . .

IKU: Cana, bird of Olofi's heavens, who always eats the dead first and carries the news of death to the supreme father. Whatever you peck turns to blood. But this death belongs to the fire. In the ashes of Shango there will be no meal for the bird of death. Silent you are and silent you will remain eternally about this death.

(The bird cries and withdraws.
Iku draws close to Shango.)

Who threw your body into the scalding flames?
SHANGO: Agayu Sola.
IKU: Who shrank back from your plaintive cry of "father"?
SHANGO: Agayu Sola.
IKU: Who has committed this crime?
CHORUS: His father.
IKU: Evil one! Evil one! This father who denies his own son.
CHORUS: Agayu Sola.
IKU: He deserves the worst of deaths.
CHORUS: Agayu Sola.
IKU: All his people, together, acting as one, should rise and strike him dead.
CHORUS: He has lost himself in the palms. He has no people. Another punishment is necessary.
IKU: I am his death. I am his other and better punishment.
OSHUN AND OYA: The wisest thing to do is to advise Olofi of what has happened.
OTHER VOICES: Go to Olofi! To Olofil! Olofi!

ABOUT THE PLAY

Shango de Ima: A Yoruba Mystery Play was produced by the Nuyorican Poets Café in its Classic Play Readings Festival with support from the National Endowment for the Arts' American Masterpieces Program. Under the direction of Rome Neal, it was given "a brilliantly orchestrated staging" according to Clive Barnes in the *New York Post*. *Shango* won eleven AUDELCO Awards, and featured music performed by Chief Bey and Grammy-nominated Wilson "Chembo" Corniel, and actors Lloyd Goodman, Robert Turner, Vinie Burrows, Karen Amatrading, Cherise Trahan Miller, Spelman Beabrun, Yaa Asantawa, Ahmat Jallo, June Sewer, Tom Southern, Patrice Johnson, Ed Sewer III, Ron Bobb-Semple, and Scottie Davis.

For further information about *Shango de Ima* contact: NC Black Rep, info@ncblackrep.org, www.ncblackrep.org.

ABOUT THE PLAYWRIGHT

Pepe Carril (1930–1992) was a Cuban director, actor, puppet designer, mask designer, costume designer, set designer, stage designer, author, and playwright who was associated with the Camejo Brothers, with whom he founded the Puppet Theater of Cuba in 1956. Their goal was to promote Cuban culture and traditions and to reach viewers of all ages. In the 1960s Pepe led Havana's Teatro Nacional de Guinol (TNG), which was initially created for children and distinguished by the use of a combination of people and puppets. Pepe wrote *Shango de Ima*, a music and dance version of the life story of Shango, one of the seven orishas (or deities) in the Yoruba oral legends, in 1969. It was translated into English by Susan Sherman. (For a comprehensive description of the play, see Dr. Lillian Cleamons Franklin's 1982 Ph.D. dissertation "The Image of the Black in the Cuban Theater: 1913–1965," Ohio State University, pp. 269–272.)

CHAIN

Pearl Cleage

1997

Chain *is a one-character play that presents Rosa, a sixteen-year-old crack addict, whose parents have chained her inside the house in a desperate attempt to keep her away from drugs.*

ROSA: DAY FOUR

Slide: "Day Four." Rosa is smoking a cigarette and pacing as rapidly as she can with the chain. She has mastered walking with it well enough so that her turns now include a practiced flip of the chain, which allows her to progress much more efficiently than she did the first few days. The chain is now less a strange imposition and more a constant irritant.

Rosa stubs out her cigarette in an ashtray that is already overflowing. She continues pacing, reaches into her pocket, takes out another cigarette, and lights it with a Bic lighter, still pacing. She inhales deeply, coughs, stubs this one out too.

My dad says I should try not to start smokin' 'cause it's bad for my health. *(Laughs)* Still trippin'. *(She lights another cigarette, inhales, makes a face)* I hate cigarettes, but I gotta smoke something. I am jonesin' like a muthafucka. My mom keeps tellin' me to just take it one day at a time and shit, like they tell you in rehab. That is bullshit. This is like a minute-by-minute trip, right? I want to get high so bad . . . damn! My fingernails wanna get high. My damn toenails wanna get high! "One day at a time." I hate that bullshit.

Jesus shoulda been lookin' for me by now. That mutha-fucka. He don't give a shit about me. He never did. He just hung around me for the . . . Shit, I don't know why he hung around me. He don't even know I'm here. I know he don't know I'm here or he woulda figured out some way to contact me. He could slide a note under the door or some shit. *(Sudden thought)* Damn! If he could slide a letter under . . .

(She goes to check how wide the space is under the door. She becomes very agitated. She tears a few pages out of a magazine and folds them like a business-size letter. She runs this under the door to see how wide a piece of something could be slipped underneath. There is plenty of room.)

Goddamn! Goddamn! *(She paces excitedly)* He could slip me some shit under there. He could slip me some shit under there every goddamn day. They'd never know it. I'll smoke it in the morning and by the time they get home, they won't even be able to smell nothin'. Shit! Why didn't I think of that before? I gotta get word to Jesus. I gotta let him know what he needs to do.

(Rosa looks around for a piece of paper and a pencil, finds them, and begins to write a letter quickly.

A slide fades in and holds for twenty seconds while she writes:

Dear Jesus,
They got me chained in the house. Bring dope.
                                        —Rosa

Rosa looks critically at the letter and makes an alteration. The slide changes to reflect rewritten letter:

Dear Jesus,
They got me chained in the house. Bring dope.
                              —Forever your girl, Rosa

The slide fades out.

    Rosa folds the letter and then looks around quickly. It dawns on her that she doesn't have any way to get it to him.)

Shit!

(She drags the chain toward the window but can't reach it. In frustration, she begins to pull and tug at the chain in a rage.)

Goddamn it! I . . . want . . . this . . . shit . . . off . . . of . . . me!

(She tears up the letter to Jesus in a rage and sits down, rocking back and forth rapidly.)

I'm not gonna make it. I'm gonna die up in this muthafucka all by myself. I feel like shit and can't do a damn thing about it. I know where the shit at. I know who got it and how to make 'em give it up and I can't get a goddamn thing. They're killin' me. They're killin' me. *(A beat, then trying to calm herself)* But it's gonna be okay. I just gotta hang in there 'til I'm eighteen, then they got no power over me no more. Jesus say when I get eighteen, I should move in wit him since he got plenty of room. I'm down wit it. I know Jesus dig me and he always got enough rock for us to get high. *(A beat)* Where is that muthafucka? He shoulda come up here and beat on the door and hollered or some shit. He could ride up the hall on a big-ass white horse like they do in the movies. I would love that shit. I love when somethin' weird happens. Somethin' you ain't seen two hundred times a day every day. Sometimes I feel like I seen everything they got to show and ain't none of it shit. Ain't none of it shit.

(A beat, then Rosa yells several times in loud succession in complete frustration:)

Jesus ain't shit. I ain't shit. Ain't none of it shit. *(Begins to laugh)* So what the fuck am I cryin' about then, right? If ain't none of it shit, who gives a fuck about it? I just wanna get high, you understand? I don't give a fuck one way or the other, I just need to get high. Goddamn, I need to get high!

When you start smokin' this shit, they don't tell you how bad your ass gonna feel when you ain't got none. They forget to tell you 'bout that shit, right?

You know the funny shit is, I was almost glad to see my daddy when he came to get me. I hadn't seen Jesus in two days and them niggas was acting crazy as shit. He told them he had the hundred he owed them at the crib and he was gonna leave me there with 'em while he went to get it so they would know he wadn't bullshittin'. He ain't said shit to me about that shit, so I said, "Say, what?" He hadn't even told me about owing nobody when we busted up in there or I wouldn't a gone in the first place. Niggas be slitting people's throat for two dollars and here he come owing some niggas I ain't nevah seen before a hundred dollas. He knew I was pissed, 'cause he said, "Don't worry 'bout that shit, baby. I'll be right back and we'll go over to the house and I'll put the rest of the niggas out and we'll get fucked up, just me and you."

Bullshit, right? But I'm so stupid, I believe the muthafucka. "Okay, baby," I say, or some stupid shit like that. I shoulda said, "No, muthafucka. You tell me where the shit is, I'll go get it and they can hold you hostage 'til I get back." But I was tryin' to hang, you know? That's where I fucked up. That muthafucka kissed me goodbye and shit and walked on out the damn door and I ain't seen the nigga since. At first them niggas had a lot of shit to smoke, so we kept getting high and they didn't say too much to me about nothin'. But then when Jesus didn't show for a long time, they started askin' me where he was. Like I knew anything about the shit! I said I didn't know where the nigga was and they said he better bring back a hundred dollars or they gonna fuck me up. I ain't even in the shit, right, but they gonna fuck me up!

So I start figuring what I'm gonna do to get out of the shit and one of 'em asks me how much would I charge him for some pussy and I say a hundred dollars and he say I must think my pussy made outta gold and I tell him I can make him get off good by just watchin' me 'cause I'm that good and he look at the other one and they both laugh and say, maybe the ho do got a pussy made a gold. "Show me," say the one who started the shit in the first place and I tell him it gotta be just me and him 'cause I don't want them to jump me or anything. Niggas get brave when they got they boys watchin'. I know I can handle one, but I ain't down wit muthafuckas tryin' to run a train and shit. So we went in the bedroom and he closed the door and told me to hit it.

So I pulled my panties to the side like Jesus showed me and started rubbin' myself and lookin' at his face and he grinned at me and started rubbin' hisself through his jeans. I always watch their faces 'cause that's how you know if they dig it or not. Then he unzip his pants so he can hold his dick in his hand and it was feeling all right to me too, even though Jesus wadn't there to call my name, and I'm thinkin' maybe this ain't gonna be so bad after all, but then the nigga reached out and grabbed my hand and tried to make me sit down on his lap while he still got his thing out and shit! And I'm tryin' to tell him I ain't down wit it 'cause a AIDS and shit and he tellin' me he ain't no faggot and we sorta wrestlin' around and I'm tryin' not make no noise 'cause I don't want his boy to come in too. That's when my dad started beatin' on the door and hollerin' and shit and all hell broke loose.

They was gettin' ready to shoot through the door at first, and I said, "No, that sound like my dad!" So they told him if he didn't pay the hundred dollars I owed them they'd blow my brains out right in front of him. My daddy just stood there for a minute lookin' at that nigga holdin' his nine-millimeter against my head and I'm thinkin', my daddy ain't got that kinda money! I'm dead! And then he reached in his pocket and took out a roll a money and handed it to the nigga who had been in the bed-room with me. The nigga counted it right in front of my daddy and it was a hundred dollars exactly. That's how I know Jesus the one told him to come get me. How else my daddy gonna be walkin' around Harlem with a pocketful of cash like he the dope man and shit.

Then that nigga told my daddy to get my little crackaddict ass outta his place and pushed me so hard I fell against his chest. My daddy didn't even look at me. He took off his jacket and put it around my shoulders and we walked the three blocks home with him holdin' my arm like you do a little kid when they been bad. He wadn't sayin' shit. When we got home, my moms was there and she started cryin' and holdin' my face up so she could look at me and shit. I know I looked like shit. I hadn't eaten in two–three days and my clothes were all twisted around from tusslin' with that nigga in the bedroom. And I know my hair was all over my head 'cause she kept smoothin' it down and I could feel it risin' right back up again and she'd smooth it down again and it would rise on back up. My head was itchin' too, but I couldn't scratch or nothin' because my mom was huggin' me and she had my arms pinned down at my sides and you can't push your mama off you, even if you want to, so I'm standin' there tryin' to get her to calm down and I catch a eyeful of my pops sittin' at the table and tears just runnin' down his face. He ain't cryin' or hollerin' or nothin'. He just sittin' there lookin' at me and Mama stumblin' around the room like we drunk.

That hurt me worse than anything. I never seen my daddy cry in my life. Never. I seen him mad plenty of times, but not over me. He be mad about some niggas actin' a fool or some crackers fuckin' over him or somethin' Mama said that didn't sit right, but he never cried. He didn't cry when his mama died. Took the phone call, drove down south and buried her, came back and never broke. So I felt real bad when I saw him cryin' over me. I love my daddy . . .

So I got away from Mama and I went over and stood in front of him and I said, "Don't worry about me, Daddy. I'm okay." And he just looked at me and tears runnin' all down his chin and he wadn't wipin' shit. Act like he didn't even know he was doin' it. I didn't have no Kleenex or nothin', but I hated to see him like that, so I just wiped him off a little with my sleeve, right? He caught my hand and held it so hard I thought he was gonna crush my damn fingers, and he just looked at me and started sayin' my name over and over and over like he wasn't sure it was even me: "Rosa, Rosa, Rosa!" And my mom on the other side of the room runnin' around hollerin' and shit.

It was almost like I was somewhere else watchin' it. It was too weird to be happenin' to me for real. When I went to bed I could still hear my mom in the other room cryin', and every time I woke up, my dad would be sittin' right by my bed, just lookin' at me like he in a dream or somethin'. Then one time I got up to go to the bathroom and he walked right wit me and stood there outside the door and waited for me and before I got back into bed he hugged me real hard and I could feel him shakin' like he was jonesin' worse than me. Scared the shit outta me. I figured my shit must be even raggedier than I thought if it making my daddy shake.

It's no way for me to tell him how it feels, you know what I mean? They don't understand nothin' about none of it so there's no place to start tellin' them anything. They shoulda kept their country asses in Tuskegee, Alabama.

My daddy used to sing when we lived down there. He can sing, too. He sound like Luther Vandross a little bit. Him and my mama used to sing in the car. Raggedy-ass car they got from somebody. We drove that muthafucka all the way up here, though. Soon as we got to Harlem, the muthafucka broke down. I used to ask my pops if the car had a broke down in Brooklyn, would he a stayed in Brooklyn, and he would laugh and say he probably would. *(A beat)*

I think that nigga was gonna rape me if my daddy hadn't busted up in there. And that wadn't gonna be the worst of it. Jesus wadn't comin' back no time soon. That's why he called my pops and told him where I was. *(Laughs)* He busted up in there, though. My daddy crazy. They coulda blown him away with his Alabama ass. *(A beat)* I don't think he'd a brought me up here if he'd a known what these niggas up here were like. They treacherous up here in New York. You think you ready for it, but you not ready. These niggas don't care nothin' 'bout you. Jesus spose to be my friend and look how he act! *(A beat)* My daddy bad, though. He was beatin' on that door like he was packin' a Uzi and he didn't have shit. Not even no stick or nothin'. He just standin' there talkin' shit about: "Where my baby girl at? Where you got my Rosa?"

And I'm hollerin': "Here I am, Daddy! Here I am!"

ABOUT THE PLAY

Chain was commissioned and developed by the Women's Project and Productions and the Southeast Playwright's Project of Atlanta in 1992, along with Cleage's one-act play *Late Bus to Mecca*. The plays were premiered at the Judith Anderson Theatre in New York City.

   Chain is copyright © 1999 by Pearl Cleage, and is published in *Flyin' West and Other Plays* (Theatre Communications Group [TCG], New York, 1999). For further information contact: Ron Gwiazda, A3 Artists Agency, ron.gwiazda@a3artistsagency.com, www.a3artistsagency.com.

ABOUT THE PLAYWRIGHT

Pearl Cleage is the author of eight novels, including *What Looks Like Crazy on an Ordinary Day*, an Oprah Book Club selection; three books of poetry, including *We Speak Your Names*, co-authored with Zaron Burnett; and her 2014 memoir *Things I Should Have Told My Daughter: Lies, Lessons, and Love Affairs*. Her most recent plays, *The Nacirema Society Requests the Honor of Your Presence at a Celebration of Their First 100 Years* (2013), *What I Learned in Paris* (2015), and *Angry, Raucous and Shamelessly Gorgeous* (2019), all premiered at the Alliance, directed by Susan Booth. Cleage was a Distinguished Artist in Residence at Atlanta's Alliance Theatre. While in residence at Just Us Theater Company, she produced *puppetplay* (1981), *Hospice* (1983), *Good News* (1984), and *Essentials* (1985). *Hospice* was also produced at the New Federal Theatre by Woodie King, Jr., and *puppetplay* was presented at the Negro Ensemble Company with Phylicia Rashad and Seret Scott. In the 1990s she produced three of her best-known works at the Alliance directed by Kenny Leon: *Flyin' West* (1992), *Blues for an Alabama Sky*, and *Bourbon at the Border* (1997). She became Artistic Director of Just Us in 1990 where she and her husband, writer Zaron W. Burnett, Jr., did ten years of performances as the award-winning Live at Club Zebra! series. *Flyin' West and Other Plays* is a collection of her works published by Theatre Communications Group. She was named Atlanta's first Poet Laureate in 2020.

MONSIEUR BAPTISTE, THE CON MAN

Roger Furman

1999

Freely adapted from Molière's Tartuffe, *this comedy of manners is set among nineteenth-century Haiti's Black community. A seemingly devout con man infiltrates a wealthy household and ends up falling in love with the lady of the house.*

THE CON

As the lights come up, the sound of church bells can be heard tolling. Music plays under. It is dusk, the sky has a reddish glow about it. Dorinea, the maid, is lighting candles, giving the room a warm glow. There is a sad, low-key atmosphere about the place. The Madame is sitting next to her daughter, Valerie. Jean Paul, the Madame's son, is pacing the floor.

MADAME: As they say on the stage, I guess "all is lost"!
DORINEA *(Hopeful)*: No Madame, we can't give up. *(Strong)* All is not lost!

(Don Pascal, head of house, enters.)

DON PASCAL: The strongbox is missing! It was left in my care for safe keeping by a person in the government. Those papers are a matter of life and death.

MADAME *(Strong)*: Well, well, Baptiste, you win again! I'm sorry you had to provoke him, knowing that he was holding the trump card over us all! Why, why?

DON PASCAL *(Angry)*: I don't ever want to see another so-called Godly person for as long as I live!

MADAME: Next time don't be so quick to be taken in by someone because they give the illusion that they are virtuous! You must learn to distinguish between the good and the evil!

JEAN PAUL *(Hugging his father)*: Papa, when Sister came and told what happened, I had a few friends standing by. They want a chance to beat him within an inch of his life. You just say the word and we'll get him tonight.

DON PASCAL *(Cutting him off)*: No, my good son, all I want from you is forgiveness. *(Hugs his son)* Don't let him sink you to his evil level. We'll work something out, my son.

JEAN PAUL: Papa, we've got to work fast! He's about to put us on the street by morning! Remember he now owns this house! *(Strong)* Something must be done!

(The doorbell rings. They all look at Don Pascal. He nods for Dorinea to open the door. The Grandmother enters with a huff.)

GRANDMOTHER: What's all this noise I've been hearing everywhere I go? Yack-a-yack! Loose tongues wagging like a dog's tail at feeding time! What's happening in this house?

DON PASCAL: Aw, sit down, Mama! My wife was almost raped by a viper! We are all about to be put out of our house and home! Other than that we've had a damn good day!

GRANDMOTHER *(At wit's end)*: Raped! Out on the street! Dorinea, get me something strong to drink. *(Loud)* Don't just stand there daydreaming! Move! *(To Don Pascal)* What is Monsieur Baptiste got to do with all this?

DON PASCAL *(At wit's end)*: Mon Dieu! *(Overreacting)* I would like to kill that man. *(Holding up his hands)* Oh, with these two hands I'd like to squeeze his neck like you squeeze the juice out of a ripe mango fruit! I'd like to cut him down like you chop sugarcane!

(Madame sits him down, patting his back.)

That Baptiste tries to rape my wife, right here on this floor!
In front of my eyes!

GRANDMOTHER: I can't believe what I'm hearing!

(Dorinea gives her a glass.)

I feel like I might faint.

(She drinks fast, holds out the glass for another one.)

Daughter-in-law, what have you got to say for yourself?

MADAME *(Very grand)*: He's telling you the truth!
    (Mopping her forehead) Dorinea, I'll have something to
calm me down. My legs are still a bit shaky.

(She sits next to Grandmother.)

GRANDMOTHER *(Holding Madame's hand)*: Courage, l'ami le
    diable est mort. A dog in heat!

JEAN PAUL: Papa, do you think he'll put us out on the street
    tonight? It looks like rain!

VALERIE *(Sobbing)*: I better get ready for the good sisters at the
    convent.

GRANDMOTHER: On the streets? Son, how can he put you out of
    your own house?

DON PASCAL: I gave him the deed to the house and the lands
    when I thought that he was going to marry Valerie. Sad to
    say this is all his. We're still a family, no matter what hap-
    pens! I have friends in high places!

*(The doorbell rings. They all look at Don Pascal. The bell
rings again.)*

The wolves are at the gates!

*(He nods for Dorinea to open the door. An older man enters,
tall and very official-looking. He speaks very authoritatively.)*

CALLER: Good evening! Is Monsieur Don Pascal Alvarez at home? I would like to have a few words with him. This is most important. It concerns his family's safety.

DORINEA: Sir, Monsieur Alvarez is very busy! If you leave your name, I'll have him get in touch with you.

CALLER *(Strong)*: I must see him now! Tell him it's on behalf of a one Monsieur Baptiste, there is not much time left.

DORINEA: Yes sir!

(She bows and comes into the room.)

(To Don Pascal, very proud) Sir, it's about that Baptiste, I think that you should hear what he has to say.

DON PASCAL: And the walls came tumbling down. Alright, show him in.

(Dorinea escorts the caller into the room. Upon entering he bows to everyone. Everyone is tense and gives him a hard look.)

CALLER *(To Don Pascal)*: Good evening, sir! *(Turning to the rest of the group)* Ladies! *(He nods to Jean Paul)* I'm sorry if I'm intruding at the wrong time, but it's most urgent that I speak to you! *(Taking out a court order paper with a seal on it)* It's a court order for you and your family to vacate this house at once.

(There is a reaction from the group.)

DON PASCAL *(At wit's end)*: Leave our house at once? Sir, how dare you!

CALLER *(Low-key)*: This house, as you already know, belongs to a one Monsieur Baptiste. He has a gift of deed legally stating that this is now his property, lock, stock, and barrel. It's all down in black and white! He has been before the high court!

JEAN PAUL: I should put a fist in your jaw! Damn the high court! *(Strong)* This is our home! We're not going no place!

DORINEA: Hay!

CALLER *(More strong)*: Young man, I suggest that you hold your tongue. This is the law of the land that you're dealing with. It can cost extra trouble for you! *(Pointing to Don Pascal)* It's this man that I'm talking to!

GRANDMOTHER *(Jumping up)*: What did you say your name is, sir? I didn't hear you say!

CALLER: I am the bailiff from the court. My name is Monsieur DuBois. I'm here to serve this writ on behalf of a one Monsieur Baptiste Jousset.

GRANDMOTHER: Oh, you did, did you!

CALLER: I have other stops to make in the course of my business. Who is the head of this household?

DON PASCAL *(Stepping forward)*: Give me the writ, sir! I am the head of this house! This is my family!

(He hands the writ to Don Pascal.)

Monsieur DuBois! It will be a long night for this family!

CALLER: May the Good Lord bless you. You had better make haste. Monsieur Baptiste and an officer of the high court will be here soon! *(Bowing to them all)* Good evening!

(He exits.)

DON PASCAL *(Holding up the paper)*: Over the hill to the poor house! Now we sit and wait for the executioner's death blow!

MADAME: We can go to the country and live with my brother. Things will work out. *(Strong)* We must stay together as a family.

GRANDMOTHER: My place is much too small. This is a grand house! To think it slipped right through our fingers like grains of sand! Oh, the sadness of it all. Years of building a family tradition, shot to hell! Dorinea, give me something to drink! I feel faint!

(There is a loud knocking on the door. They all look at Don Pascal. He nods for Dorinea to open the door. Monsieur Baptiste enters in a huff, followed by an officer of the law.)

BAPTISTE *(Hard)*: My, my! They're still here in my house. I see you've been served with the writ! That's good! I must say that bailiff is on the job! I must give him a tip!

DON PASCAL: To think that I pulled you up from the slime! You forget so soon, brother man!

BAPTISTE *(With contempt)*: How could I ever forget? But my first duty is to my government. Those papers that were in that strongbox were given to you to hold by a friend. Monsieur Don Pascal Alvarez, you should be very careful who you allied yourself with! I must say that you're a very generous man!

DON PASCAL: That strongbox was given to me to hold with the confidence of a friend!

BAPTISTE: And like the fool that you are, you gave it to me! Some confidence! I guess the Good Lord knew what he was doing.

JEAN PAUL: I should have beat you within an inch of your life!

BAPTISTE: Now you can try beating the dust! *(Laughing)* What a lot you all are! *(To the officer)* Officer, do your duty! Lodge them all in the gutter where they belong! *(Strong)* I want them out of my house!

OFFICER: I will do my duty at once! *(Taking out a pair of handcuffs)* Sir, I command you to accompany me to the prison where you will be lodged, Monsieur Baptiste!

(They all react.)

BAPTISTE *(At a loss for words)*: Prison . . . me?!

OFFICER: Yes! I'm talking to you! *(To Don Pascal)* Monsieur Alvarez, family, sit down Monsieur Baptiste! *(Strong)* I said sit!

(Baptiste sits very calmly.)

This is a small country, nothing escapes the law. The men that rule are not tyrants, they have their compassion and love and welfare for their people at heart! Don Pascal, you have been a strong public servant for years, like your late father! When this man came to the magistrate with your gift of deed, we knew that something was wrong! As for the strong box, that's another matter! Baptiste only betrayed himself! His record was in the files under another name! He has a long history of crimes that would fill volumes. *(To Baptiste)* The gift of deed, sir!

(Baptiste hands the papers over to the officer. The officer in turn gives them to Don Pascal.)

This is yours sir!
DON PASCAL *(Low-key)*: Thank you!

(Holding up the deed, the Madame hugs him.)

MADAME *(Very happy)*: Oh, how wonderful! We can live again. *(To the officer)* You have given us back our lives. Thank you!
OFFICER: The magistrate also pardons you. *(Handing him another paper)* I'm talking about the strongbox!

(They all react to this.)

GRANDMOTHER: Bless His holy name!
OFFICER: Come, Monsieur Baptiste! Your new home is waiting for you. Stand up!

(Baptiste gets up.)

Do you have anything to say to these people that you conned? Is there some word of remorse?

(Baptiste looks about the room. He starts to say something. Dorinea hums and chants in low tones. Baptiste becomes afraid and bows his head. He takes out his rosary. He has a wild, mad look on his face. He is no longer Baptiste. He is now a man possessed.)

Come, let's go! Good night, everyone.

(Baptiste is very grand as they leave. He blesses everyone . . .)

DON PASCAL: Thank the Good Lord for His mercy! We must all go to mass when the sun comes up. Now that that's over, there are things to be done! *(Hugging Valerie)* Like getting ready for one of the biggest weddings this island has ever seen! How does that sound to you?

(They all react.)

VALERIE: Oh, Papa! I'm so happy!

JEAN PAUL: I can't wait to tell André!

(They all laugh.)

DON PASCAL *(Very happy)*: All is right with the world again! God is still watching His children.

    (To Madame) Madame, you are going to be one busy woman, getting ready for that grand ball you're throwing for the Mardi Gras season.

MADAME *(Upbeat)*: Husband, it's going to be one of the best this old house has ever seen! *(Dancing about the room)* Oh yes! Tubs and tubs of Champagne from France.

DON PASCAL: The best money can buy!

MADAME: Music everywhere! They'll dance contre danses Françaises! Toe-tapping quadrilles. And a fast waltz until they fall to the floor.

(They all laugh.)

DON PASCAL: Daughter, your wedding is going to be the only true event of the social season! They will talk about it for years to come! I'm a new man!

VALERIE *(In a state of grace)*: I'll have a wedding gown with a thousand tiny white rosettes sewn on it, topped by a ruffled white veil a mile long! Flowers, Papa, everywhere you look. Red, pink, white, oh yes! *(Hugging Don Pascal)* It will be a fine wedding day!

DON PASCAL: Son, Jean Paul, you are the man of the house now!

GRANDMOTHER: Now that everything is right as rain I better get ready for sunrise mass! *(Getting up)* Monsieur Baptiste is safe in the calaboose tonight and you are all happy again. That's all that counts!

DORINEA *(Elated)*: We have won the victory! I feel the spirits all around me. I feel like dancing for joy. *(She starts swaying around the room)* I feel as light as a feather.

DON PASCAL: Dance until you fall out!

(They all laugh. The music up.)

DORINEA *(Chanting)*: I feel it! Dansez Bamboula! *(She does a bit)* Houm. Dance Calinda! Ale! Ale! The gods heard my call. Madame, I'll take back my handkerchief. I just might need it for another case. *(Very grand)* Yes, children, I'm not from Santo Domingo for nothing.

(They all laugh, as the music fills the room.)

ABOUT THE PLAY

Monsieur Baptiste, the Con Man was directed by Dr. Lundeana Thomas and performed by students from the African American Theatre Program (AATP) at the University of Louisville.

For further information about *Monsieur Baptiste, The Con Man* contact: NC Black Rep, info@ncblackrep.org, www.ncblackrep.org.

ABOUT THE PLAYWRIGHT

Roger Furman (1924–1983) was a director, actor, lecturer, and playwright who founded the New Heritage Repertory Theatre in 1964 as a street theater. Under Furman's leadership, New Heritage produced more than thirty-five plays. A co-founder of the Black Theater Alliance, an organization of performance groups, he was a 1973 recipient of the AUDELCO Board of Directors Award and was nominated in 1975 as Best Director for *Fat Tuesday*. In October 2022, Harlem-based New Heritage celebrated its fifty-eighth anniversary and is the oldest Black nonprofit theater in New York state.

RHYME DEFERRED: HIEROGLYPHIC GRAFFITI

Kamilah Forbes

2001

In his Washington Post *review (June 9, 2000) of* Rhyme Deferred, *Nelson Pressley calls the "hip-hop theatricality of this melo-drama, with its thick atmosphere and dueling rappers . . . strik-ing." There are mystical elements—a journey to the underworld, a morality tale framed in notions of authenticity versus commer-cial "rap"—that presage the ongoing fractures in a community where the debate rages over what constitutes progress and what denotes oppression. Langston Hughes's poem "Dream Deferred" is "sampled" in the title* Rhyme Deferred, *in which Kamilah Forbes highlights the lack of opportunity for people of color in Hughes's time period. But today's "evil here is exactly the opposite," Pressley states. According to Forbes, "Success . . . is killing hip-hop."*

KAIN/HERC

A flashback scene.

RECORD LABEL EXECUTIVE: Look, KAIN. We got an album to finish. And all you've given me was some damn prediction on the fucking weather. "Make It Hot"!

KAIN: I feel numb.

RECORD LABEL EXECUTIVE: You don't make money off of singles. You make them off of albums. I need songs and I need them now.

KAIN: I'm on empty.

RECORD LABEL EXECUTIVE: So you do what you need to do, smoke some reefer, drink a forty, get arrested. Write the album from behind bars. I don't give a fuck. Shoot somebody, whatever you need to do to inspire this album.

KAIN: I'm staring at a blank page.

RECORD LABEL EXECUTIVE: Kain, do you need to die and come back again? 'Cause we can market that. So you do what you do, so I can do what I do, and that's fill your pocket. Find a new sound, some new energy, some new something. Otherwise all I can say is that you are just about washed up, washed up, washed up.

(End of flashback scene; Record Label Executive exits.)

KAIN: I can't think of anything! Shit, what the fuck am I going to do? I need to get down there . . . *(Discovers Underground MC Gabe's book, starts flipping the pages)* His rhyme book!

(Herc, mythical overseer of the underground, enters.)

HERC:
New Soooouuuunnnd,
New Soooouuuunnnd,
New Soooouuuunnnd,
New Energy
His rhyme book, his energy.
You think you can hold the feelings of another in your heart,
In your hand
without getting burned?
Lessons we must learn.
Well, it's here. It's here.
Or is it here in your heart,
But somehow you lost it?
You once reigned as king.
But now you sing to the jingle and shuffle of the industry?

Commercially you thrive? Two-dimensionally, you jive us all, and yourself? Sold your soul for some gold to go platinum, to go plastic. Fake artificial MC you became, now you play a dangerous game without shame. For the key to the underground, it's in the chosen one's rhymes. By using his weapons for battle you lose your power for all time.
Some things are not meant for everyone's eyes.
You want to go to the streets? I'll take you to the streets . . .
I'll take you to the streets . . .
I'll take you to the streets . . .

(Using dance movement, the ensemble takes Kain through a mystical transition to the underworld of "the streets." This movement evokes the experience of a bad acid trip.

Kain stumbles onto the street with Herc looking on. A chorus of Headz [the ensemble, B-Dancers, Shameka, etc.] is moving in a slow-motion trance.)

KAIN: WHOA SHIT!

HERC *(Welcoming Kain)*: PEACE, BROTHER JAY!

HEADZ *(Echoing)*:
Peace, Brother Jay
Peace, Brother Jay
Peace, Brother Jay

KAIN: How did you know my name? NOBODY CALLS ME THAT!

HERC: I know who you are. I know where you've been, and I know where you're headed.

KAIN: Word, how come I've never seen you here before.

HERC: Because you never tried. I can transport my spirit from one body to another.

(Herc begins chanting the incantation and then throws his voice into the bodies of the Headz, who do the same.)

HEAD 1: I can be your sister . . .

HEAD 2: Or your brother . . .

HEAD 3: Or maybe me . . .

HEADZ: It's a spirit of duality, it's a spirit of duality.

(Throughout the following passage, Herc morphs from baby to young man to old man.)

HEADZ:	HERC:
I can transport my spirit	I am in every man
From one body to another	
I could be your sister	I am in every man
Or your brother	

HEADZ *(Cont'd)*:

    Or maybe me

    It's the spirit of duality

    It's the spirit of duality . . .

    man, man . . .

HERC *(Cont'd)*:

    I am in every man

    I am in every man

HERC: Look, what you coming back on the streets for?

KAIN: I just wanted to, you know . . .

HERC: You're not supposed to be here.

KAIN: What are you talking about?

HERC *(Shouting)*:

    You stole the rhyme book to find your way.

    You stole the rhyme book to find your way.

    You stole the rhyme book to find your way.

KAIN *(In a loud whisper)*: Yo! Shhhh, shhhh!!!

HERC: That's like stealing the Bible to get to heaven.

KAIN: Yo, chill, all right.

HERC: They can't see or hear you . . .

KAIN: What?

HERC: They can't see or hear you . . . Because you're not supposed to be here.

KAIN: If I wasn't supposed to be here, I wouldn't be here.

HERC: Aaah. Safe, first base, smart kid. So, you came back to battle?

KAIN: Battle? No, no, I don't want to battle. I just wanted to see . . .

HERC: Of course, that's it. The Invincible Suga Kain's touring, got albums and videos. People love your shit, but from what I hear, your shit is not that hot anymore. You lost it and now you coming back here to find it again through the Ashé. Am I right?

KAIN: The Ashé?

HERC: Ain't this a bitch. This nigga's on a search and don't even know what he's looking for! The Ashé, the energy source. The Ashé works through the head MC to maintain order on the streets, along with bestowing upon the head MC lyrical girth.

KAIN: Ashé.

HERC: Ashé. So, does this sound like something you might be looking for, Sherlock?

(Herc places imaginary headphones on Kain; we hear what Kain is hearing.)

KAIN: Umm, yeah. Something like that, well maybe not really looking . . .

HERC: Yeah, I think that is what it is, and according to the oracle . . .

(Herc tosses down a pair of dice. He walks confidently to their falling point; his expression changes to astonishment as he reads the formation of the dice.)

I said, "According to the oracle." *(He rolls the dice again)*

KAIN: What? What?

HERC: . . . No one will have the ability to defeat you . . . You will reign as Head MC and always be remembered and revered.

KAIN: For real? You see all that in those itty-bitty dice, huh?

HERC: That's what it says.

KAIN: See, I told you. "I'm not supposed to be here." Whatever, man.

HERC: You still ain't ready to battle.

KAIN: Wait, hold up. First of all, they play my shit on the radio. I got albums, PLURAL, out, and on top of all that, you just said that I was goin' to . . .

HERC: I know what I just said. That still don't mean nothing. What you got out there does not determine what you can do in here. You can't match up to what the Headz are doing now. They are on a whole 'nother level. You need to start training for the battle.

KAIN: Yo, just let me battle, I'll be all right.

HERC: You ain't . . . You ain't . . . you ain't ready. You ain't ready . . . You ain't ready . . .

(Herc conducts the Headz as if they are a symphony, while moving Kain across the floor.)

So, you want to start now or later? It's your choice.

KAIN *(Shamefully mumbling)*: Now.

HERC: Here, put this on.

(Herc hands Kain a hoodie.)

If the Headz knew it was you, it just wouldn't be right, ya dig?

KAIN: Oh, true, word. *(He puts on the hoodie)*

HERC: All right, all right . . .

(Herc takes Kain into a trance; we hear a heartbeat.)

Can you hear it?

KAIN: What?

HERC: Listen.

KAIN: Listen to what?

HERC: It's calling you.

KAIN: Who's calling? Calling me? I can't hear anything.

HERC: I figured you wouldn't. This is the core, the foundation.

(Headz vibing in cipher join in. They begin creating a heartbeat by pounding on stools and the floor.)

KAIN: What the hell are you dealing with, man?

ABOUT THE PLAY

Rhyme Deferred, this poetic fairy tale, was first produced by the African Continuum Theatre Company's Hip-Hop Theatre Festival 2000 at the Kennedy Center for the Performing Arts.

Rhyme Deferred is copyright © 2002 by Kamilah Forbes, and is published in *The Fire This Time* (Theatre Communications Group [TCG], New York, 2002). For further information contact: NC Black Rep, info@ncblackrep.org, www.ncblackrep.org.

ABOUT THE PLAYWRIGHT

Kamilah Forbes is an American curator, producer, and director. She created and directed the Hip Hop Theatre Festival from 2000 to 2016, and has held roles for television and theater productions such as *Holler if Ya Hear Me* (associate producer), *The Wiz Live!* (associate director), and the 2014 revival of Lorraine Hansberry's *A Raisin in the Sun* (assistant director). In 2016, she was named executive producer for the Apollo Theater. At Signature Theatre, Forbes directed the 2019 revival of Lynn Nottage's play *By the Way, Meet Vera Stark*. Other producer credits include the HBO television series *Def Poetry Jam* and *Brave New Voices*. In 2020 she directed the HBO adaptation of *Between the World and Me*, based on Ta-Nehisi Coates's book of the same title. In 2019, she was honored with the Larry Leon Hamlin Producer Award at the National Black Theatre Festival. *Rhyme Deferred* is published by TCG in the anthology *The Fire This Time: African American Plays for the 21st Century*.

HILLARY AND MONICA: THE WINTER OF HER DISCONTENT

Yvette Heyliger

2003

This one-act comedy explores what might have happened if the former First Lady and the infamous intern had a chance meeting before the scandal broke. Can Hillary save Monica from herself and secure a future run for President of the United States?

HILLARY

First Lady Hillary Clinton takes her case directly to the people:

What, tough? Everyone complains that I'm tough. Well, damn it, I have to be to stay on course, to "soldier on," as Queen Noor says! I've tried to understand it. I've examined it—taken it apart—looked at it from every possible angle. But, not for his sake, for mine! I can't take his behavior personally. I can't let his addiction rob me of my self-esteem. I can't let his weakness drag the office of the First Lady through the mud!

(Lights dim onstage. Clapping is heard. Hillary waves to the crowd as lights rise in the audience. Sound of clapping fades as Hillary delivers her stump speech, walking among the people.)

My fellow Americans, why are men the only ones for whom it is acceptable to have it all—a career and marriage? Why are you so conflicted and ambivalent about powerful women—about me as First Lady?

It was in 1877 that the term "First Lady of the Land" appeared. There has never been a job description for the First Lady. It wasn't written into the Constitution. Each First Lady has been left to define the role for herself. If you ask me, like so much of women's work, the office of First Lady is the leading unpaid job in the country, and as a result, the importance of many First Ladies' contributions to their husbands' presidencies have been hidden from history.

Abigail Adams was accused by her husband's opponents of having too much influence on the president—an accusation that would be made of many future First Ladies. Mary Todd Lincoln discovered that a seat at the dinner table could be more powerful than a seat at the cabinet table. Edith Wilson, who was mockingly dubbed "the first woman president" or "the other twenty-eighth president," almost single-handedly ran this country while her husband was laid up with a stroke, unable to move or speak. Eleanor Roosevelt became the "eyes and legs" of President Roosevelt after he was left paralyzed by polio. During the Cuban Missile Crisis, President Kennedy gave Jackie top-secret updates. In fact, the majority of the First Ladies have been politically active in their husbands' careers. You know what this translates to? Power. And there's the rub!

What are you so afraid of America—that I'm going to push Bill aside and run this country myself? As if I could do that! Oh—if only I could do that! I'll show that boy in grade school who dared say to me, "Girls can't be president," that I can be president, as good as or better than any man. To hell with the naysayers and what they think the proper role of a First Lady should be! I am no Mamie Eisenhower—a First Lady without pet projects or causes because, "I only have one career and his name is Ike." In your dreams! Me—"unladylike, unelected, and wielding political power"? You're damned right! Lady Bird said, "Though the president is chosen by the people, the First Lady is chosen by only one man." Well, history will show that you chose well, Bill; you chose well! Like Lady Bird, I too have a podium, and I intend to use it!

I am a new kind of First Lady: independent, progressive, and modern; an activist, and one who is not content with a ceremonial position executing genteel and ladylike duties such as redecorating the White House and playing hostess at state dinners. I will not be relegated to being some traditional, glorified housewife! I am living history, damn it! And I will pick out the china after I do my part to pick up this "village" called society, because it "takes a village" to prepare America to give birth to a new millennium. I am Hillary Rodham Clinton, and I approve this message!

ABOUT THE PLAY

Hillary and Monica was produced in association with Twinbiz (Yvette Heyliger and Yvonne Farrow) on the main stage at the National Black Theatre Festival and was directed by Yvette. The production stage manager was John Eric Scutchins. The cast was made up of one Black actor: Marjorie Johnson (Betty Currie); and three white actors: Heidi J. Dallin (Hillary Clinton), Jacqueline Kristel (Monica Lewinsky), and Randall England (Bill Clinton).

For further information about *Hillary and Monica* contact: twinbizny@gmail.com, 212-864-1611, https://newplayexchange.org/users/30298/yvette-heyliger.

ABOUT THE PLAYWRIGHT

Yvette Heyliger is a playwright, producing artist, activist, and author of *What a Piece of Work Is Man! Full-length Plays for Leading Women*. She has contributed to many anthologies including: *ARTemis Arts Wisdom Anthology*; *She Persisted: Thirty Ten-Minute Plays by Women Over Forty*; *She Persisted: One Hundred Monologues from Plays by Women Over Forty*; *Later Chapters: The Best Monologues and Scenes for Actors Over Fifty*; *Short Plays on Reproductive Freedom*; *24 Gun Control Plays*, *The Best Women's Stage Monologues 2003*; and *The Best Stage Scenes 2003*. Yvette has also penned theater industry–related articles for magazines, blog posts, a scholarly journal, and textbooks, including *Performing #MeToo: How Not to Look Away*. She is the recipient of the AUDELCO Award for Excellence in Black Theatre's August Wilson Playwright Award, and a Best Playwright nomination for the NAACP Annual Awards, among others honors. Along with her twin sister and producing partner, Yvonne Farrow, Yvette was honored by the National Black Theatre Festival with their inaugural Emerging Producer Award. Four Twinbiz theatrical productions: *Bridge to Baraka* (2013, Larry Leon Hamlin, Solo Series directed by Mario Giacalone); *What Would Jesus Do?* (2007); *Hillary and Monica: The Winter of Her Discontent* (2003); *Autobiography of a Homegirl* (2001), all written and directed by Yvette; and a film *I'd Rather Be Dancing* (2005), written and directed by Yvonne, were presented on the NBTF's main stage. Memberships: Dramatists Guild, AEA, SDC, and SAG-AFTRA.

PLENTY OF TIME

Dr. John Shévin Foster

2005

1997. Days after his son Ronny's death from AIDS, Corey arrives in Martha's Vineyard at the summer home of Christina, where they have met each year since they were young lovers. For the first time in their thirty-year romance, they must push beyond their physical relationship and learn to be there for each other in a real, tangible way.

TRUTH

1997. A Martha's Vineyard home. Christina, forty-six, is seated at a table, dressed in a comfortable pantsuit and scarf. She is typing steadily on a laptop computer. She stops to take a sip of wine. She thinks for a moment then returns to work. The phone rings. She crosses to answer.

CHRISTINA: Hello? *(Listening)* Is everything okay, Marie? *(Listening)* Did one of the other kids do something to her? *(Listening)* What did her teacher say? *(Listening)* All right, just take her home and I'll be back as soon as I can. Put her on please. *(Pause)* Hello, Brittany, it's Mommy. What's wrong, baby? That's not true, baby. Brittany, Mommy loves— Brittany, Mommy— Brittany, Mommy will bring you a gift when she comes home. What kind of gift? I don't know yet, but, *(Keeping her from crying)* Mommy's gonna bring you a nice dress. Okay, baby?

(Corey, fifty-one, enters, slowly, quietly. He sets down his overnight bag.)

Brittany, Mommy has to go okay? I love you. I love you, baby. Can you tell Mommy you love her? *(Pause)* That's okay. I'll be home soon. Bye.

(She stands and looks at Corey, who looks everywhere but at her.)

(Gently) I didn't think you'd be here this time.

(Pause.)

I just thought I'd use the time to do some . . . work. *(Slowly walking toward him)*

COREY: I needed to go . . . somewhere, and this was the only place . . .

CHRISTINA *(Trying to lighten the air)*: It's okay. I'm glad you're here. I've been wearing your scarf . . . the one you gave me? I know it's silly, but I feel better having a piece of you close.

COREY: I failed, Chris.

CHRISTINA: No, Corey.

COREY: It was what you said. It was my test and I failed. All of that time wasted . . . I . . . I . . .

(She embraces him.)

I should have been with him.

CHRISTINA: You were with him. When it counted. When he needed you.

COREY: In the end? To do what, feed him some soup? He didn't need me in the end. He had ten years to not need me. Ten years of my rejecting him because I needed him to be something different. My going to see him was all about me.

CHRISTINA: Don't do this to yourself.

COREY *(Holding back tears)*: I was supposed to be there when my scared seventeen-year-old boy needed me to tell him it was all right. That he was still a man. More of a man than I am.

(She listens.)

I was supposed to let him know he still had a family to come home to.

CHRISTINA: No one knew, Corey. Not you, not his mother.

COREY: He . . . he didn't want anyone to know . . . he was afraid of telling us. In the middle of his suffering he was afraid of telling us.

CHRISTINA: How did you find out?

COREY: From his brother. He called his brother the last time he went into the hospital. He was, so . . . so small. Like the little boy I used to play with. He couldn't move, but his eyes lit up like they would when I used to pick them up for the summer. I didn't know what to say. I just sat next to him, fed him some soup, and he . . . looked happy. I think. He died two days later.

(Pause.)

CHRISTINA: I came.

COREY: I saw you.

CHRISTINA: Where is Donny?

COREY: With his family. He invites me to come see them, but I don't feel . . . comfortable. Ronny was his twin. He—

CHRISTINA: Still loves you. *(Remembering)* Corey. The only connection I had to Mommy was lost when Daddy passed. Now, I visit, she and I go through the motions, being polite, with nothing to really say to each other. It was always a competition for his attention. I wish . . . I wish I had one memory of us having the kind of relationship mothers and daughters are supposed to have—one happy memory or one shared secret. Something. You've shared so much with those boys, and Donny knows all about the last ten years of his brother's life. You should let him tell you.

COREY: I don't know if I can.

CHRISTINA: You have another son, Corey. Call him.

(Corey looks at her, then crosses to the phone. He picks it up and turns to her.)

COREY: I didn't give you that scarf.

CHRISTINA: What?

COREY: I couldn't afford anything like that then. Your mother came here looking for you that day and found me lying in bed waiting for you.

CHRISTINA: And where was I?

COREY: You were late that day, remember? I told her I was just a friend, waiting for you. All she said to me was, "Please make sure my daughter gets this," and she left the box on the table. I tried to tell you then—

CHRISTINA: —I wouldn't listen.

COREY: Your father was in the car, but I think she kept your secret.

CHRISTINA: She never said . . . anything.

(Corey turns and dials the phone. A stunned Christina sits on the edge of the bed.
Music "You Are My Friend" underscores phone call.)

COREY *(On the phone)*: Hello, Darlene, this is— *(Listening)* I'm fine. I'm with a friend for a few days. Is Donny there? *(Listening)*

(Hard getting this part out) Coming to see you when I'm finished here sounds . . . fine. *(Listening)* Okay. *(Listening)* I . . . love you too. *(Pause)* Donny, it's your father. I told Darlene I would be there in a few days. Is that okay? Thank you. *(Listening)* Nothing is wrong, I just want to talk.

(Christina watches as the conversation continues, then quietly goes back to her work.)

ABOUT THE PLAY

Founded in 1998, InnerAct Productions is a theater company committed to making available to practitioners of color a greater opportunity for professional-caliber work and compensation in the theater industry. The company's objectives are to produce quality performances created by and for artists of color, and to nurture the professional craft of arts practitioners of color. InnerAct Productions' continuous mission is to produce within the central theater district of New York City, wherein the work of these artists can exist as part of the American theatrical experience. *Plenty of Time* was originally directed by Jackie Alexander and has received multiple productions, including an Off-Broadway premiere produced by Woodie King, Jr., at Castillo Theatre, and regional premieres at the Houston Ensemble Theatre, The Billie Holiday Theatre, and the North Carolina Black Repertory Company.

For further information about *Plenty of Time* contact: NC Black Rep, info@ncblackrep.org, www.ncblackrep.org.

ABOUT THE PLAYWRIGHT

Dr. John Shévin Foster (playwright/director/educator) is an August Wilson scholar who works in both academic and professional theater. Artistically, his work focuses on accurate portrayals of contemporary African American life and creates opportunities for artists of color that allow them to stretch beyond the typical roles and subjects that are afforded by non-Black theaters. His award-winning play *Flip-in: a hip-hop folk tale* debuted at the Downtown Urban Arts Festival in New York City. Other plays by Foster include *Losing the Light* and *My Name Is African American*. His company Inner-Act Productions: Quality Theatre of Color! premiered the workshop performance of the Tony Award–winning *Bridge and Tunnel* by Sarah Jones. Dr. Foster has served as President of the Black Theatre Network, and for ten years as the Education Manager and Producer at one of the world's most prestigious theater organizations, the Brooklyn Academy of Music. He has served as Artistic Director of Theater and faculty member at Shaw University and Virginia State University, and as a visiting professor, playwright mentor, and the Arts Festival Director at the Gallatin School of Individualized Study, New York University.

WASHINGTON'S BOY

Ted Lange

2007

Washington's Boy *tells the story of George Washington and his personal slave-valet, William Lee (Billy), who stood by him through the Revolutionary War and two terms as president. The play is the result of extensive research in historical records at Mount Vernon and in Pennsylvania and New Jersey.*

BILLY

Billy is at the bedside of George Washington. Washington is dying.

I don't hate you. I hate what this country you've created has become. This ain't no Camelot. You stood at the threshold of greatness and you yielded to the avarice and gluttony of others. I as a Black man have borne the scars of a land where its white citizens function from a platform of duplicity. So now you lie on your deathbed asking for my forgiveness, and you feel perfectly justified in your request . . . I have walked into danger with you, stood by you at your lowest moments, but in your precious history books will they talk of the adventures we shared? No. Why? Because I am a slave. I have lost strong friendships because they prized their freedom and had the courage to take a chance. I stand before you in your eyes not as a man, not as a compatriot, not even as a servant. I'm a cripple, drunken fellow traveler in bondage to you. A slave that watched you free yourself from the bondage of your mother country. Do you think I did not have thoughts of my own freedom when you and your friends talked of yours? Where is my justice? When you meet our Lord what will you say to Him? In your heart you know the truth of our journey together. And the eye of God can see into your soul. Your judgment day is at hand, Master George. What will you say to the Almighty Creator?

ABOUT THE PLAY

Lange Productions brought *Washington's Boy* to the National Black Theatre Festival in 2007. The play was subsequently produced by the Horseshoe Theatre at Van Nuys Community College.

Washington's Boy is copyright © 2006 by Ted Lange. For further information contact: 3langeted@gmail.com; or Entertainment Lab, angie@entlab.la, 925-575-0269.

ABOUT THE PLAYWRIGHT

Ted Lange played Isaac Washington, the affable bartender on *The Love Boat* for ten years. In the decades since, he has established a reputation as a playwright and director, creating more than two dozen theatrical works highlighting the lives of forgotten Black figures in American history. His play *The Journals of Osborne P. Anderson*, which was also presented at the National Black Theatre Festival, examines the events surrounding the death of John Brown at Harpers Ferry. Lange studied acting at San Francisco City College, where he was named Best Actor by the Black Students Association. He won a scholarship to the University of Colorado Shakespearean Festival in 1968. Lange made his Broadway debut in the musical *Hair* and was featured in the first national tour of that show. He has studied at the Royal Academy of Dramatic Art. Lange's awards include the NAACP's Renaissance Man Theatre Award for Directing, the Heroes and Legends (HAL) Lifetime Achievement Award, and the Dramalogue Award. He was the recipient of the James Cagney Directing Fellowship from the American Film Institute and the Paul Robeson Award from Oakland's Ensemble Theatre.

ASCENSION

Cynthia Grace Robinson

2009

1850. Slave quarters on the Carlisle plantation in Pike County, Alabama. Mathilda, fifties-sixties, confesses about her violent past to another enslaved woman.

MATHILDA

Lemme tell ya, when I was young, Massa used to mess wit me all da time. And dat jus' 'bout drove my Willy outta his head.

And when Willy and me ask Massa if we could git married, well, it was hard. Willy didn't wanna hafta ask Massa fer nuthin', like he was a chile, like he was da Massa's chile. He say he a man, jus' like Massa. An' he know Massa weren't gonna stop messin' wit me after da weddin'. You see, "Hafiz" mean "protector." Like my name, my REAL name, "Asimah," mean "protector." We was put on dis earth to protect each other. But weren't no protectin' from Massa. Massa messed wit me a mighty long time, and Willy, he know it was happenin', but what could he do? Massa come in our cabin, send Willy out to chop wood or collect eggs while he have his way wit me. Chile, dem was some hard times, I tell ya. So I tole Miss Amanda. I thought I could talk to 'er, thought 'cause she was always tellin' me 'bout her life an' secrets, I thought we was friends. I was a young fool. Didn't understand evil back then. So I pleaded wit her, begged her to get him to stop. She listened and jus' looked at me wit dem cold blue eyes. Den she whooped me somethin' terrible an' didn't nuthin' come outta her mouth. Miss Amanda was a fragile woman but she sho' had a way wit dat cat o' nine tails. Tore my back up somethin' wicked. Almost put me in da grave. When Willy seen my back all he could do was cry. His heart was broke. An' even though Massa let me be after dat, Willy's head was full o' poison. Men's heads is full o' poison. But I loved dat man. I loved da poison right outta him. I made him know dat I was his. Dat I was still his Asimah and he was still my Hafiz. An' I made him strong so he could walk wit his head up and den, he was a Man, a protector, 'cause I made it so.

ABOUT THE PLAY

Ascension was a Tribeca All-Access Open Stage Inaugural Event Winner. It made its world premiere in 2005 at the African American Theatre Festival, produced by Our Place Theatre Project in Boston, MA, where it earned an IRNE nomination for Best New Play. It was produced at the New York International Fringe Festival in 2008 before arriving at the National Black Theatre Festival a year later.

Ascension is copyright © 2004 by Cynthia Grace Robinson. For further information contact: info.cynthiagrobinson@gmail.com, https://www.cynthiagracerobinson.com.

ABOUT THE PLAYWRIGHT

Cynthia Grace Robinson's work centers Black women, amplifying the diversity, complexity, challenge, and beauty of their lives. Cynthia's plays include *Freedom Summer* (North Carolina Black Repertory Company); *Dancing on Eggshells* (The Billie Holiday Theatre); *Peola's Passing* (New Perspectives Theatre, Festival de Teatro Alternativo, Bogotá, Colombia); *When Night Falls* (Rising Circle Theatre Collective); *Gold Star Mother* (EstroGenius); *Ascension* (National Black Theatre Festival; FringeNYC), among many others.

Awards and honors include: Eugene O'Neill Theater Center Playwrights Conference Semi-finalist; Rising Circle Theater Collective/INKTank Residency; AUDELCO Award for Excellence in Black Theatre Nominee; and the Samuel French Off-Off Broadway Short Play Festival, among others.

Publications include *She Persisted: Monologues from Plays by Women Over 40* (Applause Theatre & Cinema Books); *The Book of Estrogenius 2012: A Celebration of Female Voices* (manhattantheatresource); *We're Not Neutral: Reset Series 2020: Collected Short Plays* (Conch Shell Press).

Cynthia is co-director of the Fire This Time New Works Lab, a member of the League of Professional Theatre Women, member of Honor Roll Playwrights, and a member of the Dramatists Guild of America, Inc.

THE LEGEND OF BUSTER NEAL

Jackie Alexander

2011

A fearless civil rights activist reappears sixty years after his supposed death to face his greatest challenge: his great-great-grandson. The Legend of Buster Neal *tells the story of four generations of African American men and the challenges each faced. A powerful drama examining legacy, friendship, and fatherhood, the play questions the true definition of manhood.*

PAPA MELVIN

Boy, you don't know the first thing about bein' broke. And as far as flippin' burgers go, I'll just share this with you. 'Fore the war, I was a mechanic; that was good work for a Black man in those days, respectable work. But after I come back from Vietnam, in my condition, the only job I could find was shinin' shoes down there at the train station. White folks treated me like a carnival monkey most days. I swear I hated that job with every fiber of my bein'; my only savin' grace I thought was the fact I couldn't see myself when I looked in the mirror. But times was tough, and I got up and took that streetcar downtown every day; shined them white men's shoes with a smile on my face from sunrise to sunset. I was so ashamed, I ain't tell Daddy 'bout the job for over a month. When he found out I was workin' down there and asked me 'bout it, I told him I was sorry; said I know I was embarassin' him doin' that sort of thing, but I couldn't find no other work. Well, he sat me down and told me he had never been more proud of me in his life. He said just being a

Black man in this country meant the deck was stacked against me, and havin' lost my eyesight in the war like I did, some might say I had good reason to expect pity from the world, and just give up my manhood. But he said my taking that job left no doubt in his mind that he hadn't raised a quitter, but a man worthy of respect. He explained to me that the type of job I got up and went to every day didn't matter; it was the fact that I got up and went that defined me as a man, because there was honor in any honest work. But there is no honor in what you're doing, son. You killin' your own people, and I won't allow it.

ABOUT THE PLAY

The Legend of Buster Neal was produced by The Billie Holiday Theatre at the National Black Theatre Festival. Other productions include ETA Creative Arts in Chicago, IL; the African Continuum Theatre Company in Washington, DC; the Booth Playhouse at the Blumenthal Performing Arts Center in Charlotte, NC; and An Appalachian Summer Festival at the Valborg Theatre in Boone, NC.

For further information about *The Legend of Buster Neal* contact: www.jackiealexanderproductions.com; or NC Black Rep, info@ncblackrep.org, www.ncblackrep.org.

ABOUT THE PLAYWRIGHT

As a producer, Jackie has brought fifteen world premieres to the stage. The Obie- and AUDELCO Award–winning Billie Holiday Theatre in New York devoted its entire 2010–2011 season to Jackie's work, commissioning him to write three new plays and making him the only playwright in the storied history of the theater to receive that honor. The Black Theatre Network honored Jackie with its 2018 Presidential Pathfinder Award, which is presented to an artist or an institution that illuminates a path to innovations and new concepts in Black theater. In February 2019, Jackie was honored by North Carolina Governor Roy Cooper for his theatrical contributions to the state. At the forty-ninth annual AUDELCO Awards in November 2021, Jackie was honored for Outstanding Achievement in Black Theatre.

THE BALLAD OF EMMETT TILL

Ifa Bayeza

2013

A month after his fourteenth birthday, Emmett Till, "Bobo," a confident Chicago youth, a boy on the threshold of manhood, embarks on a summer trip to Mississippi. His saga changes the course of a nation . . . but what of his journey?

BOBO

*Emmett Till, "Bobo," turns. He is perhaps by himself, looking in
the bathroom mirror, or on the street corner with his buddies.*

New suit . . . traveling shoes
The rumble of the El
The sounds of the city
Awakening
Call me Bo! Bub-Bobo!
Emmett Louis Till, fir-first class!
The birds announce my arrival
Thou didst make me
Show me my rival!
Brim upturned
Blond Panama straw
With a green exotic feather
Still say caw
New pants

Never been worn
White buck shoes!
Not a scuff on 'em

New shoes! Man!
White bucks! D__m!
Uncle Mose say, "Uh uh Mississippi?
This is someone you should know.
This my nephew, Buh-BoBo!"

"So, so, so," she say.
"So how long you gonna be around?"

Uh cuh-cuh—Uh Uh ck-cuh-uh ck-cuh cuh, uh ck-ck uh ck
    cuh cuh-cuh—((o))
A couple of weeks . . .
Okay, okay, Oh oh oh KAY!
So you're short and you stutter.
Duh-deal with it or let it get in your way.

"Duh-Don't look." Mah-Mama duh-don't know. Okay, 1 prom-
ise, I won't look . . . Look, my eyes are closed. "Duh-Don't look."
Mah-Mama duh-don't know. I'm from Chicago! Girl watchin'—
in the summuh? ((o)))! Wear a brother out! You die and go to
heaven every day! Ow! A national pastime—the girls bloom
like flowuhs inna summuhtime! Man! You got Tulips. Roses.
Daffodils. Bluebells. Buttercups. Venus fly traps! . . . I step out.
Hair pressed flat, pantsline pat. A ripple and a sheen, with a dip
that's mean! . . . I met this guh-guh-girl, last May. Of of of all
play-places, Argo! Church went up to a carnival . . . Heluise,
Heluise Woods. Hello, hello, hello Hellooooo Heluise! Okay,
okay, okay, I bought a ticket at the carnival to ride on the thing.
We was standing in line, getting on two by two, Noah's ark. I'm
movin' right along beside her, counting to make sure we end
up together in the same car. And! "CURTIS, BABY!" I mean
Curtis?! Jumps the line. I-I-I push past him, just make it. POW!
And I'm sittin' right next to her! Our own kah, an aerial car-
riage. Chains rattle the seat. Then then then it started up. Up up

we went, up up we goin'. She draws close. One hand round my, round my girl and you're praying yes, yes, yes and it stops at the very top. The stars out, carnival lights below, the kah swinging in the breeze. Wooo-Weeee! Just her and me—and—*Mama*—w-wants to go on a road trip. I tell you, I had to write the girl a letter. "Dear Heluise. I am not coming out in Argo Saturday because my mama—

"Want(s) me to go tuh tuh—to Detroit . . . I liked when I was out there and we went out to that carnival. Cutest little thing. Beautiful brown skin. Like a piece uh milk chocolate. Long pretty hair."

(He improvises a song, debonaire in his mind, singing to Heluise.)

> Met a little girl named Heluise,
> Wrote her a letter to be my squeeze,
> Sorry baby, I can't come to town,
> But I sure wanna see you girl, next time I'm around,
>
> Remember M, remember E,
> Put 'em both together so you'll remember me.
> You're the last thing I see,
> Hey, pretty baby, remember me,
>
> E-M-M and a E-T-T,
> Hey, pretty baby, remember me,
> Emmett Louis Till from Chicago,
> Buh-buh-but you can call me Buh-Buh-Buh-Bobo . . .

Wanna know the truth? We finished the ride, I stood up there. All he could say was—Bye. Now how-how-how not-not cool could you be? Haven't heard back from her yet. Only been three months. But I will. Put two carnival tickets in the envelope. Labor Day weekend. Church picnic. You know a cat's got nine lives.

ABOUT THE PLAY

The Ballad of Emmett Till received a Eugene O'Neill Theater Center National Playwrights Conference fellowship and premiered at the Goodman Theatre in Chicago in 2008, winning the Mystery Writers of America Edgar Award for Best Play. *The Ballad* made its West Coast premiere at the Fountain Theatre in Los Angeles in 2010, garnering six Ovation Awards, including Best Production; four Drama Desk Critics' Circle Awards, including Best Production; and the Backstage Garland Award for Best Playwriting. Acclaimed productions followed, including Ion Theatre, where it earned top honors at the San Diego Theatre Critics Circle's Craig Noel Award, including Outstanding Dramatic Production.

For further information about *The Balled of Emmett Till* contact: Susan Gurman, Gurman Literary Agency LLC, www.gurmanagency.com, 212-749-4618.

ABOUT THE PLAYWRIGHT

Ifa Bayeza is an award-winning theater artist, novelist, and scholar. Her works, through both creative nonfiction and fictional lenses, explore pivotal intersections of race. The Till Trilogy (*The Ballad of Emmett Till, Benevolence,* and *That Summer in Sumner*) interprets the epic civil rights saga of Emmett Till. Her novel *Some Sing, Some Cry,* co-authored with her sister Ntozake Shange, chronicles two hundred years of African American music through seven generations of women. Her drama *String Theory,* in a quartet of voices, relives the voyage of the slave ship *Amistad,* and the tragicomedy *Welcome to Wandaland* portrays, through a child's magical realism, the experience of desegregation in St. Louis post–*Brown v. Board of Education.* Commissioned by the National Trust for Historic Preservation in 2018, she is collaborating with eleven local Black writers to reconstruct the historic narrative of Shadows-on-the-Teche, a former sugarcane plantation in New Iberia, Louisiana. A graduate of Harvard University, Bayeza holds an MFA from the University of Massachusetts Amherst. She is a 2022 MacDowell Fellow and the inaugural Humanist-in-Residence at the National Endowment for the Humanities.

HOW I FEEL

Dennis A. Allen II

2015

Across seven monologues written by seven Black playwrights, Hands Up *depicts the realities of Black America from the perspective of varying genders, sexual orientations, skin tones, and socioeconomic backgrounds.*

In this monologue, a Black male attempts to express how it feels to live as a Black man in America and be relatively conscious.

HANDS UP!

Actor enters. He takes a moment to "take in" the audience.

I'd like to start with a showing of solidarity. If you would please raise your arms straight up in the air. Everyone. Everybody please. Hold them up just like this. Keep them up. Now we're going to do a call and response. I'm going to say, "Hands up," and you respond with, "Don't shoot!" So when I say, "Hands up!" you all say, "Don't shoot!"

Hands up. Hands up. Hands up! Hands up. Hands up! Hands up!

I'd like you ALL to keep your hands up with me. Some of you won't, but try. I'm asking you to be uncomfortable with me for a moment, for this moment in time let's attempt to experience the same experience together.

A few days into the protests in Ferguson, I was at my fiancée's apartment, lying on her bed, watching the news coverage and following the Twitter updates. We both had been following the events closely for the past few days on almost a 24/7 vigilance and the room was filled to the ceiling with our angst and anger, fear, and depression; so we decided it was time to take a break. Turn off the television and go offline. We sat silently for a second, and then she turned to me and said, "Baby, we've never talked about how to handle if we're out together and the police harass you. Like what do you think I should do?"

(A moment.)

I'm looking at a woman I love, a woman for whom, as cliché as it sounds, I would literally give my life for. I look at her and I see and feel her fear and it is a fear that I am all too familiar with. It is a fear that I was introduced to at the very moment of my conception; surrounded by it for nine months and nurtured and loved unconditionally by it my entire life. This fear is all too familiar.

My mother has shared with me on a couple of occasions that when she was pregnant with me she would find herself praying that I wouldn't be a boy. Each time she admits this she cries tears heavy with the burden of guilt that only a mother can fully comprehend. She cries tears filled with a helplessness and anger that only someone born into a world that doesn't value Black life can truly know. She said, "I prayed that you wouldn't be a boy because I knew that from the time you were born, you'd be born with a bull's-eye on your back." This fear is all too familiar.

So when I look at my girlfriend and she asks what's the best strategy to keep me safe from police, from keeping them from violating my rights; keep them from injuring and possibly killing another unarmed citizen—because that's what I would be. I don't carry any weapons, never broke any jail-worthy laws, but I am obviously Black and THAT has been reason enough to kill me for hundreds of years now.

I'm not interested in giving you a history lesson, there are scholars out there way more knowledgeable than I am; don't want to talk politics or sociology; economics or psychology; again there are social justice professionals, activists, and doctors that have given lecture after lecture, have written book after book, blog after blog—tons of information out there that you can help you contextualize this world we live in. Google it. I want to share how I feel.

I think about Mike Brown. I think about him being shot to death and then left in the street for four point five hours, uncovered for the entire neighborhood to see. I think about the countless other names—the ones we know and the ones undocumented—beaten, tased, violated, shot, murdered at the hands of our so-called servers and protectors. I think about my fiancée and my mother worried night after night—hoping and praying that when I go out I come home because they know it's open season out there and I'm the prey. Love and Worry seem to always go hand in hand but it is a very specific "worry," the fear that comes with knowing that you're not protected by those that are hired to protect you—not only that but they are targeting you and it is illegal to protect yourself against those that are hired to protect you.

So how I feel.

Fuck you, is how I feel. I know that's not a very sophisticated or in-depth response but, Fuck you. I'll write something eloquent for another play. I wanted to write some inspirational, soul shaking, "I done seen the mountaintop," type monologue. Something that could heal the four hundred years of untreated trauma; cure us from the disease of white supremacy; humanize us in a way that we've never been humanized before. But, Fuck you, is all I could come up with.

Your shoulders are probably burning a bit, feeling fatigued. Keep them up for me.

There are some people, of all races, colors, and creeds, that believe that it is MY responsibility through "proper living" to combat white supremacist thinking. Some that use the terms, "post-racial" and "color-blind" as if they were real things. Since we're on this magical mystical fantasy ride let's imagine together. Imagine a world where every single Black or brown American only wore their Sunday best; all prayed to a Christian God; never said a cuss word; didn't do any drugs—not even prescription; and broke no laws. Never engaged in any violence whatsoever, unless of course they were being good patriots and killing Black and Brown people in some other country. All worked and never got on public assistance, no matter what the state of the job market or economy was; every Black person was married if they had children and were one hundred percent faithfully monogamous. All graduated high school regardless of the poor school funding and poor living conditions and at the very least had a bachelor's degree and was never in debt. Imagine if Black people were morally, spiritually, and financially better than any and every white person that has ever walked the earth. Perfect. Better than any human being has ever been.

Then and only then could we rid our society of institutionalized racism, prejudice, and bigotry in America. Then and only then will white people see us as valuable human beings. Then and only then will we be able to see ourselves as valuable human beings. Imagine this world. What if I told you, if you could just keep your hands up high we could create this utopia together. But you can never drop your hands. Hands up. For the sake of Black people here in America and abroad, keep your hands up!

No one can do it. No human can keep his or her hands up forever and this bullshit fantasy isn't the answer either. I am human. My life is valuable and I shouldn't have to keep my hands held high to prove it, and time and time again keeping our hands held high hasn't gotten us treated like human beings should be treated. So how do I feel? Fuck you is how I feel.

I will not allow you to take away my humanity. Every time you tell me not to be angry. That I'm "too aggressive"; that I shouldn't be out at night; that I shouldn't wear a hoodie and that I need to pull up my pants and when I comply to your orders and reach for my wallet you kill me anyway. When I drop to the ground and allow you to handcuff me you shoot me anyway. When you put me in the back of your paddy wagon you break my neck anyway! Fuck You. Fuck you for coming into our neighborhoods telling us that our "no snitching" culture is stopping justice from being done, stopping you from keeping us safe, but then turn around and subscribe to the exact same No Snitching policy within the precinct.

Mike Brown was shot six times and he had NO WEAPON. His brains were blown out in broad daylight. His blood all over the concrete. And was left there in the street uncovered for over four fucking hours. There's not language strong enough to convey what the fuck I feel about that. Fuck you for not feeling what I feel. Fuck you for shutting down because I'm using "strong" language. I'm not safe, my father's not safe, my brothers and sisters, my fiancée; my mother is not safe because none of you value our lives. Police don't. Whites don't. Blacks don't. But I will not allow you to take away my rights, my humanity.

You indiscriminately killing me is a display of your power. Me giving zero fucks if you kill me is an exercise of mine.

Hands up! Hands up. Hands up. Hands up. Hands up. Hands up!

(A moment. Actor looks at the audience. He raises one arm in the air and balls up his fist.)

ABOUT THE PLAY

In 2015, The New Black Fest commissioned a script in response to the police killing of Michael Brown, an unarmed Black teenager from Ferguson, MO. The themes and stories the play (written by seven Black playwrights) tells still ring true today. In late 2019, Spelman College students reimagined the original monologues as a full ensemble performance, and it was produced in the Alliance Theatre's 2020–2021 season, under the co-direction of Keith Arthur Bolden and Alexis Woodard.

How I Feel, part of the collection Hands Up: 7 Playwrights, 7 Testaments is copyright © 2016 by Dennis A. Allen II, and is published by Concord Theatricals. For further information contact: Concord Theatricals: info@concordtheatricals.com, www.concord-theatricals.com.

ABOUT THE PLAYWRIGHT

Dennis A. Allen II's play The Mud Is Thicker in Mississippi won the thirty-fifth annual Samuel French Off-Off Broadway Festival. His play When We Wake Up Dead is published by Samuel French (Concord Theatricals). He is the recipient of Atlantic Theater Company's Launch Commission and National Black Theatre's I Am Soul Playwrights Residency. Allen is an alumnus of the Djerassi Resident Artist Program, and he has developed and produced plays with The New Black Fest, The Lark Play Development Center, the Classical Theatre of Harlem, the Fire This Time Festival, New York Madness, Jack, 48 Hours in Harlem, and the National Black Theatre of Harlem.

As an actor, Dennis helped to develop and performed in Reid Farrington's Tyson vs. Ali and the world premiere of Kate Benson's A Beautiful Day in November on the Banks of the Greatest of the Great Lakes. Directing credits include Theater Masters' Take Ten, Iowa New Play Festival, Bring a Weasel Festival at The Public, Playwrights Horizons, Poetic Theater's The Taproot Festival and Conscious Language. He is an associate professor at LaGuardia Community College, Montclair State University, and Brooklyn College. Dennis received his MFA from Brooklyn College.

SWEET TEA: BLACK GAY MEN OF THE SOUTH TELL THEIR TALES

Dr. E. Patrick Johnson

2015

Giving voice to a population rarely acknowledged, Sweet Tea *collects more than sixty life stories from Black, gay men who were born, raised, and continue to live in the South. Playwright Dr. E. Patrick Johnson challenges stereotypes of the South as "backward" or "repressive" and offers a window into the ways Black, gay men negotiate their identities, build community, maintain friendship networks, and find sexual and life partners—often in spaces and activities that appear to be antigay. Ultimately,* Sweet Tea *validates the lives of these Black, gay men and reinforces the role of storytelling in both African American and southern cultures.*

In this monologue, Stephen represents one of the voices of this often-unrecognized community. Here he speaks from the heart about his identity and becoming a father.

STEPHEN

Stephen enters, singing "Sometimes I Feel Like a Motherless Child" in a somber tone. During the last line of the song, he sits on the floor center stage, his knees pulled to his chest with his arms wrapped around them.

> Sometimes I feel like a motherless child
> Sometimes I feel like a motherless child
> Sometimes I feel like a motherless child
> A long way from home

(Projection: "Stephen—Tuscaloosa, Alabama.")

(To himself) I was just wired differently, just was wired differently. And, I felt that I was being punished for being this way. And so from every angle, I was being told, "You've got it wrong." *(To audience)* I vividly remember my mom saying, "Don't you grow up to be no faggot." I vividly remember hearing that. I was

really, really effeminate, and would get beat up a lot because of that. You're getting beat up at school 'cause you're a faggot, you're a little girl, you're a little sissy. And my mom was like, "Everybody is telling you this is wrong." And I struggled and I really wanted to kill myself. I wanted to die rather than continue to displease the God that I loved so much. Since I can't stop these feelings that I've been told are wrong, I would really prefer to die and be able to say, "I'm going to Heaven," than continue to live this way and go to Hell because of this. *(Beat)* And, it got to the point to where I made the realization that I believe in the God who is all-knowing. I believe in a God that doesn't make mistakes. I believe in a God that has created me. I believe that I'm not a mistake. I believe that this is the way that I was created. *(Beat)* I didn't choose it. *(Beat)* Who would choose it? *(Beat)* It used to frustrate me so much being in the closet early on, and hear people say, "It's a choice. It's a lifestyle change." *(Angrily)* It's like you really don't understand my struggle. I've tried that. I've tried that. I read up on ex-gay therapies. I have tried to be what you thought Stephen should be, and I'm exhausted. *(Beat)* I was headed for destruction. I was gonna have to come to terms with this 'cause it was something that I was ignoring for a long time, ignoring this fight within myself, that was killing me. And it got to the point to where it was like, "No. No. From now on, what I believe is gonna be something that I find to be true for me and who Stephen is, not something that I've been fed since I was smaller."

(Beat.)

It is so easy to be loved for something that you're not, rather than to be hated for something that you are. You know what I mean? It's so easy.

(Beat.)

I guess the first time when I honestly stopped to think about it I was about seventeen years old and had a girlfriend. I really wasn't interested in a physical anything with her. I really wasn't.

Sex was always an issue until finally, I thought, "Well, for me to prove myself as a man, we need to have sex." And it was the first time I had sex. I fathered my son. And it's like, although he is something that motivates me, someone, when I get exhausted, or when I really start to be like, "What am I working towards," he motivates me past those moments. But it's one of the earliest moments where I was like, "You came to this point being something that you're not."

(Beat.)

Right before I got my first professional job doing theater in college, I had to leave for the summer. So, the day before I had to leave, I spent all day with my four-year-old son, Ledarius, and I explained to him who I was. *(Rising to one knee and speaking to his son)* "The same way that your mom loves her husband, I feel the same way about other men. I don't know if you understand this or not. More than likely, you'll probably be angry because you don't completely understand it, but come to me with that anger. Let's talk about it."

(Long pause. Stephen rises to his feet.)

It was surreal. It was like, *(Beat)* here I am *(Beat)* coming out to my son, the only person in my family that I've truly *(Beat)* truly *(Beat)* come out to.

(After a beat, Stephen sings the last line of "Sometimes I Feel Like a Motherless Child":)

A long way from home

ABOUT THE PLAY

The staged reading of *Pouring Tea: Black Gay Men of the South Tell Their Tales* is based on Johnson's book *Sweet Tea*. In 2009, Johnson adapted the staged reading into a full-length stage play, *Sweet Tea —The Play*, which premiered in Chicago and toured throughout the country. *Sweet Tea* won a Black Theatre Alliance Award for Best Solo Performance. In 2011, the show ran at Signature Theatre in Arlington, VA, and at the Durham Arts Council in 2014. In 2010, Dr. Johnson was awarded the Leslie Irene Coger Award for Distinguished Performance by the National Communication Association; the Randy Majors Memorial Award for outstanding contributions to LGBT scholarship; and he was inducted into the Chicago LGBT Hall of Fame. In 2014 Johnson received the Otto René Castillo Award for Political Theatre.

Since 1993, the International Colloquium (IC) has been an integral component of the National Black Theatre Festival (NBTF). A collaborative effort between Winston-Salem State University, the Black Theatre Network (BTN), and the NBTF, the IC is coordinated by Dr. Olasope Oyediji Oyelaran, who states that the IC's objectives are "to cultivate and enhance the artistic consciousness and sensibilities of the public and audience to and through Black theater." In 2015 *Sweet Tea* was presented at the NBTF as an example of the scholar/artist model that the IC celebrates.

For further information about *Sweet Tea* contact: NC Black Rep, info@ncblackrep.org, www.ncblackrep.org.

ABOUT THE PLAYWRIGHT

Dr. E. Patrick Johnson is Dean of the School of Communication and the Annenberg University Professor at Northwestern University. He is a 2020 inductee into the American Academy of Arts and Sciences. Johnson is a prolific performer/scholar, and an inspiring teacher, whose research and artistry has greatly impacted African American studies, performance studies, and gender and sexuality studies. He is the author of *Appropriating Blackness: Performance and the Politics of Authenticity* (2003); *Sweet Tea: Black Gay Men of the South—An Oral History* (2008); *Black. Queer. Southern. Women. An Oral History* (2018); and *Honeypot: Black Southern Women Who Love Women* (2019); in addition to several edited and co-edited collections, essays, and plays.

BREATHE

Javon Johnson

2017

Andre, a Black teenager, killed a boy for taking his bike, and he has been sentenced to life in prison. "In three minutes my life changed forever." In this poetic monologue, he asks Case, a white adolescent murderer, unanswerable questions.

ANDRE

What is it about me, Case? My skin tone blankets my soul like the deceased. My heart beats like feet pounding concrete. Steam rises from my mind as my tears draw heat. I'm four hundred years old, you're seventeen. I'm one billion and one souls lost in a sea of dreams. Three of those Black souls I know got dropped by the cops unarmed. I don't know one of your kind who got popped by the cop's nine. Somebody please tell me what's going on. What is it about me that can't be free? My speech, my flav, my creep? My slang, my thang, my beat? What is it about my talk, my style, my walk? Why should I be hung because I'm so hung and so deep? I don't stink do I? Is it my scent that makes you flee? Perhaps it is the shit that I've been through that makes you mistreat me. Perhaps channel five lies about me on TV. Perhaps America don't want me to be me.

ABOUT THE PLAY

Breathe was developed at The Lark Play Development Center in 2006 with director Rajendra Ramoon Maharaj and dramaturg Sybil Robert. It had its world premiere at the Greenway Court Theatre in Los Angeles in 2016 under the direction of Levy Lee Simon.

For further information about *Breathe* contact: NC Black Rep, info@ncblackrep.org, www.ncblackrep.org.

ABOUT THE PLAYWRIGHT

Javon Johnson is a native of Anderson, SC, and a founding ensemble member/resident playwright of Congo Square Theatre in Chicago. His awards include the 2009 Black Theater Alliance Award for Best Play, the 2004 Lorraine Hansberry Award for Best Play, the 2003 New Professional Theatre Playwriting Award, and numerous others. As a writer, his work has been produced at The Lark, Queens Theater in the Park, and HERE Arts Center in New York; Grahamstown Festival in South Africa; Victory Gardens, Congo Square, and ETA Theatre in Chicago; as well as Studio Theater, Kuntu Rep, and many more. His extensive credits as an actor, aside from stage work, include stints on the Hallmark Channel, work for Tyler Perry Studios, BET, STARZ, the CW, and TBS. He is a member of the Dramatists Guild, SAG-AFTRA, and AEA. Javon earned his undergraduate degree at South Carolina State College and his MFA from the University of Pittsburgh.

ANNE AND EMMETT

Janet Langhart Cohen

2019

An imaginary conversation between Anne Frank and Emmett Till, this one-act play has been widely produced in educational and regional theater, opening space for dialogue and empathy. Frank is the thirteen-year-old Jewish girl whose diary provided a gripping perspective of the Holocaust. Till is the fourteen-year-old African American boy whose brutal murder in Mississippi sparked the modern American civil rights movement. The beyond-the-grave encounter draws the startling similarities between the two youths' harrowing experiences at the hands of societies that could not protect them.

EMMETT

Emmett whistles.

When I whistled at her, she just pointed a finger at me. My cousins scattered and ran for the car. They knew we were in trouble. They were so scared they didn't say a word all the way home. None of us could sleep that night. The next day, nothing happened, so we thought everything was okay. But a couple of nights later, some men come looking for me at my Uncle Mose's place. Took me to an old barn. Said they going to teach me a lesson.

Some lesson . . . Took an ax to me . . . gouged out one of my eyes, blinded me in the other . . . Mama!!

My eye sockets feel like red-hot coals have been poured into them. Everything spinning around in my head, I can't breathe . . . The pain so great I think my whole body's on fire. I can't see them . . .

Can't tell where they were going to hit me again. Even

though I'm scared and hurtin,' I didn't back down. I keep swinging my arms trying to fight back. Just makes them madder.

All the time I know I'm dying. Things flashing through my mind. No more pranks, playing baseball, jumping in swimming holes. No more doo-woppin' and singing with my cousins. No more sweet hugs from Mama . . . Finally, they tie a big cotton-gin fan around me, shoot me in the head, and throw me in the Tallahatchie. Everything starts going blank . . . The last thing I could hear was them laughing, and my body splashing in the water . . .

Funny, all the time they were beatin' and cuttin' me up, scared as I was, I kept hoping that no one would ever find my body. All I could think of was what would happen to my mama if she ever saw what they had done to me. I could bear the dying easier than the thought of her crying . . .

ABOUT THE PLAY

Anne and Emmett has had educational productions around the world, including the United States Supreme Court. The play has been produced in theaters such as St. Louis Black Rep; Crossroads Theater in New Brunswick, NJ; the Atlas Theater in Washington, DC; the African-American Performing Arts Community Theatre in Miami, FL; the Haymarket Theater in Lincoln, NB; Martha's Vineyard Theater, and in numerous educational institutions, including the Duke Ellington School of the Arts in Washington, DC, and the Baltimore School for the Arts, among many others.

For further information about *Anne and Emmett* contact: NC Black Rep, info@ncblackrep.org, www.ncblackrep.org.

ABOUT THE PLAYWRIGHT

Janet Langhart Cohen is a native of Indianapolis, where she grew up in a segregated housing project. In the 1960s she was an Ebony Fashion Fair model who became the first Black woman in America to host a nationally syndicated show, *Good Morning*. She has worked for both ABC and NBC, Entertainment Tonight, BED, the Armed Forces Network, as well as in print journalism for the *Boston Herald*. Over the course of her twenty-five years in broadcast journalism, she interviewed some of the most influential newsmakers in the world, including presidents Bill Clinton and Jimmy Carter, Margaret Thatcher, Rosa Parks, Senator Ted Kennedy, Oprah Winfrey, and Barbara Walters, to name a few. Her life's work is to raise awareness around issues of race and reconciliation and to spur thoughtful conversation that can lead to a new national dialogue about race and equality in America. In 2004 she wrote her memoir, *From Rage to Reason: My Life in Two Americas,* and in 2007 she and her husband (former defense secretary William Cohen) co-wrote *Love in Black and White.*

Larry Leon Hamlin and Cicely Tyson, 1989.

August Wilson, Dr. Maya Angelou and Larry Leon Hamlin, 1989.

All photos courtesy of the North Carolina Black Repertory Company Archive.

Herman LeVern Jones; Larry Leon Hamlin; Lou Gossett, Jr.; Micki Grant; Antonio Fargas and Esther Rolle, 1989.

Dr. Maya Angelou, Oprah Winfrey and Larry Leon Hamlin, 1989.

Mable Robinson, Dr Maya Angelou and Roscoe Lee Browne, 1989.

Ossie Davis and Ruby Dee, 1992.

*Starletta DuPois and
Sherman Hemsley,
2005. Photo:
Bruce Chapman.*

Larry Leon Hamlin, Amiri Baraka and Festival guest, 1997. Photo: Michael Cunningham.

Malcolm-Jamal Warner (left), 2005. Woodie King, Jr. (right), 2005. Photos: Michael Cunningham.

Larry Leon Hamlin, 2005. Photo: Michael Cunningham.

Sylvia Sprinkle-Hamlin, 2011.
Photo: Bruce Chapman.

Hal Williams (right), 2013.
Photo: Bruce Chapman.

Closing Night Processional, 2017. Photo: Bruce Chapman.

Chester Gregory, Art Evans, André De Shields, Michael Colyar and Keith David, 2019. Photo: Bruce Chapman.

Stephen Byrd, Jasmine Guy, Alia Jones-Harvey and Jackie Alexander, 2019.

Jackie Alexander, 2019.

(From left to right) Adarian Sneed, Asha Duniani, DeWitt Fleming, Jr. and L. G. Williams, Jelly's Last Jam, *2019.*

PART 2
FULL-LENGTH PLAYS

MAID'S DOOR

Cheryl L. Davis

2015 and 2017

PRODUCTION HISTORY

Maid's Door was presented at the 2015 and 2017 National Black Theatre Festival. The director was Jackie Alexander; the set design was by Patrice Davidson, the costume design was by Helen L. Collen (2015) and Helen L. Collen and Frenchie LaVern (2017), the lighting design was by Avan (2015) and Arthur Reese (2017); the stage manager was Normal Small (2015) and Taylor Murrell (2017). The Producing Company was the Billie Holiday Theatre (2015) and the North Carolina Black Repertory Company (2017). The casts were:

2015

IDA	Sandra Mills Scott
BETTY	Melissa Joyner
SARA/YOUNG BETTY	Joan Anderson
CASE	Nathan James
ANGELA/ADELA/MRS. LEWIS	Madeleine Lodge
DR. PATEL	Kimberlee Monroe

2017

IDA	Sandra Mills Scott
BETTY	Melissa Joyner
SARA/YOUNG BETTY	Nikyla Boxley
CASE	Jacobi Howard
ANGELA/ADELA/MRS. LEWIS	Rachel Buckland
DR. PATEL	Anja Lee

CHARACTERS

IDA FARRELL—Elderly African American woman. Solid, old-fashioned. The type who can manage her home and her community without breaking a sweat.

BETTY FARRELL MCKAY—Ida's daughter, early to mid-forties. A lawyer; type-A personality.

CASE MCKAY—Betty's husband. More easygoing than his wife.

SARAH MCKAY—Ida's granddaughter, early teens. Energetic and curious.

MRS. LEWIS—White, twenties. Ida's former employer. Nervous, tries to appear controlled.

ADELA—White, twenties. A recent immigrant, works as a cleaning lady for Betty's family.

ANGELA—White, twenties. A graphic designer.

DR. PATEL—South Asian, male, age indeterminate. Ida's doctor.

ACT ONE

1

An apartment kitchen. A door is seen in the back.

From the side, Mrs. Lewis, a young white woman dressed in fifties-style clothes, enters. She is followed by Ida, a middle-aged African American woman. Ida is dressed in an old-fashioned coat and hat and carries a handbag.

MRS. LEWIS: And this is the kitchen.

IDA: It's very nice, Ma'am.

MRS. LEWIS: This is the newest model refrigerator. We try to stay up to date with our appliances. Cassie did tell you that, didn't she?

IDA: Yes, Ma'am, she did.

MRS. LEWIS: And see right here, we have one of those new dishwashing machines. Have you ever used one of those before?

IDA: I haven't, but I'm certainly willing to try.

MRS. LEWIS: Before you do, you make sure and read the directions carefully and go through them with me first. It took me long enough to get Bob—Mr. Lewis—to buy it, I don't want it getting broken right off.

IDA: Yes, Ma'am.

MRS. LEWIS: Please don't "yes" me unless you mean it. Cassie used to do that and it drove me up a tree.

IDA: I'll only "yes" you when I mean it, Ma'am.

MRS. LEWIS: Good, good. *(Pause)* I didn't mean to snap. I've had a rough morning. Angela would *not* let me put her down for a minute, and Joseph kept pulling on me, "Mommy, look at this, Mommy, watch me do that."

IDA: I understand just how you feel, Ma'am. Would you like a cup of tea?

MRS. LEWIS: I'd love one. But we haven't finished discussing, I mean, I haven't actually . . .

IDA: Wouldn't you like a cup of tea while we keep on discussing things?

MRS. LEWIS: Yes, I suppose. *(She sits)* The kettle's on the stove, the tea is in that ceramic jug over there. Careful with it please!

IDA: I'll be careful, Ma'am.

MRS. LEWIS: Bob—Mr. Lewis—brought that back all the way from Amsterdam. That's in Europe, you know.

IDA: I've heard tell, Ma'am. My brother was over there in the war.

MRS. LEWIS: The cups are up on that second shelf. Bob went over for business. His law firm has an international practice. He just made partner this year.

IDA: You must be very proud, Ma'am.

(Ida reaches up for the cup.)

MRS. LEWIS: We are, thank you. Oh, good, you're tall enough to reach it. We can get rid of that stepstool that Cassie had cluttering up the kitchen.

(Ida prepares the tea throughout the following.)

Do you have children of your own?

IDA: Yes, Ma'am. Three girls.

MRS. LEWIS: I don't know how you handle it. I need another pair of hands just for my two. But that's why you're here, isn't it?

IDA: Yes, Ma'am.

MRS. LEWIS: So since you have children of your own . . .

IDA: I won't be sleeping in, that's right, Ma'am.

MRS. LEWIS: Hmmmm.

IDA: I'll make sure and get here early enough to make breakfast and get little—Joseph?—off to school, though.

MRS. LEWIS: And if we need you at night?

IDA: Some nights, if you let me know in enough time, I'll fix it so I can stay late.

(Ida serves the tea and remains standing.)

MRS. LEWIS: Oh, thank you. *(Sipping gratefully)* You have no idea how much I need this.

(She sips another few moments, ignoring the standing Ida.)

(When she notices her) Please, have a seat.

IDA: Thank you, Ma'am.

(Ida sits, still in her coat and hat.)

MRS. LEWIS: Would you like anything? A glass of water, a cup of tea?

IDA: No, thank you, Ma'am.

MRS. LEWIS: Fine, fine. *(Pulls out a list)* I think we discussed most of these points. Salary, time off . . . you said you have daughters, didn't you?

IDA: Yes, Ma'am.

MRS. LEWIS: Would you like to have any of them help you out? We wouldn't pay her the same as you, of course, but . . .

IDA: No thank you, Ma'am. All my girls are in school.

MRS. LEWIS: Oh. If you think that's best . . . all right. If you change your mind . . .

IDA: I'll let you know, Ma'am.

MRS. LEWIS: Good, good. *(Pause)* I'm sure Cassie told you about me, about our family. *(Smiling)* And since you came here anyway, I'm hoping what she told you was good.

IDA: Nothing but good, Ma'am.

MRS. LEWIS: Has she gone yet?

IDA: Just last Friday. They finally finished packing up the apartment and set out for Virginia.

MRS. LEWIS: We'll all miss her.

IDA: We'll miss her too.

MRS. LEWIS: Joseph just wailed when I told him she wasn't coming back. *(Pause)* Not that he's a "wailer," mind you. No more than any other little boy.

IDA: I'm sure he isn't, Ma'am.

MRS. LEWIS: He's not. Well, Ida. You've seen the apartment, you've met me and the children. Do you think you might like to work here?

IDA: I don't think I've seen all the apartment yet, Ma'am. Is that a laundry room back there? *(Pointing to the door)*

MRS. LEWIS: Oh, no. That's your door.

IDA: I beg your pardon, Ma'am?

MRS. LEWIS: If you decide to work here, I mean. Surely you must have used . . . I mean, did you come in and out through the front door in the other places you've worked?

IDA: Yes, Ma'am. There's only been the one door in the other apartments.

MRS. LEWIS: Oh, well, that explains it. I hope that won't be a problem. Cassie never had a problem with it.

(Pause.)

IDA: No Ma'am, it won't be a problem.

MRS. LEWIS: I'm so glad.

(She stands and puts out her hand.)

Welcome to our home, and our family, Ida. I hope you'll enjoy it here.

IDA *(Shaking her hand)*: Thank you, Ma'am. I'm sure I will.

MRS. LEWIS: Why don't you take off your coat and hat and get started. *(Checking her watch)* You can get lunch together while I get Angela up from her nap. You'll find some cold cuts in the refrigerator, and over lunch, we can discuss the menu for the rest of the week.

IDA: Yes, Ma'am.

(Mrs. Lewis exits. Ida stands looking at the door. After some time passes:)

SARAH *(Offstage)*: Gramma? Gramma?

(Sarah enters from the side. She is an early teenaged—or tweenaged—African American girl, dressed in contemporary clothing.)

What are you doing in the kitchen?

IDA: Just looking around.

SARAH: Well come look around the other rooms, they're much nicer. Mama says we have to remodel in here anyway, rip out this old junk, install all new appliances.

IDA: Get everything nice and "up to date."

SARAH: This place so totally rocks. Have you ever seen an apartment like this?

IDA: I've seen a few.

SARAH: It'll cost like mad bucks to remodel it, but Mama says now that she's a partner at this new firm, we can splash out a little more.

IDA: That's wonderful, baby.

SARAH *(Looking at the door)*: And the kitchen even has a back door! Hey, that could be like my door, and me and my friends could come in and go out whenever.

IDA: Sarah, don't you ever use that door.

SARAH: But Gramma, I could decorate it, and make it like my own entrance. None of my friends have their own door.

IDA: Did you hear me? I don't want you using that door!

SARAH: It's just a door! Jeez!

IDA *(Soothing)*: I don't see why you'd worry about some old door when you have a brand-new room to fix up. Did you pick a color yet?

SARAH (*Happy again*): I'm between the yellow with orange accents or the blue with purple accents. Because yellow means energy, but blue's so pretty, and they say it's calming?

(*Betty, a mature African American woman, enters.*)

BETTY: *Here* you are.
SARAH: I found Gramma.
BETTY: I see. Mama, are you okay?
IDA: Why do you keep on asking me that?
BETTY: Just checking, you know me. Sarah, why don't you go help figure out how your room will be laid out.
SARAH (*While running out*): Not against the wall! The bed can't be against the wall!
IDA: She still scared of monsters under the bed?
BETTY (*Nods yes*): But you didn't hear that from me. But moving the bed away from the wall is actually good feng shui, so we don't make a fuss about it.
IDA: Fung who?
BETTY: Nothing. (*Looking at the hat and coat*) Aren't you planning on staying awhile?
IDA (*Absently; as if speaking to Mrs. Lewis*): Yes, Ma'am.
BETTY: What?
IDA: What, what? Yes, I plan on staying.
BETTY: Then why are you still wearing your coat and hat?
IDA: Just hadn't gotten around to taking it off is all.

(*She starts to do so.*)

This is a beautiful apartment, Betty. Real, real nice.
BETTY: We thought so. And we got a great deal too.
IDA: You mean *you* got a great deal. You the one paid for it.
BETTY: Case pulls his weight.
IDA: Ain't nobody said a word against Case. You know I could eat that boy up with a spoon. Just doesn't seem right to me, a grown man staying at home all day.
BETTY: *Working* at home. Case *works* at home.
IDA: If it was work, it wouldn't be at home.

BETTY: Besides, he's going to handle all the renovations, and that way we won't have to pay another architect.

IDA: Renovate? But you just moved in.

BETTY: First, we're going to tear out all this old stuff. It looks older than dirt.

IDA: These appliances look just fine to me. Almost good as new.

BETTY: That settles it. We are getting you new glasses first thing tomorrow.

2

Betty and her husband, Case, are in the bedroom.

CASE: It's not about that.

BETTY: Then exactly what is it about? The money? Because I can certainly afford to help her keep up the place all by myself, you don't need to worry about that.

CASE *(Interrupting)*: Don't put words in my mouth! I'm not one of your witnesses.

BETTY: Then talk to me. Tell me . . . why.

CASE: It's . . . the way she's been acting lately. You must have noticed.

BETTY: She's fine. She's old, but she's fine. She just needs new glasses is all.

CASE: You remember how my mother was after my father passed. Moving into assisted living ended up being the best thing for her.

BETTY *(Interrupting)*: See, I knew this was about your mother. She had those kind of issues from the beginning, you know that.

CASE: But they got worse.

BETTY: "Worse" implies an admission that yes, the problems existed before. Otherwise they could not have gotten "worse."

CASE: I'm not playing this game with you.

BETTY: Game? You think this is a game?

CASE: I think you're mad, and when you get mad, one of us better stop talking before this gets out of hand.

(Betty calms herself down.)

BETTY: My mother is fine. And if she is ever not fine, we will deal with it then. In the meantime . . .

CASE: Everything is "fine." I got it.

(Betty starts to walk out of the room, then turns around and hugs Case, who hugs her back.)

It's okay. It'll be okay.

BETTY: It's just when she gets tired. And only sometimes. Everyone forgets things sometimes. Sometimes, I've been in court, and had a huge brain fart, and forgotten the name of a key case. It happens. It . . . happens.

CASE: I know it does.

BETTY: I know you know. Many times as you've forgotten my birthday, you better know.

CASE: She's like a mother to me, you know that.

BETTY: She loves you too. Better than me sometimes, I think.

CASE: Not true. You know she's never gotten over my leaving the firm and going out on my own.

BETTY: Thank God. Because otherwise, I think she'd put you on a pedestal so high none of us could touch you.

CASE: You know you always have permission to kiss my feet.

BETTY: And you can feel perfectly free to kiss my ass.

(They kiss.)

It would be different if Dottie or Clara were here. But no, everything always gets dumped on me.

CASE: Baby, don't pick at the scars. Never does anybody any good.

BETTY: Telling the truth isn't the same as picking at scars. *(Beat)* Do you have any idea how long she's lived in that house? We all grew up there. It's *home.*

CASE: I know that.

BETTY: You heard her criticizing the way we want to renovate. She's still every bit as sharp as she ever was.

CASE: Oh, yeah, she's sharp all right. And I'm not saying anything needs to be done now.

BETTY: Right. Because nothing needs to be done. Not now.

CASE: Case closed?

BETTY: Case, you are so closed.

(They kiss. She is the first to pull away.)

CASE: Work?

BETTY: Need to pay for this beautiful new apartment.

CASE: You work. I'll cook.

BETTY: And Sarah will complain about cleaning up afterward.

CASE: And everything in the McKay family is "status quo."

BETTY: Yes, it is.

CASE: Res ipsa loquitur.

BETTY: Don't talk Latin. You know it's not cute when you talk Latin.

CASE: Veni, vidi, vici.

BETTY: So not cute.

(She starts to exit, and he follows her.)

CASE: Or, as they say down the way . . .

BETTY *(Overlapping)*: You are the anti-cute!

CASE *(Overlapping)*: "I came, I saw, I kicked serious ass!"

(After a moment Ida enters. She looks around, shakes her head, and starts cleaning.)

IDA: A grown man and a woman who cannot pick up after themselves. I swear I don't understand it. If I don't put this in some kind of order, who will?

(Mrs. Lewis enters from the master bathroom wearing a robe. She is surprised, turns her back, wipes away tears, and tries to compose herself.)

MRS. LEWIS: You shouldn't sneak up on someone like that, Cassie.

IDA: I'm sorry, Ma'am. It's Ida, Ma'am.

MRS. LEWIS: What?

IDA: You called me Cassie, Ma'am. I'm Ida.

MRS. LEWIS: Yes, of course you are. I "misspoke." That's what Bob always says. He "misspoke." Lawyers have their own language sometimes. *(Bitterly)* Come to think of it, men have their own language.

IDA: Ma'am? Are you all right?

MRS. LEWIS: Of course I am. Why would you ask?

IDA: No reason. Would you like me to clean in here later? After you've gotten yourself together?

MRS. LEWIS: Yes, thank you.

IDA: Yes, Ma'am.

MRS. LEWIS *(Just as Ida is about to leave)*: Ida? Are you married?

IDA: Yes, Ma'am. For almost twenty years now.

MRS. LEWIS: Really? I never . . . It's true what they say about how you people age.

IDA: Yes, Ma'am.

MRS. LEWIS: How old would you think I am?

IDA: I wouldn't like to say, Ma'am.

MRS. LEWIS: Please. I really want to know.

IDA: I'd say round about twenty . . . *(Feeling the situation out, going for the lower number)* two, Ma'am.

MRS. LEWIS *(Relieved)*: I'm twenty-nine.

IDA: I never would've known.

MRS. LEWIS: You see? I still look young. And pretty, if I do say so myself. And we have two beautiful children.

IDA: That's all true, Ma'am.

MRS. LEWIS: Then why . . . why . . . would he need somebody . . . *(Covering)* it seems like I hardly ever see him anymore. He leaves before I'm up in the morning and only gets home after the children are asleep. And when he is here, it seems like he's just halfway here.

IDA: He is a hard worker, Ma'am.

MRS. LEWIS: I know that. And I'm not complaining, mind you.

(She blows her nose.)

It's just that . . .

IDA: Why don't you come on in the kitchen and I'll make you a cup of tea just the way you like it. Not too hot, and not too cold. It'll make you feel better.

MRS. LEWIS: I would like a cup of tea.

IDA: My mother always used to say that the world always looked a whole lot better after a good cry and a cup of sweet tea.

MRS. LEWIS: I haven't been crying.

IDA: Of course not, Ma'am. I was just making conversation.

3

Ida, in a maid's uniform, with a pencil in her hand. As she draws, a sketch of a Black baby girl appears, superimposed over the door.

IDA: Black and white is simplest. Easiest, some say. But they don't know squat. Squeezing a rainbow into a shade, life into a line. Putting what's in your head on paper. Ain't nothing easy about any of that.

(She starts to draw outside the shape of the door, and erases.)

Betty always had funny-looking ears. Used to pick out her braids and pull her hair down to cover them. Child walked around looking like birds nested on her head until I gave in and came up with a style that suited us both. I thought the braids were cute, myself. Used to draw them to myself all the time. Clara, now, she had that Franklin nose. Had a ball at the tip. Dottie, now Dottie had the dimple. Both Betty and Clara tried to draw dimples in their own cheeks 'til they dug too hard and poked a hole in Clara's face. Then Clara had what she called the Scar. No human eyes could see it, though. One day, I drew her with a real scar on her face? The Scar died right quick after that.

I used to draw before them. I know I did. I remember I always had a pencil in my hand, at least as much as I had time. Seems like the first time I touched Betty's skin, I wore out a ton of pencils trying to draw how it felt. If you sketch light enough and small enough, you can fit a whole bunch of pictures on a piece of paper.

(Ida takes a piece of paper from her pocket and reads it. Her face changes.)

Betty Louise Farrell! You get your behind in here right now!

(Young Betty enters, played by the actress who plays Sarah. Young Betty is dressed in 1950s garb.)

YOUNG BETTY: Mama, I can explain.

IDA: You better explain. Just what are these grades supposed to mean?

YOUNG BETTY: You said I could try out for softball.

IDA: Did I say you could get a B in Latin?

YOUNG BETTY: I don't need Latin.

IDA: You need an A in it a lot more than you need that softball.

YOUNG BETTY: Softball is good exercise, it helps hone hand-eye coordination, and team activities are good at promoting community spirit.

IDA *(Interrupting)*: Stop talking at me like a Philadelphia lawyer. Either you get an A next semester, or you can kiss that softball goodbye.

YOUNG BETTY: You said!

IDA: And now I'm saying different!

YOUNG BETTY: Mama, I'm on the team now, and everybody thinks I'm going to be really good.

IDA: Then I guess you better get real friendly with that Latin then.

YOUNG BETTY: It's not fair!

IDA: Who lied to you and told you life was fair? Not me. You want some fair? How about instead of softball, you come to work with me?

YOUNG BETTY: You *said*.

IDA: Picking up and dusting their European china will teach you some "hand-eye coordination." Working with your mother will help your "community spirit"!

(Young Betty turns away, hurt. Ida starts to soften but resists.)

Either you keep those As coming, or else it's "Goodbye softball" and "Hello Mrs. Lewis."

YOUNG BETTY *(Softly)*: Yes Ma'am.

IDA: I don't think I heard you.

YOUNG BETTY *(Louder)*: Yes, Ma'am. I'll do better next semester.

IDA: That's right. *(Beat)* Here.

(She hands her a pretty blue sweater.)

Mrs. Lewis was tired of it, and I was never partial to blue.

YOUNG BETTY: It's beautiful.

IDA: I thought so. You can wear it to that party you think you're going to on Saturday.

YOUNG BETTY: Thank you, Mama.

IDA: You're welcome. Now go on and tell your sisters that I brought some of that strudel back home

YOUNG BETTY *(Yelling)*: Dottie! Clara!

(Young Betty exits. Ida sets the strudel on the table, cuts a piece, and puts it on a plate. Older Betty enters.)

BETTY: I'm leaving now.

(Silence.)

Mama? Mama!

IDA: Who you yelling at?

BETTY: You. I said I'm leaving now.

IDA: What time is it?

BETTY: Almost eleven. I told you to put batteries in that clock. I'll bring them next time.

IDA: I can get my own batteries.

BETTY: But you don't. *(Looking at the strudel)* You know that sweet stuff isn't good for your sugar.

IDA *(Savoring the strudel)*: Don't you worry about me. I'm doing just fine.

BETTY: Not according to your doctor, you're not.

IDA *(Singing)*: "Jesus is my doctor, and He writes out all of my prescriptions."

BETTY: Then maybe Dr. Jesus needs to have a talk with Dr. Jones. I wonder if Jesus takes Blue Cross?

IDA: Sure you don't want any of this?

BETTY: Very. I haven't been able to get to the gym lately.

IDA: You worry too much. You always were too hard on yourself.

BETTY: I wonder where I got that from.

IDA: Must be your father. He always complained about how I spoiled you girls.

BETTY: My memory must just be playing tricks on me.

IDA: Must be. *(Beat)* Where's Sarah?

BETTY: I left her at home, with her tutor.

IDA: Her what?

BETTY: We got her a tutor. She needs to ace her PSATs if she's going to have any hope of getting into a decent school.

IDA: She's smart enough to get into any school she wants.

BETTY: Smart's the least of it these days, Mama. All her friends are smart. Sarah needs to be the smart*est*.

IDA: Don't you pressure that child. A child needs time to be a child.

BETTY: I'm sorry, who are you and what have you done with my mother?

IDA: It's a wonderful thing being a grandmother. You just get to watch all the mess and smile. *(Beat)* Why don't you go tell Dottie to come have some of this strudel? You know how much she loves strudel.

BETTY: Mama, Dottie's not here.

IDA: Where is she, then? Out with that boy again?

BETTY: Dottie lives in North Carolina now, with her family.

IDA: Of course she does. She moved there round about Christmas six years ago. What are you going on about Dottie for?

BETTY: Because you . . . nothing. I must have heard wrong.

IDA: Best clean your ears out then. Or at least have some of this here strudel.

(Ida keeps eating the strudel, as Betty watches.)

4

The kitchen. Ida sits chopping vegetables.
Sarah enters and gets a soda.

IDA: You're home early.

SARAH: The other team didn't show so we won by default. *(Flatly)* Yay.

IDA: Last time I looked, winning was winning no matter how it happened.

SARAH: I wanted to kick serious butt. It's never as much fun if you don't kick serious butt.

IDA: I'm sure you'll beat their butts another time, baby.

SARAH: I hope so.

(Sarah exits.)

IDA *(Calling after her)*: That friend of yours, the one with the eye? Came by looking for you. You better call her or tax her, or something.

(The actress playing Mrs. Lewis enters in contemporary garb. She is now the heavily accented Adela.)

ADELA: Hello?

IDA: How did you get . . . Sarah, did you leave the door open?

ADELA: Mrs.?

IDA: Can I help you?

ADELA: No, I Adela. I help. *I* . . . help.

IDA *(More slowly)*: Miss, can I help you? Did you need something?

ADELA *(More slowly too)*: I. Help.

IDA *(Smiling, yelling)*: Sarah? Did you let a crazy lady in the apartment?

(Sarah enters.)

SARAH: Adela, you can start in my room.

ADELA: Yes, Miss Sarah.

(Adela exits.)

IDA: Who's that?

SARAH: Adela. She's our cleaning lady.

IDA: I beg your pardon?

SARAH: Our cleaning lady. She comes on Thursday afternoons. I guess you haven't been here on a Thursday before.

IDA: Y'all have a maid? Why? Can't you help your mother pick up? It's not that much of a mess around here.

SARAH: Mom has work, I have school and soccer. Daddy's got a lot of building stuff to draw.

IDA: Well, I wouldn't expect your father to clean a house.

SARAH: That's sexist, Gramma.

IDA: That's life, baby. *(Picking up)* Why didn't you tell me she was coming? I would have picked up a bit around here.

SARAH: Why? You just said it's not that much of a mess.

IDA: Enough of a mess for y'all to pay somebody to clean it for you. Did you make your bed?

SARAH: Why can't Adela do it?

IDA: You go and make your bed! And make sure to put all your underwear in that hamper you keep missing! That girl is not your personal slave!

(Sarah slouches out.)

(Yelling) Miss Adela? Miss Adela? Would you like something?

(Adela enters.)

ADELA: You want me in here?

IDA: I just wanted to know if you wanted something to drink or to eat.

ADELA: I clean in here now?

IDA *(Smiling, yelling)*: Sarah? Does this girl speak American? Sarah!

SARAH *(Yelling)*: I'm on the phone!

(Ida motions to a chair.)

IDA: Would you like to sit down?

ADELA: Is something wrong? I not do good job?

IDA: No, nothing's wrong. I'm sure the job you do is just fine. I just wondered if you might like to sit for a minute.

(Adela gingerly sits.)

Would you like a glass of water, or a cup of tea?

(Adela starts to rise.)

ADELA: You want tea?

IDA: No, would *you* like . . . you sit. I'll get.

(Ida gets two cups of tea and puts one in front of Adela.)

Would you like some sugar?

ADELA: No. Thank you.

(They both sip their tea, awkwardly.)

IDA: So . . . how long have you been here?

ADELA: I get here ten minutes.

IDA: No, I mean . . . America, here.

ADELA: Six months. I join sister. She is nanny across town.

IDA: Looking after children. That's one hard job.

ADELA: So she says. Cleaning? Calm.

IDA: Did you clean in your country?

ADELA: Teacher.

IDA: Really? What'd you teach?

ADELA: English. *(Beat)* Joke. Ha ha. *(Beat)* You have joke in America?

IDA: We do, but I didn't know you . . . so what did you teach?

ADELA: History. Not much use here.

IDA: So are you going to try to be a teacher over here?

ADELA: Maybe. First I am study English, then see what is next.

IDA: Sounds like a plan.

ADELA: Yes.

IDA: Then no more cleaning for you.

ADELA *(Nervous)*: I am like cleaning. Cleaning is good job.

IDA: I know it is, Adela, I didn't mean to say . . . I used to clean folks' houses myself.

ADELA: Really? You are not from here?

IDA: I'm from here all right. But it was the best job folks like me could get in those days.

(Adela changes her costume and becomes Mrs. Lewis.)

MRS. LEWIS: Ida, if you can't sleep in, I just don't know how this is going to work.

IDA: Ma'am, you said your mother was going to be staying with the children during your trip.

MRS. LEWIS: That's Mr. Lewis's mother, Ida. And much as I love and adore her, she cannot be the only one looking after the children. Not at night.

IDA: I see. If it's only for the two weeks then, Ma'am . . .

MRS. LEWIS: Just two weeks. Unless Bob's trip gets extended, of course.

IDA: You wouldn't come back without him?

MRS. LEWIS: No. Not since . . . Bob likes for me to be at his side as much as possible.

IDA: I suppose *two weeks* would be fine then, Ma'am.

MRS. LEWIS: Ida, you are a godsend. And we will absolutely, positively, bring you—and your girls—something back from Italia.

(Mrs. Lewis becomes Adela again.)

ADELA: Mrs.? Hello?

IDA: More tea?

ADELA: I think I must clean now.

IDA: Sure, sure. You start in Sarah's bedroom, and I'll pick up in my daughter's room. We'll meet up in the living room.

(Ida exits, putting the cups in the sink. As Adela starts to wash them, Sarah enters.)

ADELA: Miss Sarah? You want something?
SARAH: No thanks.
ADELA: Mrs. . . . She is your family?
SARAH: My grandmother. My mother's mother? *(Sarah motions a family tree with her hand)*
ADELA: Ah. She is not cleaner?
SARAH: Of course not. Gramma doesn't work.
ADELA: She is . . . okay?
SARAH: Sure she is. Why would you ask?
ADELA: Nothing. I clean now.

5

Betty sits working. Sarah is watching her.
After a moment:

BETTY: Ask already. You're making me nervous and I need to finish this brief.
SARAH: Is there something wrong with Gramma?
BETTY: No. Why would you ask that? Did your father say something?
SARAH: No. Adela said something.
BETTY: Is Adela a doctor?
SARAH: No, but . . .
BETTY: Does Adela even know your grandmother well enough to tell if there's something wrong?
SARAH: I guess not.
BETTY: There, then. *(Beat)* Just what did Adela say?
SARAH: She asked if Gramma was a cleaner, and if there was something wrong with her.
BETTY: She asked if Gramma was a "cleaner"?
SARAH: I know? It's totally random, right? Maybe there's something wrong with Adela.

BETTY: I guess your grandmother must've started talking to her about the old days.

SARAH: Hold up. So Gramma used to clean people's houses?

BETTY: And mind their children, and . . . I must've told you all this before.

SARAH: Uh . . . No.

BETTY: Well what did you think Gramma did all her life?

SARAH: Look after you and Aunt Dottie and Aunt Clara. And Grampa when he was alive.

BETTY: And how did you think she paid for me and Aunt Dottie and Aunt Clara to eat and go to school?

SARAH: I don't know. I guess I figured Grampa left her money. My friend Kim's grandfather left her grandmother a whole lot of money and now she spends her winters in Florida.

BETTY: Well *your* grandmother was a maid.

SARAH: You mean like in a shorty black uniform with an apron, like the Halloween costume?

BETTY: Trust me, your Gramma never wore a "French maid's" uniform. She was an entirely different kind of maid.

SARAH: Oooh! Was Gramma part of the Montgomery bus boycotts? We read about them in school.

BETTY: Your grandmother worked in New York City, and there were not a lot of boycotts in Manhattan.

SARAH: So she went from apartment to apartment like Adela?

BETTY: Nope. She primarily worked for one family, the Lewises. *(Thinking)* Now that I think about it, they lived somewhere around here. *(Teasing)* You could even be going to school with a Lewis.

SARAH: What?

BETTY: The family had a couple of kids. By now, they could have their own kids who could be going to school with you. Granddaughter of a maid going to school with the granddaughter of her employer. Only in America.

SARAH: So they were a family? Like a regular ordinary family? Not rich, or anything?

BETTY: They were rich enough to afford a maid back in the day.

SARAH: But their kids could seriously be in an ordinary school like mine? Not in the Sorbonne, or something?

BETTY: Your school is extremely expensive, young lady. And need I remind you, we have someone who cleans up after *you* and we are not rich.

SARAH: No, we're not. *(Beat)* So one day, maybe I could end up going to school with one of Adela's kids too?

BETTY: If Adela can afford to send her children to St. Michael's, we are obviously paying her too much money.

SARAH: So what were they like, the family Gramma worked for?

BETTY: Lord, I don't remember. Just regular people, I suppose.

(Ida stands holding a baby in her arms, while on the phone with Young Betty.)

YOUNG BETTY: I hate them.

IDA: You do not hate anybody. Least of all . . . *(Looks around and lowers her voice)* them.

YOUNG BETTY: If you didn't have to stay with their stupid kids, I could spend the night at Michelle's LIKE YOU PROMISED!

IDA: You lower your voice!

MOTHER LEWIS *(Mrs. Lewis's mother-in-law; offstage)*: Girl? Who are you talking to? Do you have company out there?

IDA: No, Mrs. Lewis.

MOTHER LEWIS *(Offstage)*: Don't lie to me, girl! I can hear you talking plain as day! I told Bobby to get one of the *good* Coloreds.

IDA: Mrs. Lewis, your daughter-in-law said I could use the phone once a night to talk to my family.

MOTHER LEWIS: Then keep your voice down while you do it.

IDA: Yes, Ma'am.

BETTY: I hate her.

IDA: *Her* you can hate. With her "Girl this" and "Girl that." Even being called Cassie would be better than that.

(The baby whimpers. Ida softens and sweetens her voice.)

It's alright, baby, nobody hates you.

BETTY: What if I'm home by curfew, *before* curfew?

IDA: I told you, I don't want you leaving your sisters alone while your father is on the road.

YOUNG BETTY: Mama, please!

IDA: No means no! Now wrap this up so I can put this baby to bed.

YOUNG BETTY: You like them better than us.

IDA: Girl, don't you make me reach out through this phone and slap you.

YOUNG BETTY: You do everything they want! When they say jump, you ask how high!

IDA: Do you like eating, and wearing nice clothes and having someplace to live? Do you?

YOUNG BETTY: You draw pictures of them. You never draw pictures of us.

IDA: What are you doing going through my sketchbook?

YOUNG BETTY: It didn't used to be a secret.

IDA: Well put it right back where you found it! *That's* why I couldn't find it when I was packing my overnight bag. *(Beat; defensive)* Mrs. Lewis likes when I draw pictures of the baby. And I drew plenty of pictures of you girls when you were little.

YOUNG BETTY: Not in a really long time. Not like the ones you draw of her baby.

IDA: You leave who and what I draw out of this. And put Dottie and Clara on the phone so I can say good night to them.

YOUNG BETTY: They're already in bed and I don't want to wake them up.

IDA: Betty!

YOUNG BETTY: They need their rest as much as Mrs. Lewis's baby does. Night, Mama.

IDA: Betty Louise, don't you hang up this . . .

(But Young Betty has already hung up the phone. She pulls out a battered sketch pad and flips through it. She pulls out a pencil and starts marking up one of the drawings. After she's done, she transforms back into Sarah.)

SARAH: I don't think I like it.

BETTY: Like what?

SARAH: Gramma being somebody's Adela.

BETTY: Why? Don't you like Adela?

SARAH: Yeah, but Adela's . . . She's . . .

BETTY: She is a young woman trying to make her way the best way she can. Don't you dare look down your nose at her.

SARAH: I don't!

BETTY: You better not! *(Beat)* And you make sure and make your bed and pick up after yourself before she comes. She's not your personal slave.

SARAH: You sound just like Gramma!

(Case enters, sipping from a mug and reading from his iPad.)

Daddy, do we pay Adela to clean or don't we?

CASE: Is this a trick question?

SARAH: I just need a yes or no.

BETTY: We do not pay her to walk around after you and wipe your behind.

SARAH: Making my bed is not the same thing as wiping my behind! Daddy?

CASE: If you think I'm getting in the middle of this, "you crazy."

SARAH: Daddy. That doesn't even sound right coming from you.

CASE: Prejudice. I am the victim of prejudice in my own family. I ought to sue.

BETTY: You go on and do that. And tell your daughter to make her bed while you're at it, since she's obviously not listening to me.

SARAH: Listening is not the same as agreeing.

CASE: Sarah, you know better than to argue with your mother when she's in one of her moods.

BETTY: I am working, I am not in a "mood."

CASE: Working moods are even worse. She will whip out eight different kinds of Latin on your ass.

SARAH: "She do dat, don't she"?

BETTY: I can hear you two ganging up on me.

CASE: That's because you have the ears of a bat, baby.

BETTY: Then bat yourselves on out. Working lawyer here. And stop encouraging her to speak Ebonically! I don't want that mess slipping out at St. Michael's!

SARAH: LOL.

CASE: SMH.

BETTY: No textspeak either!

6

Ida and Adela are talking in the kitchen.

ADELA: It's not true!

IDA: It most certainly is. The mother-in-law used to eat them all the time.

ADELA: The . . . how you call them . . . chitlins?

IDA: She didn't call 'em that, though.

ADELA: Stuffed with the blood?

IDA: Could have been. They looked and smelled nasty enough to be stuffed with anything.

ADELA: I didn't know rich people eat that. Not in America.

IDA: Rich folks eat whatever they want in America. That's what makes it America.

ADELA: So you cook and clean?

IDA: And mind the children, and the mother-in-law . . . whatever they asked—and paid—me to do.

(Adela starts to take the garbage through the maid's door.)

Adela, don't . . .

ADELA: What? Oh, I take garbage, it is fine. "No big deal."

(Adela takes the garbage out and returns.)

IDA: Do you know what that door used to be?

ADELA: Part of the wall?

IDA: It used to be a maid's door.

ADELA: Maids, they had own doors?

IDA: So they didn't have to use the same door the family used.

ADELA: Oh. *(Realizing)* Oh. And you, you used to . . .

IDA: Just about every day. Some days I found ways around it. "Mrs. Lewis, I just couldn't fit all the packages through my door." "Ma'am, my door is squeaking so bad the neighbors are complaining, and I just knew you didn't want to bother them."

ADELA: And this, this is what you did always?

IDA: Only for round about two hundred years. Then Lincoln freed the maids. *(Beat)* I wanted to be a painter when I was a girl.

ADELA: I too wanted . . . did want . . .

IDA: Wanted is right.

ADELA: I wanted to make art. But art, it does not feed you. Not like teaching.

IDA: Or cleaning.

ADELA: Do you still? Paint?

IDA: Oh, no. I used to sketch some when I was younger. I could tear up a piece of paper with a pencil. Even won a blue ribbon for one of my drawings, back when I was in school.

ADELA: Shut your mouth!

IDA: What did you say?

ADELA: "Shut your mouth." It's like you say. I didn't say it right?

IDA: No, you got the words right. They just . . . don't sound right coming out of your mouth.

(Adela transforms into Mrs. Lewis.)

MRS. LEWIS: Bongiorno, Ida. That's how they say "Good morning" in Italy.

IDA: Is that right, Ma'am?

MRS. LEWIS: It most certainly is. And I swear I must have gained twenty pounds, what with all the spaghetti they keep pushing on you over there.

IDA: You look just the same to me, Ma'am.

MRS. LEWIS: Thank you, Ida. *(Beat)* I do hope the children and Mother Lewis weren't too tiring.

IDA: Everyone was just fine, Ma'am. Cup of tea?

MRS. LEWIS: Espresso, if you don't mind, Ida. I learned to adore it in Italy.

IDA: I'll do my best to make it, then, Ma'am.

MRS. LEWIS: The baby's sleeping awfully late this morning.

IDA: I expect she tired herself out last night. She just about tipped her way all around the apartment.

MRS. LEWIS: "Tipped"?

IDA: Walking, Ma'am.

MRS. LEWIS: She walked? Angela took a step? And I missed it?

IDA: She barely took a step, Ma'am. More like a tip.

MRS. LEWIS: I was in Italy when my baby started walking? What kind of terrible mother am I?

IDA: Walking's really not the word for it, Ma'am. She tried her little heart out, but she mostly just fell.

MRS. LEWIS: She didn't hurt herself, did she?

IDA: Of course not. And she and your mother-in-law got on like a house afire. I did one of my sketches of the two of them together.

MRS. LEWIS: Wonderful!

IDA: I'd've done more, but I forgot and left my book home last week. I remembered to bring it with me today, though.

(Mrs. Lewis takes Ida's sketch pad and flips through it.)

Ma'am, I can find you the page . . .

MRS. LEWIS: Oh, I don't mind.

(She finds the picture.)

Oh, Ida, this is just darling.

IDA: Thank you, Ma'am.

MRS. LEWIS: Are there any . . . ?

(She flips the page and stops.)

Ida?

(She shows a sketch of the baby with horns, a mustache, and a big black X over her face.)

What is this? *(Beat)* Ida? Did you hear me? Ida, what is the meaning of this?

IDA: Ma'am, I didn't mean for you to see that. I just . . . I messed up that picture so bad, I couldn't stand it. So I crossed it out to remind myself not to do that again.

MRS. LEWIS: Really.

IDA: Yes, really, Ma'am.

MRS. LEWIS: I suppose I understand. But it is really very disturbing, Ida. You must see that. You see that, don't you?

IDA: I do see that, Ma'am. And I'm sorry you had to see it too. And to prove to you just how sorry I am . . .

YOUNG BETTY: I said I was sorry!

IDA: You don't act like it!

YOUNG BETTY: Her baby is stupid-looking, anyway!

IDA: And thanks to you, I have to look after that "stupid-looking baby" and her brother next week instead of going to Aunt Marjorie's shower.

YOUNG BETTY: I'm sorry.

IDA: So am I.

YOUNG BETTY: You want me to babysit? So you can go to the shower?

IDA: No. You don't need to go to that place.

YOUNG BETTY: It's just babysitting.

IDA: It ain't "just" anything. You set one foot through that door and you'll never get back out again. You think I work this hard just so you can be like me? You stay home and look after your sisters, and keep your grades up. You do your job, and I'll do mine.

(Young Betty disappears.)

Half the time, they don't know how much they take. You just have to stay strong. My mama was strong up till the day she died. Strong in body and in mind.

MRS. LEWIS *(Hands Ida the baby)*: Thank you so much for this, Ida. We won't be back any later than ten o'clock. Eleven at the latest. *(To the baby)* Night, precious Angela. "And flights of angels sing thee to thy rest." That's Shakespeare, Ida. From *Romeo and Juliet*.

IDA: From *Hamlet*, Ma'am. *(Beat)* My daughter just studied it in school, went reading it out loud around the house.

MRS. LEWIS: Did she? I suppose Shakespeare speaks to all of us.

(Mrs. Lewis exits.)

IDA *(Cooing to the baby)*: Hey there, sweet thing. It's not your fault your mommy's a baby and your daddy cats around. You and your brother are the only ones have reason to act like children, and you're the best behaved of the bunch.

(As Ida sings to the baby, Betty enters.)

BETTY: Mama? What are you doing?

IDA: Singing Sarah to sleep. What does it look like? Hush now, I just about got her down.

BETTY: Mama, that's a doll. That's one of Sarah's dolls.

7

Dr. Patel's office. He is examining Ida.

IDA: I'm real sorry to trouble you, Dr. Paddle.

DR. PATEL: Don't worry about it, Mrs. Farrell. It's why I'm here. Follow my finger, please.

IDA: My daughter and son-in-law insisted I come. His family has a house on Martha's Vineyard, and they just call doctors at the drop of a hat.

DR. PATEL: Is that right?

IDA: I told you that, didn't I? That they have a house on Martha's Vineyard?

DR. PATEL: He's the architect, right? Have you had any problems with your balance lately?

IDA: Yes. No. Maybe a little.

DR. PATEL: How would you say you've been feeling lately?

IDA: I'd say I'm feeling just fine.

DR. PATEL: Your daughter said there was an incident with a doll? You thought it was your granddaughter?

IDA: I was just joking. Betty never could take a joke. She gets that from her father.

DR. PATEL: Glad to hear it. I like a joke just as much as anyone else. But just to make your daughter feel better, I'd like you to take a few tests.

IDA: Betty's the one for tests. Used to pass them with flying colors. Smart as a Philadelphia lawyer. She passed the bar first time out.

DR. PATEL: Great. Well, this is a really simple test. *(Hands her a piece of paper and a pencil)* I want you to draw a few things for me.

IDA: Did Betty put you up to this?

DR. PATEL: Excuse me?

IDA: She's always on me about getting back to drawing. I haven't drawn in years.

DR. PATEL: This is a simple diagnostic test. First, I'd like you to draw me a clock.

IDA: Grandfather? Cuckoo?

DR. PATEL: Just the face of a clock, writing in the numbers.

IDA: All right.

(As Ida sketches, we see her periodically draw lines and erase them out.)

Clocks. He wants me to draw clocks. Who can't draw a clock?

MRS. LEWIS: Time, time, time, Ida. You've got to keep your eye on the time.

IDA: Don't rush me, Ma'am.

DR. PATEL: Mrs. Farrell?

(Ida finishes the circle and starts writing in the numbers. She transposes the three and nine, sees her mistake, and corrects it.)

IDA: I could've drawn you a grandfather clock, back in the day. My grandma used to have one in her hallway. She got it from the family she used to work for.

DR. PATEL: Just a plain clock face is fine, Mrs. Farrell. Now, please draw in the hands so the clock says five minutes after eleven.

IDA: What happens at five past eleven?

DR. PATEL: Nothing happens then, I just want you to draw in the clock hands.

YOUNG BETTY: Come on, Mama! I have to get to school! I can't wait for you to fix the hem!

IDA: Betty, can't you see I'm busy? Mrs. Lewis wants me to draw a picture of the baby that she can put in a frame and give it to her husband for his birthday. I got to get this just right.

(Ida draws the clock hands to show five minutes before one.)

There. *(Beat)* What?

DR. PATEL: Nothing, it's fine. Now, I'd like you to copy this drawing.

(We see a picture of a cube.)

IDA: If you're sure.

DR. PATEL: Just do the best you can.

IDA: Gonna be a mighty boring picture if you ask me.

(Ida labors to sketch accurately, but the lines don't meet at the right angles and the product is a mess.)

DR. PATEL: Okay, that's good.

IDA: I'm much better at faces. Give me a face to draw, and you'll see.

DR. PATEL: You did a great job, Mrs. Farrell. Let me just take these and review them along with your other tests.

IDA: I told you, Sarah's the test taker. Passed the bar the very first time.

DR. PATEL: Sarah?

IDA: What about her?

DR. PATEL: You said she passed the bar? I thought your granddaughter was still in school.

IDA: She is. Don't you try to trick me. I know my granddaughter's name. Sarah Felicia McKay. Felicia for her grandmother on her father's side. They have a house on that Martha's Vineyard, you know.

8

Dr. Patel's office. Betty, Case, and Ida are there.

BETTY: So what are our next steps, Dr. Patel?

DR. PATEL: We monitor the situation.

IDA: "Situation." I am not a "situation." I'm *fine*. Why doesn't anybody believe me?

BETTY: We believe you, Mama. We just want to take care of you is all.

IDA: I take care of myself just fine!

CASE: We know that, Mrs. Farrell. But let us and the doctor take care of you just a little, okay? Just for a change.

IDA: A change would be nice, Case honey. Thank you for thinking of it.

BETTY: I don't believe this. Just because Case says something does not make it gospel.

CASE: Dr. Patel, what are our next steps?

BETTY *(Hissing to Case)*: I asked exactly the same question! You couldn't even come up with a different question?

CASE *(To Betty)*: The answer is what's important—what does it matter who asks the question?

DR. PATEL: As I said, we monitor. Mrs. Farrell, you start coming in on a regular basis.

IDA: I don't want to bother you, Dr. Paddle.

BETTY: It's *Patel*, Mama, and it's the man's job.

IDA: He's a busy doctor, Betty. We don't need to be all up in his face with our little problems.

BETTY: Your health is not a little problem!

CASE: Mrs. Farrell? Let's listen to Dr. Patel, okay?

(Ida nods, folds her hands, and acquiesces. Betty glares at her and Case.)

DR. PATEL: You still retain extremely high levels of cognitive function, which is very good. The best way to maintain it is to continue to stay mentally active.

BETTY: What about your artwork, Mama? Maybe you could take an art class?

IDA: Oh, that's nothing.

BETTY: No, it's not. *(To Dr. Patel)* Doctor, my mother used to be a talented artist. Please tell her to start doing it again.

DR. PATEL: I do recommend that you engage in mentally stimulating activities, Mrs. Farrell. Do you have any games you like to play, any groups you like to attend?

BETTY: He means art, Mama.

DR. PATEL: If you like. There are any number of activities that we've found to be helpful. Music, for example.

CASE: "Music hath charms to soothe," and all that?

DR. PATEL: Exactly.

BETTY: She's really more of an artist. Wouldn't taking up an activity she used to do be the best thing?

DR. PATEL *(Getting annoyed with Betty)*: It's really up to your mother, Mrs. McKay. Whatever she wishes to do.

BETTY: Oh, I understand. But maybe you could clarify your answer. For my mother's benefit.

CASE: Babe, I think she understands.

DR. PATEL: Mrs. Farrell, do you understand what I'm recommending?

IDA: I think so.

DR. PATEL: Nothing seems to need clarification, Mrs. McKay.

BETTY: The doctor thinks you need to stay mentally active, Mama. Engage in activities, keep yourself busy. If you don't want to draw, Mama, then what would you like to do to keep yourself busy?

IDA: I don't need to keep busy. I *am* busy. I do plenty. I do plenty! I look after you girls, I look after the Lewises, I stay plenty busy!

BETTY: Mama, Clara and Dottie and I have our own families now. And you retired from working for the Lewises, remember?

IDA: Of course I remember! Stop trying to trick me! I know what year it is, and who the president is, and all those things! Ask Dr. Paddle if you don't believe me.

DR. PATEL: As I said, your cognitive abilities are still quite high.

IDA: All this "head" business, nerves and cognitives and what-not—that don't have a thing to do with me. It's for *(Lowering her voice) white* folks who don't have enough real things in their lives to worry about. I'm fine.

BETTY: That's absurd, Mama. Your condition has nothing to do with race.

CASE: Don't you remember my mother, Mrs. Farrell?

IDA: Of course I do, Case. And your mother may not have been white—but she was rich. Same thing when it comes to most things. Who knows but if she hadn't had so much time to think about being sick, she might not have gotten sick?

CASE: That's not . . . that's just wrong, Mrs. Farrell. My mother did not *think* herself into mental illness.

BETTY: Doctor, would you please explain to my mother? This has nothing to do with race.

DR. PATEL *(To Betty)*: Actually, many of my patients are African American, Mrs. McKay. I'm afraid they're—you're more likely to develop Alzheimer's than most other populations.

IDA: I have the Alzheimer's?

DR. PATEL: I'm sorry, I shouldn't have . . . let's just monitor the situation. See how things develop. Watch and be there when things change.

BETTY: If. If things change. They might not.

DR. PATEL: Mrs. McKay, I don't want you to leave with false hope.

BETTY: I'm not your patient, Doctor. Please don't worry about me. Just treat my mother. For whatever disease she may—or may not—have.

9

The kitchen. Betty is writing. Case enters sleepily.

CASE: Still working on that brief?

BETTY: Looking up names of doctors for my mother. We need a second opinion.

CASE: Dr. Patel was the second opinion.

BETTY: The second right opinion. I emailed some attorneys I know who specialize in elder law, and I've started doing my own research.

CASE: I know you feel like you need to do this. Lord knows we went through a laundry list of doctors for my mother.

BETTY: Oh, here we go, back to your mother again. The almighty "Felicia McKay."

CASE: Now what the hell is that supposed to mean?

BETTY: You always held her up to me when she was alive, and now that she's dead, you're holding her up to my mother. And I'm not having it.

CASE: I never held . . . the woman is dead, for Christ's sake. My mother is dead. This beautiful, vital woman.

BETTY: She was beautiful, and she was vital, and she was perfect, I know that!

CASE: Goddammit, are you still jealous of my mother? After all this time?

BETTY: I'm sorry. I'm just . . . I'm sorry.

CASE: I watched her lose every bit of herself. I lost her months, years, before we buried her.

BETTY: And that is not happening to my mother! It is not. We are getting a second . . . second opinion.

CASE: Nothing's definite, okay? These things, this disease, it takes time. Nothing may change for a really long time.

BETTY: And it's not going to. Because nothing is wrong with my mother. Nothing that the right doctor can't fix.

CASE: There is no "right doctor." If there was, don't you think we would've found one for my mother?

BETTY: Well I'm finding one for mine. Because I'm not waiting for someone to come up to me with life on a silver platter like some kind of a McKay. The Farrells worked and struggled all their lives. Nobody ever gave us a thing.

CASE: Oh, here we go again. The poor little "maid's daughter" who had to walk uphill to school both ways.

BETTY: Don't you make fun of me. And don't you dare make fun of my mother.

CASE: I know you're scared. You'd have to be a fool not to be scared, and my baby ain't nobody's fool.

BETTY: You sound so wrong when you go all . . . ethnic.

CASE: Yeah, well, Scarsdale and the Vineyard do not a gangsta make.

BETTY: Yeah, we know that all right. *(Beat)* Oh, babe? Remember Mitch Wilkins?

CASE: Should I?

BETTY: You met him at Dave and Lisa's. He's one of the elder law specialists I contacted. We got to talking, and it turns out that they're looking at renovating their offices. I told him you'd give him a call.

CASE: Why would you say that?

BETTY: Because it's a job. And his firm has a lot of money and ugly offices in need of a great architect. Sounds like a match made in heaven. Call him tomorrow, okay?

CASE *(Beat)*: I can find my own jobs, okay?

BETTY: Nobody said you couldn't.

CASE: So we're agreed. My jobs are my jobs. My career is just that—mine.

BETTY: I was just trying to help.

CASE: Help is great. I can always use help.

BETTY: But?

CASE: Help and ordering me around? Not quite the same thing.

BETTY: I didn't order . . . okay so maybe my suggestion could've maybe sounded, in a way, like an order.

CASE: And?

BETTY: And . . . I'm sorry. If you interpreted my suggestion as an order.

CASE: Semi-apology semi-accepted.

BETTY: It just seemed like such an easy thing to do. To pick up the phone and call, and maybe get a paying job. Sorry if I "overstepped."

CASE: That's not what it was and you know it. *(Beat)* I know you've been under a lot of stress, what with your mother.

BETTY: Not everything is about my mother.

CASE: It's getting late. Your mother and Sarah are probably done with their movie. I'll take her home, and we can talk . . . [later]

BETTY *(Interrupting)*: You don't have to. She started drifting off, so I told her to lie down in that spare room.

CASE: The maid's room?

BETTY: The what?

CASE: That's what it's called on the plans. Didn't you see that when you looked at the plans for the apartment?

BETTY: I just looked at the size of the rooms. You're not serious.

CASE: Nothing's meant by it, it's just what it's called.

BETTY: I don't believe this.

CASE: It doesn't make any difference what it's called. We always intended to have it fixed up as her room whenever she stayed over anyway. So, she'll stay over tonight. And tomorrow, I'll take her back home.

(Ida is asleep on the bed in the maid's room. Mrs. Lewis opens the door and Ida awakens.)

IDA: Ma'am?

MRS. LEWIS: I'm so glad you decided to stay, Ida. Now you'll really be like one of the family.

ACT TWO

1

Ida is sketching a series of rectangles.

IDA: Left right top bottom. Just a bunch of straight lines. Nothing scary about a bunch of straight lines. Nothing scary 'bout that. Left right top right. No, that's not right. Left right top. Top. Top. Ain't nothing scary about a rectangle. Ain't nothing interesting either. Why's he want a rectangle? Doors, now. That's a little bit more interesting.

(The rectangles start to resemble doors.)

Doors need something. Handles, knobs.

(She draws the maid's door.)

No. Don't like that door. No door.

(She scribbles over the drawing.)

DR. PATEL: Mrs. Farrell? Is something wrong?

IDA: I didn't like that one. Let me draw you a fresh one.

DR. PATEL: Whatever you like. Remember you don't have to push yourself.

IDA: Remember. I remember.

DR. PATEL: Just draw the rectangles as best you can. No hurry. No pressure.

(Ida starts a new drawing.)

IDA: No pressure. No pressure. Who don't have "no pressure"? What kinda life's he had? "No pressure"? Probably had every door he ever wanted swing open for him. Doctors have it that way. Men have it that way.

(The doors get more and more out of proportion and stop resembling doors.)

DR. PATEL: Okay, Mrs. Farrell. Just try drawing a circle now.

IDA: Circles. Knobs. Doors need knobs. Look at the knob. Focus on the knob. Work on the knob. Just a circle. No pressure. All he wants to see is a circle. Just give 'em what they want to see, and it'll be fine. Everything will be fine.

(She draws circles—but they're not where doorknobs should be.)

They changed my door the other day. Tried to tell me it was my front door. Who did they think they were fooling? As if I wouldn't know my own front door. What kind of person doesn't know their own front door? Doors, doors, doors, doors . . . this is a . . . this is a . . . I know I know the word.

DR. PATEL: Don't agitate yourself, Mrs. Farrell.

IDA: Don't you tell me what to do. I know the word.

DR. PATEL: I told you, it's all right. There are going to be times you don't know, and that's to be expected.

IDA: I told you, I know the fucking word!

2

The McKay apartment.

BETTY: So meet with them someplace else.

CASE: Where? They're only going to be in town for a few hours.

BETTY: Take them to the Princeton Club or the Yale Club.

CASE: How's that going to look?

BETTY: Like you're meeting them at the Princeton Club or the Yale Club.

CASE: You know what I mean. If I don't have an office space I can bring them to, I don't look "settled." Besides, I can't exactly bring all my models to the Club. This is a potentially massive project, babe. I cannot screw this up.

BETTY: And you won't. You just can't meet them here is all.

CASE: For how long?

BETTY: Just for a bit.

CASE: I've started locking my designs away since that time she drew on them.

BETTY: And I appreciate that.

CASE: I'm doing what I can, but . . .

BETTY: But what.

CASE: Her temper . . . it's starting to get out of hand.

BETTY: I'll ask Sarah to take her out for a walk after school. How long do you need?

CASE: I need for you not to "solve" this, okay? I need you to hear what I'm saying to you.

BETTY: Like I said, she has good days and bad days. The good days aren't over yet.

CASE: I'm not saying that they are. I'm saying that . . . "good" means something different every day where this disease is concerned.

BETTY: I know good is a relative term, I'm not an idiot.

CASE: That's not what I'm saying!

BETTY: She'll be fine. She just needs to get a few more good days strung together.

CASE: Last week, she didn't recognize her own front door.

BETTY: With this new medication . . .

CASE: You saw how many medications my mother went through. And none of them kept her from walking into a dinner party topless because she forgot what clothes went where.

BETTY: Your mother. Not mine.

CASE: How come, when I was going through this, *we* went through it together? But when it's your mother, I'm the enemy?

BETTY: I don't know why, Case. Why don't you tell me? You seem to have all the answers.

CASE: I don't have the answers. Hell, I barely even know the questions.

BETTY: Really? Because it seems to me that when it comes to my mother, you have all the answers, and the questions, and the sun, and the moon, and the baby Jesus wrapped up in every single word you say.

CASE: Why is it my fault that your mother trusts me?

BETTY: More than me. She trusts you more than she trusts me.

CASE: Maybe because I don't try to control her the way you do.

BETTY: Control? I'm trying to create a sense of structure and order for my mother and her life. That's exactly what the literature says you're supposed to do.

CASE: And you know what every single word of the literature says, don't you?

(He pulls out some files.)

Alzheimer's. Dementia. Your mother's symptoms cross-referenced with other possible diagnoses. *Every* possible diagnosis.

BETTY: So I did some research.

CASE: And that's fine! But all the time you spend figuring out ways around what's happening to your mother is time you're not spending with her. Time you will never get back.

BETTY: My mother spends more time with us than yours ever did. Is that what's going on here? Don't dump your guilt on me, Case, and call it mine.

CASE: You want to handle this all by yourself, you go ahead and do it. You want to throw dirt on my dead mother's grave, you do it. It make you happy? Huh? Does that make you feel better?

BETTY: That's right, put it on me. Every single solitary thing is on me. Tell me something I don't know.

CASE: I am trying to be here for you. I am trying to give you what you need. You don't want it? Fine with me.

BETTY: Is this really giving me what I need? Always reminding me of what's happening to her? What's going to happen to her?

CASE: There are three of us in this family other than your mother. She cannot be the only one you think about.

BETTY: That's right, I need to think about your clients too. You want to rent a separate office, Case? You go right ahead. Just tell me who to make the check out to.

(Case storms into the kitchen, where Ida is alone.)

IDA: Hi, Case. You off to work, baby?

CASE *(Appeasing her)*: That's right, Mrs. Farrell.

IDA: You tell that firm not to work you too hard.

CASE: I will. How are you feeling today?

IDA: Fine, just fine. You want me to fix you something before you go? Cup of tea?

CASE: No thanks, Mrs. Farrell.

IDA *(After a moment, just seeing him)*: You off to work now, Case?

CASE: Yes, Mrs. Farrell.

IDA: Let me fix you up something.

CASE: Okay, sure. Fine.

(Ida doesn't move.)

Mrs. Farrell?

IDA: Hi there, Case. You want something, baby?

CASE: I can get it myself. I don't want to bother you.

3

Adela and Ida in the kitchen, both washing dishes. Adela is surreptitiously watching Ida, moving plates and dishes when Ida misplaces them.

ADELA: My sister, she says if the baby sticks her with a fork one more time, she is quitting.

IDA: Some folks just don't know how to raise children.

ADELA: Your three, they come out fine. Here, Mrs., let me take that.

IDA: I've washed more plates than you've had . . . than you've had . . . *(Searching for the word)*

ADELA *(Filling in the gap)*: Hot dinners. You have washed more plates than I've had hot dinners.

IDA: That's right. Where were we?

ADELA: Children. You raised three beautiful children.

IDA: I raised more than three. I raised Joey and Angela Lewis right up until they went off to college.

Don't you let them tell you boys aren't any different from girls. Joey, he used to hit the other little boys something fierce. Girls scratch more than they hit, and you can usually cut their nails to stop them doing that.

ADELA: How do you stop the hitting? Especially with the fork?

IDA: Tell your sister to take the fork away and replace it with a spoon. *(Looks at the maid's door)* What's through there?

ADELA: Mrs.?

IDA: What's that door to? Has Betty been putting in new rooms?

ADELA: That's the maid's door, Mrs.

IDA: The what?

ADELA: That is what you tell me it's called.

(Silence.)

Mrs.?

IDA: If he keeps hitting, take the spoon away too. He'll get frustrated—they do when you take their toys from them. But you have to draw the line and keep it steady. Consistent.

(Adela becomes Mrs. Lewis.)

MRS. LEWIS: How do you do it, Ida? He doesn't listen to me.

IDA: He listens to you, Ma'am. He just takes his time about it, is all. Remember that time you told him to give little Angela back her doll and he did?

MRS. LEWIS: That's right, he did. I suppose I'm not too bad a mother, at that.

IDA: No, Ma'am.

MRS. LEWIS: Do you like me, Ida?

IDA: Of course I like you, Ma'am. What's not to like?

MRS. LEWIS: Now you sound like Mother Lewis. She says that all the time.

IDA: I like you just fine, Ma'am.

MRS. LEWIS: I don't like being called "ma'am." I never have. It makes me feel . . . old.

IDA: Then what would you like me to call you . . . Mrs. Lewis?

MRS. LEWIS: I suppose that's not much different from "ma'am," is it?

IDA: I suppose not, Ma'am.

MRS. LEWIS: What do you think of this place? Do you like this place?

IDA: It's a very nice apartment, Ma'am.

MRS. LEWIS: It is, isn't it? For an apartment. Bob keeps talking about moving to the suburbs, to a house and a lawn. But we never do it.

IDA: Lawns are nice, Ma'am.

MRS. LEWIS: Do you have one, Ida?

IDA: Yes, Ma'am. A little bit of one, but a lawn just the same.

MRS. LEWIS: Our house had a lawn. My mother used to have a garden. She loved it so. One year, she grew a tomato.

IDA: You mean a tomato plant, Ma'am?

MRS. LEWIS: No, one tomato. It was a big one though, so she took pride in that. The next year, she went back to flowers.

IDA: Since you can't stand tomatoes, Ma'am, it was a good thing for you your mother only raised the one tomato. Our tomatoes have just about taken over our yard.

MRS. LEWIS: I didn't know you raised tomatoes, Ida. Bob loves tomatoes.

IDA: I'll make sure and pick up some at the market when I go out shopping.

MRS. LEWIS: Of course, I didn't mean . . . I wasn't asking for any of *your* . . .

IDA: I know you didn't mean anything, Ma'am. We were just talking about tomatoes.

(Ida steps away from the sink and Mrs. Lewis becomes Adela.)

ADELA: Mrs.? Can I get you something?

IDA: I'm just headed home, Ma'am. Got to take care of my tomatoes.

ADELA: Mrs.? Mrs.? I will get you tomatoes.

IDA: I can tend to my own tomatoes.

ADELA: Please, sit down, Mrs., calm down.

IDA: I'm not giving you any of my tomatoes! I'm going home!

ADELA: Miss Sarah? Miss Sarah, your grandmother!

(Sarah runs in.)

SARAH: Gramma? Gramma, what's wrong?

IDA: Betty, what are you doing here? Why aren't you at school?

SARAH: Gramma? Gramma, I'm Sarah.

IDA: I asked you a question, Betty, why aren't you at school?!

SARAH: Gramma, it's okay. Mom said when you get like this, you just need to sit and calm down.

ADELA: I ask her to calm down, she doesn't. We call your mother?

IDA: Why does everybody want me to calm down? I ain't nothing but calm! I just need to get home is all!

ADELA: Mrs., please, sit down.

(Adela grabs Ida's arm. Ida hits her.)

IDA: Get your fucking hands off me!

SARAH: Gramma!

IDA: Stop calling me that, Betty! I am your mother!

SARAH: You're my Gramma! Gramma, it's Sarah! I'm Sarah, your granddaughter?

IDA: Sarah?

SARAH: Sarah, Gramma. I'm Sarah.

IDA: Course you are, baby. I just . . . I just need to go home. I just have to leave the Lewises' apartment and go on home.

SARAH: Okay, Gramma? Okay. I'll call Mom, and she'll . . . I'll call Mom, okay.

IDA: You do that, baby.

(Sarah steps away, takes out her phone, and dials.)

SARAH *(Trying her best not to lose it)*: Mom, it's Gramma. Mom, she's . . . she's . . . she didn't know me. She didn't know *me*. *(Failing)* Mommy. Mommy, please come home.

4

Ida in Dr. Patel's office.

DR. PATEL: It's really all about the tomatoes, Mrs. Farrell. The tomatoes in your brain.

IDA: The tomatoes?

DR. PATEL: No, the *tomatoes*. The to-ma-toes. *(Off Ida's blank expression)* Do you understand?

IDA: Yes, yes, I understand.

DR. PATEL: The tomatoes aren't firing the way they should, and the sideways that give you gas—do you still have the gas?

IDA: Yes.

DR. PATEL: You need to gas the car when you get back home. You need to remember to gas the car, after you take the blue pill.

IDA: The blue pill and the gas.

DR. PATEL: Exactly. So we're going to cut back on the blue pills, and increase the greens. Betty hates greens, but Dottie loves them, so you'll need to get okra for Betty for dinner.

IDA: Yes.

DR. PATEL: Did you pencil?

IDA: Did I what?

DR. PATEL: Did you pencil?

IDA: I . . . I don't understand.

DR. PATEL: Did. You. Pencil? It's okay if you didn't. These things happen.

IDA: Why? I go to the doctors, I take the, the, the . . . little circles, and they still happen. Why?!

5

Ida and Betty are seated in the kitchen. Ida is dressed in her coat and hat.

BETTY: You want some more tea, Mama?

IDA: No, thank you. We don't want to keep the folks waiting. When are we leaving?

BETTY: In a little while. We've got time. *(Beat)* It's a very nice place.

IDA: I'm sure it is. We used to go and visit those homes when you were little. Back when your father used to give the shut-ins communion. Remember?

BETTY: No. Did we?

IDA: Did we what?

BETTY: Visit . . . never mind.

IDA: Aren't we supposed to go someplace today?

BETTY: Yes, Mama.

IDA: When are we leaving?

BETTY: In a little while. You sure you don't want some more tea?

IDA: You want some tea?

BETTY: No, do you . . . I'll pour us both some more tea, okay?

IDA: Okay. If you want some tea, I'll join you.

(Betty takes Ida's cup, pours her some tea.)

BETTY: There you go, Mama. Let me get you some sugar.

IDA: Got any milk?

BETTY: Milk?

IDA: For the tea.

BETTY: You don't put milk in your tea.

IDA: Shows what you know. My mother always put milk in her tea, and so do I.

(Betty gets the milk and pours it in Ida's tea.)

BETTY: Gramma Taylor used to put milk in her tea?

IDA: That's how she showed me how to fix tea. She'd hold out her hand and say, "Put in just enough milk so the tea matches the back of your hand. Then it'll be just right."

BETTY: I never knew that.

IDA: I must've told you that. You probably just forgot. You always did have a terrible memory. You get that from your father's side.

BETTY: I probably do.

IDA: I got to go see Mama one of these days.

BETTY: Mama, Gramma Taylor passed on.

IDA: I know. I haven't been to visit her grave in ages.

BETTY: Oh.

IDA: What did you think I meant?

BETTY: Nothing.

IDA: Always acting like I'm senile. I remember things. I'm not a vegetable yet.

BETTY: Of course you're not.

IDA: Aren't we going someplace today?

BETTY: Yes, Mama.

IDA: When?

BETTY: In a little while.

IDA: You got anything to drink around here?

BETTY: Your tea is in front of you, Mama.

(Ida sips her tea and makes a face.)

IDA: Tastes nasty. What's this you put in it, milk?

BETTY: I made it the way Gramma Taylor used to make it.

IDA: That's right. Her tea always used to taste milky and nasty.

BETTY: Let me get you a fresh cup of tea.

(She does so.)

IDA: Thank you, baby.

BETTY: You're welcome, Mama.

(Ida looks at Betty's hands.)

IDA: You still making them fists.

BETTY: What?

IDA: Your fists. You always used to make those fists. Used to sleep like that. Angry little face, with those fists. You and that temper.

BETTY: I never had a temper. Clara had a temper. And I didn't sleep with . . .

IDA: The word is fists. And yes, yes you did. Not Clara. *You.* That's why we gave you that stuffed rabbit to sleep with. Taught you to pet it before going to bed. Can't pet something with a fist, now can you?

BETTY: Boogie Bunny. That's why you gave me Boogie?

IDA: Boogie, that's the name.

BETTY: I remember Boogie.

IDA: You loved that bunny rabbit.

BETTY: I did.

IDA: I'm glad. You fought so much in the daytime, I thought you should stop fighting and get some rest at night.

(Ida pats Betty's hand.)

You got to learn to relax sometime, baby. Can't pet with a fist.

BETTY: I know.

IDA: I thought we were going someplace today.

BETTY: We are, Mama.

IDA: When?

BETTY: In a little while.

IDA: Good, good. Don't want to sit around here all day.

(Sarah enters.)

SARAH: Hi, Gramma.
IDA: Hi, baby. You want something? Let me fix you up something.
SARAH: No thanks, Gramma.
BETTY: Sarah, you keep your Gramma company while I check and make sure everything's packed.

(Betty leaves the kitchen and sees Case with a suitcase.)

CASE: I, I just came to pick up a few things.
BETTY: For the Princeton Club.
CASE: You always said we kept up that membership for a reason.

(He sees Ida's packed luggage.)

What's going on?
BETTY: You were right.
CASE: Oh. My God. You're taking her today.
BETTY: In about half an hour. It's a lovely facility, she's going to get the best of care. I don't even know why I made such a big deal out of it.
CASE: Look, do you want . . . do you want me to . . .
BETTY: What? Come with me? Hold me and tell me this is all a really really bad dream and I'm going to wake up tomorrow and fight with my mother and everything is going to be all right?
CASE: What do you want?

(Betty goes into his arms, hands fisted, and holds on for dear life.)

BETTY: I want my mommy.
CASE: You're right, baby. What you're doing is right.
BETTY: I don't wanna be right.

6

The nursing home. Ida is drawing, but her picture is completely abstract.

IDA: That's it. Mama's house. Picture Mama's house. Finally right.

(Ida draws a childlike stick figure.)

Dottie pretty one. The pretty. Pretty. Hole in her face. Betty smart. Clara . . . something. What is Clara? My daughter is Clara. Clara is . . . my daughter. Draw Clara. Draw Clara.

(Ida looks at the pencil.)

Sticks. Sticks that draw. Draw the picture. Pencils! That's the word. Pencil! Pencils give you picture. Part of picture. Pieces you want to see, to save. The other side . . .

(She turns the page over.)

Nothing.

(She looks at the pencil blankly.)

7

Betty, Sarah, and Adela are in the kitchen.

ADELA: You want me to come next Wednesday instead of Thursday?
BETTY: If you could, Adela. We're going to see my mother.
ADELA: I know. Can you wish her well from me too please?
BETTY: Of course.
SARAH: Why? She won't know the difference.
BETTY: We'll send her your regards, Adela.
ADELA: Thank you, Ma'am. Miss Sarah, I'll do your room now?
SARAH: Thanks, Adela.

(Adela exits.)

BETTY: I don't want you talking about your grandmother like that.

SARAH: Why not? It's the truth.

BETTY: I don't care if it is. And don't you dare say anything like that tomorrow.

SARAH: Do I have to go?

BETTY: I don't want you asking that question. How can you ask me that?

SARAH: Because she won't know . . . I have to study.

BETTY: I told her you were studying last time.

SARAH: Please don't make me. Please.

BETTY: Oh, baby, I'm sorry. I know this is hard. Believe me, I know.

SARAH: Am I a bad person?

BETTY: You're not a bad person. My daughter could never be a bad person. I'll tell Gramma you'll be there next time.

(Betty starts to exit.)

SARAH: Mom? Gramma Felicia—and Gramma. Is this going to happen to you and Daddy too?

BETTY: Please don't ask me that. I don't have an answer. I wish to God I did.

SARAH: Is it going to happen to me when I get old?

BETTY: No. Do you hear me? Not if I have to . . . No. No!

(Betty exits.)

SARAH: Mom? Mom, I'm sorry! Mom!

(Sarah runs after Betty.
    Ida enters the kitchen. She is again neatly dressed, hair done. She looks around the kitchen, shakes her head, and starts organizing things.
        Over her actions, we hear the following:)

YOUNG BETTY: Mama! Dottie and Clara won't listen to me!

(Ida looks toward the voice, then turns back to her work.)

MRS. LEWIS: Oh, Ida. What would we do without you?

BETTY: You worry too much, Mama. I'll be fine.

CASE: Mrs. Farrell, that meal was delicious. But you shouldn't be working so hard. You're our guest.

SARAH: Come on, Gramma, the movie's about to start!

BETTY: Thank you, Mama. I love you.

(Satisfied with her work, Ida walks to the maid's door, opens it, and exits.)

8

Betty is dressed in black. She keeps making fists with her hands, until she catches herself. She opens her hand and looks at it wistfully. Sarah enters.

SARAH: Aunt Dottie says the limo isn't big enough.

BETTY: It's big enough for the immediate family. Her . . . "psychic" will just have to take his own car. And if he were any good at his job, he'd've known that to begin with.

SARAH: I'm not telling her that.

BETTY: Just take your father and sit in the limo and . . . take up space. If that psychic sticks his foot in, slam the car door on it.

(Sarah exits, Case enters.)

CASE: Was Dottie always this crazy?

BETTY: Always. The flowers?

CASE: We're taking them to the gravesite first, then the hospital, so . . .

BETTY *(Speaking along with him)*: "So the living can enjoy them." Good. The repast, I need to check on the repast.

CASE: Babe, you don't have to.

BETTY: If I don't, who will?

CASE: When you're right, you're right.

BETTY: You're yessing me, aren't you?

CASE: Yes, dear.

BETTY: Good.

(He holds her. She weakens for a moment, then pushes him away.)

Go sit in the limo with Sarah and save me a spot.

CASE: I'm not sitting next to that psychic, I'm telling you that right now.

BETTY: Sarah has orders to slam the door on his foot.

CASE: That's my girl. My little girl.

(He kisses her.)

That's my girl.

BETTY: Limo. Now.

CASE: Yes, Ma'am!

(Case exits.
A tearful young white woman dressed in black [Angela] enters. She is played by the same actress as Mrs. Lewis/Adela.)

ANGELA: Excuse me? You're Betty, aren't you? Her daughter?

BETTY: Yes. Can I help you?

ANGELA: I'm Angela Gaines. It used to be Lewis?

BETTY: Angela Lewis?

ANGELA: Yes. Your mother practically raised me and my brother Joe.

BETTY: Joe. Angela and Joe Lewis, I remember. Your family sent flowers, you didn't have to come.

ANGELA: Of course we had to come! Joe's getting the car, for the drive to the cemetery. Your mother was . . . well, you know what she was.

BETTY: Yes, I do.

ANGELA: My mother kept that picture Ida drew of me on the wall until the day she died. She swore no one ever captured me as well.

BETTY: Mama did love to draw. When she could find the time.

(Sarah enters.)

SARAH: Mom, we can't find Aunt Clara.

BETTY: She'll be in the bathroom fixing her face. I'm half tempted to leave without her.

ANGELA *(To Sarah)*: You made a lovely speech about your grandmother. Just lovely.

SARAH: Thank you. Did you know her?

BETTY: This is Angela Lewis. Used to be Angela Lewis, I mean.

SARAH: I'm pleased to meet you. *(Beat)* Wait. From the family Gramma worked for?

BETTY: Yes.

SARAH: Oh. Okay.

BETTY *(Warning)*: Sarah.

SARAH: I'm sorry, I just . . . my grandmother used to work for you. She was your maid, right?

ANGELA: She was more than that to us.

SARAH: Yeah, right.

BETTY: Sarah!

SARAH: I guess if she hadn't, my mother wouldn't have gone on and become a lawyer. My mother's a lawyer, you knew that, right?

ANGELA: I did. Ida—your grandmother told us. My father was a lawyer, too.

SARAH: My father's an architect. He went to Yale.

ANGELA: That's wonderful. I'm a graphic designer, myself. Part time. And Joe's a therapist. Joe, would you just double-park the damn car and get over here!

BETTY: Angela, would you and Joe like to come join us at the repast? You're certainly welcome.

ANGELA: We'd love to.

(Angela exits.)

BETTY *(Looking at Sarah)*: What?

SARAH: I don't like her.

BETTY: She's not as bad as you think.

SARAH: You don't like her either.

BETTY: I never said that. And we've got no reason not to like her. She didn't do anything wrong.

SARAH: I'll be good.

BETTY: You do that. *(Beat)* But make sure and tell them you're going to Harvard. Make Gramma proud.

SARAH: I will. *(Beat)* Did you check on the repast?

BETTY: I meant to! But your father insisted "somebody" would handle it.

SARAH: Daddy should know better. If we don't do it, who will?

BETTY: I know! *(Looking at Sarah)* Just like . . .

(Sarah takes her mother's fisted hand and puts her hand in it. Betty gathers herself.)

Limo.

SARAH: Now.

(They exit.)

END OF PLAY

ABOUT THE PLAY

Maid's Door received its world premiere at The Billie Holiday Theatre in Brooklyn, NY, in 2014. That production received seven AUDELCO Awards, including Best Play. It was a finalist for the Francesca Primus Prize. *Maid's Door* was presented at An Appalachian Summer Festival and the 2015 and 2017 National Black Theatre Festival. It was further developed at Red Mountain Theatre's Human Rights New Works Festival in Birmingham, AL (Keith Cromwell, Executive Director).

Maid's Door is copyright © 2022 by Cheryl L. Davis. For further information contact: Ricki Olshan, Buchwald Literary and Talent Agency, ricki@buchwald.com, 212-867-1200.

ABOUT THE PLAYWRIGHT

Cheryl L. Davis received the Ed Kleban Award for her work as a musical theater librettist. Her musical *Barnstormer*, written with award-winning composer Douglas J. Cohen, received a Jonathan Larson Performing Arts Foundation Award under the auspices of The Lark Play Development Center. *Maid's Door* was produced at the Billie Holiday Theatre to excellent reviews, received seven AUDELCO Awards, and was presented at the National Black Theatre Festival; it was also a finalist for the Francesca Primus Prize. Her musical *Bridges* was commissioned and produced by the Berkeley Playhouse. It was a finalist for the 2018 Richard Rodgers Award. *Don't Stay Safe,* the short film musical based on *Bridges,* was nominated for a Drama Desk Award, and was screened and won awards in several film festivals. Her short play *Now I Lay Me Down to Sleep* starring Patina Miller streamed as part of #WhileWeBreathe and received a glowing write-up in the *New York Times.* Cheryl writes for *Law & Order: SVU* on a freelance basis, and her episode "Garland's Baptism by Fire" is available On Demand. She received a Writers Guild Award for her work on the daytime dramatic serial *As the World Turns* and was nominated for a Daytime Emmy Award for her work on that show as well, and has also written for *Days of Our Lives.* She was a Maven Media Fellow at Stowe Story Lab for her pilot *Swimming Uptown,* 2021.

BERTA, BERTA

Angelica Chéri

2019

PRODUCTION HISTORY

Berta, Berta was presented at the 2019 National Black Theatre Festival. The director was Reginald L. Douglas; the set design was by Luciana Stecconi (original set design, Contemporary American Theater Festival, CATF), the costume design was by Sarita Fellows, the lighting design was by John Ambrosone (original design, CATF), the sound design was by David Remedios; the stage manager was Jeremy Phillips. The Producing Company was Contemporary American Theater Festival. The cast was:

BERTA	Bianca La Verne Jones
LEROY	Benton Greene

CHARACTERS

LEROY, African American, a smoldering wanderer

BERTA, African American, a young widow

SETTING

Berta's home in Mcridian, Mississippi.

TIME

May 1, 1923.

NOTES

The play is inspired by the prison work song "Berta, Berta" that originated on Parchman Farm, Mississippi State Penitentiary. It is an imagination of the love story behind the song's origins.

Some lyrics from the actual song appear in the dialogue. They are presented in bold type. This is not that those lines should necessarily be sung, but particular attention and weight should be given to their delivery.

Leroy's song on page 234 should reference the melody of the actual song, but should have a more relaxed, intimate quality.

The play should be performed without an intermission.

"BERTA, BERTA" ORIGINAL LYRICS

O Lord Berta Berta O Lord gal oh-ah
O Lord Berta Berta O Lord gal well now

Go 'head and marry don'tcha wait on me oh-ah
Go 'head and marry don'tcha wait on me well now
Might not want ya when I go free oh-ah
Might not want ya when I go free well now

O Lord Berta Berta O Lord gal oh-ah
O Lord Berta Berta O Lord gal well now

Raise 'em up higher, let 'em drop on down oh-ah
Raise 'em up higher, let 'em drop on down well now
Don't know the diff'rence when the sun go down oh-ah
Don't know the diff'rence when the sun go down well now

Berta in Meridian and she livin' at ease oh-ah
Berta in Meridian and she livin' at ease well now
I'm on old Parchman, got to work or leave oh-ah
I'm on old Parchman, got to work or leave well now

O Lord Berta Berta O Lord gal oh-ah
O Lord Berta Berta O Lord gal well now

When you marry, don't marry no farmin' man oh-ah
When you marry, don't marry no farmin' man well now

Everyday Monday, hoe handle in your hand oh-ah
Everyday Monday, hoe handle in your hand well now

When you marry, marry a railroad man oh-ah
When you marry, marry a railroad man well now
Everyday Sunday, dollar in your hand oh-ah
Everyday Sunday, dollar in your hand well now

O Lord Berta Berta O Lord gal oh-ah
O Lord Berta Berta O Lord gal well now . . .

SCENE 1—TWO A.M.

Open to the sound of silence. Out of that silence creeps in the subtle hum of a prison chain gang in the rhythm of labor.

Leroy is revealed in the rising of the light, standing in front of a worn-in couch in the midst of a solemn but charming living room. He wears an undershirt and trousers, soiled from daily labor.

Leroy is a sturdy, well-built Black man with piercing eyes. He is undeniably handsome, yet overwhelmingly troubled. His feet are planted firmly in the floor as if to keep him from falling over or being blown away.

Leroy's gaze intensifies, as does the rhythm of the chain gang as it clangs over and over in his mind. The clanging overtakes him with panic.

LEROY: Berta? Berta?!

(Thick silence.)

Berta where you went?! BERTA?!

BERTA (Off): What you say?!

LEROY: I say where you went woman?! You makin' me nervous!

BERTA (Off): I say hold on now! Stop all that hollin'!

(Leroy exhales deeply as Berta enters, carrying a white button-down shirt stained with blood. Berta is a voluptuous, stately Black woman with a striking countenance. She looks majestic yet intimidating, wearing a long robe and a sleeping bonnet. The robe clings to her every curve as she enters, carrying a kerosene lamp in her free hand. She sets it on a table. Berta is beautiful yet marred by hardship. Her steps are always heavy.)

BERTA: I set it in the bleach for a hot second.	LEROY: Why you take so long?

BERTA: What you say?

LEROY: Why you leave me in here—

LEROY: —so long woman? It too quiet in this house.	BERTA: I say I goin' to get the blood out! It ain't come out all the way.

BERTA: What you say?!

LEROY: I say it too quiet in this house. Give me a funny feelin'.

BERTA: That don't mean you got to go hollin' and carryin' on. Steppin' on my sweet potatoes.

LEROY: I don't like the quiet.

LEROY: It's too quiet. So quiet it's loud.	BERTA: Ya betta be glad ya missed my watermelons!

BERTA: If ya had a squashed my watermelons, I would a had ta kill ya. You got your nerve, you know that? Makin' tracks through my crops. Bangin' on my door like you the sheriff. Done nearly scared me half to death. And this! (Holding up the shirt) Where all this blood come from?

LEROY: Know what I mean? When it get too quiet? So quiet you can hear things. Like a ringin' sound goin' over and over in ya mind.

BERTA: Man, what is you talkin' 'bout?

LEROY: And you can't make it stop . . .

(Leroy stands frozen, in a hypnotic daze.)

BERTA: Leroy? Leroy!

LEROY: Huh?

BERTA: You hearin' things? What things you been hearin'?

LEROY: Nothin', nothin'.

BERTA: You got the devil in you?

LEROY: Woman, please.

BERTA: Don't tell me I done let the devil in my house.

LEROY: Always talkin' 'bout the devil.

BERTA: You on that stuff? I don't welcome no dope in my house, neither. No dope and no devils!

LEROY: I ain't on no dope, woman.

BERTA: If it ain't dope, then what in the world you got goin' on?

LEROY: Never mind all that noise—

LEROY: —I just had to see ya.   BERTA. Got me washin' God-knows-whose blood outta your shirt.

BERTA: And do ya know what time it is? Do ya? You comin' up in my house half past hell's bedtime.

LEROY: Hell this, devil that. Talk about the devil so much. He your new boyfriend?

(She throws the shirt at him.)

BERTA: G'on get outta here with all that.

LEROY: Ha ha ha! That's my Berta gal!

BERTA: Boyfriend . . .

LEROY: You ain't changed, baby girl. Ain't changed one bit.

BERTA: Still cleanin' up behind your mess.

(Leroy inspects the shirt.)

LEROY: You did it again. Worked your magic.

BERTA: Whose blood is it Leroy? Don't see you bleedin' from nowhere.

LEROY: My Berta touched it. That's all that matters. Don't care if the stain ain't came out all the way.

BERTA: Well 'scuse me Massuh. Maybe one of ya lil girlfriends could do a better job.

LEROY: Girlfriends?

BERTA: You heard me. Your girlfriend. Shouldn't she be the one you botherin' in the middle of the night?

LEROY: Don't start now, it's too early.

BERTA: Too early, too late.

BERTA: Same story with you.	LEROY: Try to talk sweet nothin's, and you always gotta make 'em sour.

BERTA: Give it here.

(Berta takes the shirt and drapes it over a chair. Leroy looks around.)

LEROY: So this is it, huh? Alberta's house. Never thought I'd see it. The inside of it.

BERTA: Well here you are.

LEROY: Done seen the front so many times. Ain't what I thought it would look like on the inside.

BERTA: What that mean?

LEROY: He done a good enough job. Good floors. Good strong floors.

(Leroy looks down at the floors, stomping on them.)

I know he don't approve a my feet walkin' on his floors.

BERTA: Don't make no diff'rence now.

LEROY: Couple lil holes here and there. Could use another coat a paint or two.

(Leroy spots a small box positioned in a corner of the room. A lit candle and a white rose sit atop the box. A Bible is nearby. Leroy approaches the box, curious.)

This your little prayer corner or somethin'?

BERTA (*Running over to him*): DON'T YOU TOUCH THAT! (*Steps in Leroy's way*) Ain't it enough for you to barge up in here unannounced, walkin' 'round like you own the place?! Ain't you got no respect?!

LEROY: Well damn, can I sit down then?!

BERTA: Sit?!

LEROY: I was waitin' for permission! Since you think I ain't got no manners!

BERTA: G'on head, hell, ya makin' me nervous just standin' there!

(*Leroy sits down on the couch. Berta watches with her arms folded.*)

LEROY: Thank you.

(*Having looked him up and down, Berta goes back to Leroy's shirt, rubbing the blood out with her hands. Her nervous energy seeps into the stain. Leroy watches.*)

BERTA: You never could keep a shirt nice. If it wasn't blood, it was dirt or gravy or some kind a grease.

LEROY: You lookin' good, Berta Ann.

BERTA: What you say?

LEROY: Say you lookin' good. Mighty good.

BERTA: Don't start now, Leroy!

LEROY: First I'm fussin', now I'm—

BERTA: —Meddlin'.

BERTA: 'Cause I's half-dressed,   LEROY: Now *you* the one fussin'.
just like you like.   No matter what I do, you
                                                          fussin'!

LEROY: Can't win with you.

BERTA: And you can't win no fight neither, from the look of things.

LEROY: I ain't got a scratch on me.

BERTA: Not one I can see.

LEROY: Awww hush up, gal. Come on now, I been missin' ya.

BERTA: My foot.

LEROY: Yeah ya foot, ya hips, ya lips—

BERTA: Don't start, Leroy!

LEROY: A man can't miss his sweetheart?

BERTA: Sweetheart . . .

LEROY: My sweet, sweet Berta Ann.

BERTA: What happened this time?

LEROY: Awww, baby girl.

BERTA: Come on now. Tell me.

LEROY: I can't. Not now.

BERTA: Why not? You got somewhere else to go at this hour?

LEROY: It's a lot. It's a whole, whole lot.

BERTA: I deserves an explanation. My sweet potatoes deserves
an explanation!

LEROY: I just had to see ya. Honest. Been too long.

(Berta looks at him, struggling to read his face.)

BERTA: Was it Rosa?

LEROY: Rosa?

BERTA: Don't play dumb with me.

LEROY: Woman, whatcha talkin'?

BERTA: Rosa Lee; don't play dumb with me.

LEROY: Rosa?

BERTA: *Rosa Lee*, the gal whose husband just got let outta
Parchman!

LEROY: I ain't messin' with Parchman!

BERTA: Fool, I'm talkin' 'bout Rosa's husband! Bet he heard
you was sniffin' 'round his woman while he was locked up,
pickin' cotton.

(Leroy tenses up, slowly fuming.)

Mmm-hmm, I knew it! That man been gone four, five
months. Sweatin' his time away in the fields, chained to six
other men. Countin' down the days 'til he can get back to
his fast, tail-waggin' wife. Know she been leavin' her back
door open while he been gone. Lettin' the tomcats in and

out. Did her husband come home and find your finger in his sugah bowl? Huh Leroy? You give that man somethin' to bleed about?

LEROY: You talkin' 'bout **Parchman** like it's some kind a playground. It ain't no play-pretty.

BERTA: I know what **Parchman** is—

LEROY: —What you talkin' to me 'bout **Parchman** for? **Parchman**? That's where they take the Colored man to kill him from the inside out.

BERTA: I done heard the stories Leroy!

LEROY: Wring out his soul like it ain't nothin' but blood on a washrag. Then hang it out to dry. Paint a black film over his eyes so it feel like he 'sleep when he wide awake. Film so dark it color nightmares over his dreams.

BERTA: What the hell is you—I don't give a lick 'bout **Parchman**—

BERTA: I'm talkin' 'bout you and that woman!	LEROY: And he **can't tell the diff'rence when the sun go down.**

LEROY *(Standing up)*: Hear me? Said ya **don't know the diff'rence when the sun go down**!!

BERTA: Man, what the hell is wrong with you?!

(Leroy exhales, composing himself.)

LEROY: What you talkin'?

BERTA: Is you drunk?

LEROY: Naw, I just—I just got a lot on my mind . . . It's a whole lot on my mind.

BERTA: Sit your drunk ass down. What you been drinkin'?

LEROY: I ain't drunk, woman, damn! And I ain't been messin' with nobody's wife!

BERTA: Just full a the devil. Betcha Rosa know well as I do now.

LEROY: I don't be creepin' 'round with nobody wearin' a ring. Not Rosa Lee, not *nobody's* wife. Even the devil himself gotta tip his hat to that.

BERTA: The devil can't wear no hat; his horns too big.

LEROY: I swear I ain't seen Rosa since 'fore the weddin'.

BERTA: Hers?

LEROY: Yours.

BERTA: Oh . . .

(Silence. Berta looks away.)

LEROY: Mmm-hmm.

BERTA: *Mmm-hmm*, what? Don't you *mmm-hmm* me.

LEROY: I'm just sayin'.

BERTA: I know what you sayin', and I don't feel like sayin' nothin'
'bout it. Not right now.

LEROY: That's all I'm sayin'.

BERTA: Well say it to yourself.

LEROY: **Oh Lord gal.**

*(Berta retreats to the kitchen. Leroy returns to his seat on the
couch.*

*As he sits, **the sound of a single cicada** pours in for a brief
moment. Leroy jerks at the sound, looking to the window.
Berta reacts as well, moving toward the box and candle.*

The sound dissipates.

*They both halt in the aftermath of the sound, checking
each other's reaction. Both choose to play it off as if they've
heard nothing, as if it was only in their minds.)*

BERTA: What?	LEROY: What?
Nothin'.	Nothin'.

BERTA: You uh . . . you hungry?

LEROY: What?

BERTA: I got some greens I can warm up for ya.

LEROY: I ain't got no appetite right now.

BERTA: Not even after walkin' from Nellieburg in the dark?

LEROY: Nellieburg ain't nothin' but a hop, skip, and a jump away
from **Meridian.**

BERTA: You need to eat Leroy. You ain't ate in a while; I can tell.
Can smell it on your breath. Got that hollow smell.

LEROY: You studyin' my breath again, woman?

BERTA: I'm fixin' ya a plate a greens.

LEROY: In a lil bit. Just sit. Sit with me Berta. You been runnin' back and forth all through the house since I walked in the door.

BERTA: If I sit I'm a fall back to sleep.

LEROY: Please, baby. Sit with me. I got somethin' I gotta tell ya.

(Berta sits, cautiously.
Berta exhales. Leroy inhales.
He takes her in.
She glares at him with expectation.)

BERTA: *And?*

LEROY: What?

BERTA: G'on now! Say what you gon' say!

(Leroy takes a breath, preparing his thoughts. Then he abandons them.)

LEROY: You smell nice. Smell like that rose cream you been usin' since forever.

BERTA: You smell like . . . outside.

LEROY: I'd bathe, but why bathe and get back in the same dirty clothes?

BERTA: I'd give ya some of Ernie's, but—

LEROY: —Naw, that's bad luck. I need all the luck in Mississippi on my side right now.

BERTA: Leroy what did you do? What kind a trouble you done found yourself in this time?

LEROY: If I tell you, you might throw me out this house.

BERTA: I might throw you out anyways.

LEROY: In a minute. I'll tell you in a minute. Just let me look at you, Berta. Been so long. I seen your face in my mind more than my own reflection, but feel like it been a dozen lifetimes since I—

(Leroy gingerly reaches out and tries to touch Berta's face, but before he can reach it, she swats his hand away. She shoots up from the couch.)

BERTA: A dozen and a half damn lifetimes it's been. Three long years! Waitin' for you to come outta whatever hole you been in and stop by for one hot second to check on me. Say hello, goodbye, Merry Christmas, or at least see if I'm breathin'! But nooooo. Not a cotton-pickin' word! Not a word, hair, or prayer from Leroy Grant for *three years*. And for somebody that's s'posed to loooooooooooove me like you say, I think that's pretty cotton-pickin' rotten! I been searchin' all over **Meridian** for one lone word from you, but did nobody have nothin' for me. Not the pastor, not the butcher, not the man sellin' cigarettes on 4th Street. Not nobody had a word from Leroy Grant to give to Alberta Watkins. Let alone you writin' me a letter. Or a telegram, Western Union, somethin'. You just disappeared on me!

LEROY: You got married, Berta.

BERTA: He's dead! Been dead.

LEROY: You went and got married on me.

BERTA: It's too early for all this. Too late!

LEROY: Course I love you.

BERTA: Mmm-hmm, my foot.

LEROY: Love ev'ry bit of you I could get my hands on. Wanted to get a hold of your hand. But you went and gave it to someone else!

BERTA: My hand would a gone limp if I'da left it hangin', waitin' for you to be ready enough to take it!

LEROY: I had some things to take care of. Things to get out the way, our way.

BERTA: Things. Women.

LEROY: That ain't the whole story.

BERTA: I said I ain't wanna talk about this.

LEROY: Me neither.

(Berta sits back down, arms folded.)

BERTA: Ernie loved me enough to marry me. He ain't let nothin' stop him. You always got you a fresh-baked excuse. Hot and ready!

LEROY: Yeah, he loved you enough to die on you.

BERTA: Shut yo' mouth! God rest his soul.

LEROY: That the only way a Colored woman own a house and a farm on her own? Her husband gotta die and leave her in it?

BERTA: I'm a slap you in a minute.

LEROY: If I could a bought you a house I would a.

BERTA: Just seem to me like if a man wanna do somethin' bad enough, he go 'head and do it. He don't spend his time thinkin' 'bout whether or not he can.

LEROY: Ernest was a different kind a man than me. A **farmin' man**. He knew how to plant seeds and help 'em grow. **Railroad men**, we cursed. We gotta follow the tracks wherever they take us. But we find our way home. One way or another.

(Leroy looks deeply at Berta.
   She turns her head.)

BERTA: I done heard this before, Leroy. Same story, different day. That all you got?

LEROY: You think I ain't wanted to come check on you after he passed? Think I ain't wanted to stop by with some eggs—?

BERTA: —I got my own eggs—

LEROY: —Check on your grass, chop up some wood for the stove? Fix the holes in the wall? Fill the empty hole in your bed? But that's *his* stove. *His* walls. And *his* bed!

BERTA: Here you go.

BERTA: "Pride come before the fall."	LEROY: But it ain't all 'bout Ernest. I ain't studyin' him. It was *me*.

LEROY: I been through some things Berta. Things I can hardly put words to. Every time I try, dirt come out. And I ain't wanna spit my dirt on you, so I waited. I waited for God to clean me out. I waited for Him to tell me I was ready.

(Berta looks at Leroy in disbelief.)

BERTA: You tellin' me God told you to come to me in the middle of the night?

LEROY: I'm tellin' you I been waitin' and waitin' 'til I couldn't wait no more. Tonight, I jumped ahead of God's mouth.

BERTA: You been waitin'. Three years you been waitin'. Waitin' on *God* to tell you when you to come to me. But you know your ass don't wait on God for nothin' else!

LEROY: You could a wrote me! But you ain't wanna see me bad enough!

BERTA: You don't know the half of it!

(Berta retreats to the chair where the shirt is hanging. She smells it.)

Like sweat and sweet nothin's. That's how you smell. That's what come outta your skin.

(Berta holds the shirt against her body.)

Ya know, your shirts always did look better on me.

LEROY: I look better on you.

BERTA: Hush your mouth!

LEROY: Tell me I'm lyin'.

BERTA: I don't know. Been so long, I done forgot.

LEROY: You ain't forget one bit of me.

BERTA: I reckon I have.

LEROY: Swear 'fore Lord.

BERTA: Don't bring the Lord into your drawers!

LEROY: You called His name enough when you was in 'em.

BERTA: Leroy! Lord forgive us.

LEROY: Tell me I'm lyin'.

BERTA: I forgot. On purpose.

LEROY: You forgot me?

BERTA: Them nights. You, me, and your snake. Eatin' from the tree 'fore its time.

LEROY: Why you wanna go forgettin' me?

BERTA: I couldn't have you in my head with Ernie in bed next to me . . . But it happened anyway.

LEROY (*With a smile*): You a lie.

BERTA: Don't get to goin' now.

LEROY: Poor ole Ernest.

BERTA: I'd be lyin' there some nights and feel hands goin' down my back, my legs. Thought they was his hands, but they was yours. He'd be sound asleep.

LEROY: You sho' that wasn't no ghost?

BERTA: I think he could tell too sometimes. By the look on his face when he woke up.

LEROY: Can't every man be Leroy Grant.

BERTA: Thank the Lord.

LEROY: Ernest and his triflin' self.

BERTA: What you talkin'?!

LEROY: You know he had his head all up and through his ass. Thinkin' he had me beat. Marryin' you. He knew 'bout us, how I felt. Wanted to throw it in my face, like he done beat me or somethin'.

LEROY: Sho' he had me beat.   BERTA: Ernie wasn't studyin' you.

LEROY: Even beat me to the grave.

BERTA: You goin' to hell!

LEROY: What's goin' send me to hell first, my mouth or your legs? Don't think I can't see them through that robe.

BERTA: Boy . . .

(*Berta self-consciously adjusts herself.*)

LEROY: I miss them legs, Berta.

LEROY: Them thighs.   BERTA: Don't say it, Leroy, don't—

(*Leroy slowly approaches Berta from behind.*)

LEROY: Strongest thighs God ever put on a woman. Made to squeeze life out, head first. And just as easily squeeze some life back into me. After I go dead. You put life back into me

Berta. Squeezed it in me. Dripped it on me. Watered my roots. I swear after makin' love to you I ain't had to read the Bible to know what Eden was like. Felt like Eden rained down from heaven with you. You and your thighs. You was Eve. Singin' as you watered my garden.

(Berta is fully encased in Leroy's embrace.)

BERTA: I remember . . . these arms.
LEROY: Stop hidin' Berta. Lemme see ya.

(Leroy removes Berta's sleeping bonnet, revealing her hair pulled back into a long French braid.)

There she is. There's my Berta gal.

(Leroy caresses Berta's hair, smelling her.)

You remember what you used to say to me? Just before you'd call out to God?
BERTA: I do.
LEROY: Say it.
BERTA: "You ain't s'posed to feel this good."
LEROY: Say it again, Berta Ann.

(He kisses the back of her neck.)

BERTA: You ain't s'posed to feel this good, Leroy.
LEROY: I know. You ain't neither.

(Leroy turns Berta and kisses her. It's not a short kiss, but it wants to be longer. Berta interrupts it.)

BERTA: Now you just stop, you stop it! Get off a me!
LEROY: What's the matter?!
BERTA: With me? Or with you? What's the matter with you, Leroy?!
LEROY: Me?!

BERTA: That's what you came here for? Some tail?! Some good ole Berta tail!

LEROY: I ain't meant no harm by it!

BERTA: I ain't seen as much as your shadow since Ernie's funeral. *Three long years!* Now you jump God's mouth so you can come for my panties?! Lowdown good-for-nothin' Negro!!

LEROY: Hey! You watch yourself!

BERTA: That's what I'm doin'! I'm watchin' myself 'fore a piece of me float off while I ain't lookin'. *"Keep thy heart with all diligence."* That's what I'm doin', Leroy, I'm keepin' my heart. You can't run off with it again. Not even if you hide it in your drawers!

LEROY: Ain't nobody tryna take nothin' from you, Berta, it's *me*! I be the one tryna give you somethin'. Some of me. You got more of me than I'd ever dare take from you!

BERTA: Then why you come in here runnin' sweet words down my back?!

LEROY: What else I'm a do when I get this close to you? What else have I ever done? That's what kept me away! I knew where my hands would go soon as they saw you. Like butter to bread.

BERTA: My foot!

LEROY: Come on, baby; don't do me like that.

BERTA: Ain't like I just been sittin' here twiddlin' my thumbs, Leroy; I was *workin' on somethin'* before you ran up in here! Somethin' *important*. Somethin' you wouldn't know nothin' about. Not to mention *my crops*. Grass. Chickens! I got my own whole world goin' on that ain't got nothin' to do with Leroy Grant. The sun don't rise and fall on your name like it did when we was kids. So if all you wanted was to come in here and light my fire, then—

BERTA: —you can take your ass right back through that door!!	LEROY: I got in trouble alright?! Just like you say!

BERTA: What you say?

LEROY: I say I got in trouble, woman! Good God!

BERTA: Trouble!

LEROY: This ain't no kind a backwards business 'bout gettin' in your panties!

BERTA: You got in trouble! I know you did!

LEROY: Well there it is!

BERTA: What kind a trouble?

LEROY: It's pretty ugly. Ugly trouble.

BERTA: Over what? What you do this time?

LEROY: *This time?* You make it sound like I be in the business of doin' this sorta thing all the time!

BERTA: What *happened*, Leroy?! I ain't got time for all this back-and-forth mess!

LEROY: Curtis Wilburn.

BERTA: Who?

LEROY: Bald-headed. Curtis Wilburn from Daleville. His mama make them pies 'round Thanksgiving. She grow them apples in her backyard. Say that why Curtis ain't got no more hair left on his head. His mama kept prayin' for apples 'til his head turned to one. Shine just like one.

BERTA: Oooohhhhh *him*. Bald-headed Curtis Wilburn!

LEROY: He sho' know you.

BERTA: Ain't nobody studyin' ole bald-headed Curtis.

LEROY: He got a mouth on him.

BERTA: What he got to do with this? Y'all done got into some mess?

LEROY: Somethin' like that.

BERTA: Lord.

LEROY: You got somethin' you wanna tell me, Berta?

BERTA: Whatchu talkin'?

LEROY: I'm a ask you one time, and I need you to put your grown-woman panties on and tell me the cotton-pickin' truth! How well you do know this nigga?!

BERTA: Who in the hot hell you think you talkin' to like that?!

LEROY: Answer me!

BERTA: Leroy, get your head out your ass and talk right!

(Leroy takes a deep breath.)

LEROY: He say he been friendly with you. More than friendly.

BERTA: Friendly how?

LEROY: You know friendly. *Friendly*-friendly.

BERTA: He a *lie*! He a cotton-pickin' lie!

LEROY: He better be.

BERTA: His old bald-headed behind tried for my spare key, but hell if I'd give him anything!

LEROY: How you mean?

BERTA: He call himself offerin' to buy me a new couch. I say, "The one I got work just fine." Then he call himself gettin' loud. Got to yellin' at me 'bout how, "Colored women won't take to nobody bein' neighborly these days," and somethin' or other that ain't made no kind a sense. I told him, "Don't nobody get loud with Alberta Watkins!" Then he call himself tryna grab a hold of me!

LEROY: DEVIL!

(The ostinato pulse of the prison chain gang returns to Leroy's mind.)

BERTA: I slapped him so good his mama felt it! Felt it while she puttin' one of them pies in the oven. I ain't seen or heard of him since.

(Berta sees the intensity in Leroy's face.)

Why? What he told you?

LEROY: You wanna talk about the devil? *He's* the devil! He knew what he was doin'. 'Cause they done marked me. I'm a marked man!

BERTA: What is you talkin' 'bout?

(Leroy jolts up.)

LEROY: They marked me like they own me. Like I'm cattle. So no matter where I go, no matter how far I get, they can claim me and lead me back to pasture. And he knew it! He wanna see 'em make a nigga outta me. A cotton-choppin' nigga. They gon' put a **hoe handle in my hand**!

BERTA (*Overlapping with above*): Leroy! Hey! Hey!! Leroy!!!

(*Berta grabs Leroy, trying to calm him. He shakes her off, inadvertently tossing her to the ground. The sight of a fallen Berta brings Leroy back to his senses.*)

LEROY (*Trying to help her*): Berta!! You alright?! Baby, you alright?

BERTA (*Pushing him off*): Get away from me! You crazy! I swear you crazy. Got the devil in you. The devil is in you, Leroy! Don't care what you say!

(*Berta gets up off the ground.*)

LEROY: I don't wanna talk about it, alright?! That ain't what I came here for.

BERTA: You ain't got that right no more. Not at this hour. You don't get to raise hell and high water in my house, boil my blood with your breath, yellin' to the skies or the earth below like it's some kind a devil speakin' through you, and then turn around and say to me that you don't want to talk about it! It's too late for that, Leroy. Too early in the mornin'! The dew is fallin' and the sun ain't gon' be far behind! Now get to talkin'!

LEROY: I'm tryna tell you; damn! Just let me get a good breath in!

(*Leroy sits down.
  Berta just looks at him, arms folded.
  Leroy takes a deep breath.*)

You know I could smell that rose cream soon as I got to the front door.

BERTA: I know you not startin' up again.

LEROY: I know that smell like I know my own voice. Always stuck to me. Never could get it outta my clothes. Never wanted to.

BERTA: 'Cept for when it got you caught. One of them women sniffin' 'round you.

LEROY: One day you gon' let that go.

BERTA: Women talk, Leroy.

LEROY: Which means they lie.

BERTA: What this got to do with nothin' now?!

LEROY: What about all them men knockin' your door down?
A widow with windows. Bet she'll look my way if I keep
walkin' by.

BERTA: I keeps my curtains closed.

LEROY: Then how Curtis Wilburn get behind 'em good enough
to see that your couch is fallin' apart?

BERTA: He stick his nose where it ain't s'posed to be!

LEROY: You wouldn't give him the time of day would ya? Would
ya, Berta?

BERTA: Don't be a fool; you know I ain't studyin' him.

LEROY: I was! I was bein' a fool. I doubted myself. For the quickest second in the world. But deep down I knew. Not my
Berta gal.

BERTA: What did you do, Leroy?!

LEROY: I can still see his face, Curtis Wilburn's face. I can see
that greasy gum look on it when he say he done had you in
the back of his bossman's Studebaker.

BERTA: SAY WHAT?!!!

LEROY: He said you gave it all to him. All up and through that car.

BERTA: He a cotton-pickin' LIE!

LEROY: I couldn't figure out what the bigger lie was: you lettin'
him put a single one of his fat fingers on you, or the fact
that any white man with good sense would give Curtis's
cross-eyed self a job drivin' a nice car. Lie or not, he got me
smokin' mad. Talkin' 'bout how he loved it, but how you
loved it more. I liked to sweat blood, mad as he got me.

BERTA: He know he ain't no good! Spreadin' lies. LIAR! I oughta
kill that nigga!

LEROY: He said it only for me. Thought he'd get my blood boilin'.
He knew 'bout me and you. And he knew I been hopin' for
your heart again.

BERTA: You told him that?

LEROY: Everybody knows that.

BERTA: Oh . . .

LEROY: I ran into Curtis leavin' the Town Hall or wherever he
say he was comin' from. Comin' down Whippoorwill Road

to pick up his bossman from a meetin'. Thinkin' he somebody in that car. Seen me walkin' from the railroad. Had
the day's sweat pullin' me down. That's when he seen me
and thought he could get me to goin'. Spoutin' that non-
sense. He was right.

(Berta picks up the shirt.)

BERTA: Y'all got to tusslin' then. Fightin' and carryin' on. You
drew blood?
LEROY: I say, "You a lowdown filthy lie, Curtis! You know you
a lie!" I say, "Don't nobody soil my Berta's honor. Don't
care who it is. Where it is. When it is. That be the road
you don't wanna walk on. 'Cause it don't matter how long
it been since I last lay my eyes on her, she still the seed of
my heart. She my mornin' and my midnight. She wake up
with me and she put me to sleep. She like the sky; she ain't
even gotta touch me, all she gotta do is shine her face off
the river, and I know she there. You wanna talk about my
mornin' and my midnight like it's some cheap piece a tail
you done flipped around?" I say, "You might as well blow a
kiss to hell, 'cause that's exactly where you goin'!"
BERTA: And?! What he do?!
LEROY: Nothin'. I kill't him.

(Blackout.
    The candle is the only light that remains. In the darkness,
*we hear the sound of **a single cicada, making its way to a***
***nearby tree**.*
    Shift.)

SCENE 2–HALF AN HOUR LATER

Lights up on Berta's kitchen. The kerosene lamp now sits on the
end table beside the Bible.
    Leroy sits at the table with a bowl of collard greens in front of
him. Berta sits across from him with a large cup of coffee. She now
wears an apron over her robe.

Berta stirs. Leroy eats. They avoid eye contact. Tension pervades the space. Not a word has been spoken since the last.

Berta tries to take a sip of coffee. She puts the cup down just as it touches her lips.

LEROY: Hot?
BERTA: What?
LEROY: Your coffee. It too hot?
BERTA: Oh no. No . . . Bland. Lil bland.
LEROY: Needs some sugah.
BERTA: Yeah . . . yeah. Sugah.

> *(Berta spoons in a little sugar from the dish on the table. She stirs.*
>   *Silence.*
>   *Leroy chomps into the greens.)*

They cold?
LEROY. The greens? No. They perfect. Just right.
BERTA: Good.
LEROY: Mmm-hmm. Real good. I was hungry.
BERTA: Yeah. I could tell.

> *(Leroy continues eating.*
>   *Berta takes a full sip of coffee.)*

LEROY: Better now?
BERTA: Mmm-hmm. Much better.
LEROY: Good.
BERTA: Yeah, real good.
LEROY: Mmm-hmm.

> *(They continue in silence.*
>   *Berta takes another small sip and Leroy takes another big bite.)*

This ham hock?
BERTA: Huh?
LEROY: You got ham hocks in these greens?

BERTA: Turkey necks.

LEROY: Oh yeah?

BERTA: Better for your heart.

LEROY: Hmm.

BERTA: You like 'em?

LEROY: Taste just as good.

BERTA: It's Mama's recipe. She say the pig ain't got no more favors to give us. We ain't slaves no more.

LEROY: I still likes my bacon, slave or not. Your mama can't do away with that.

BERTA: Mama don't eat this and Mama don't eat that. She gon' live forever.

LEROY: Don't nobody live forever. If one thing don't kill 'em, somethin' else will.

BERTA: Somethin' like you.

(Leroy looks up at Berta from his greens.)

Dammit Leroy! *(Slamming down her coffee)* Dammit! Dammit, dammit, DAMMIT! *(She shoots up from the table)* Why you let the devil get in you like that?!

LEROY: I done told ya, I ain't got no business with the devil! This 'bout me and you. Me lovin' you.

BERTA: 'Til it make you crazy. You done gone crazy!

LEROY: Don't nobody spit on your honor!

BERTA: They just words Leroy. Who cares 'bout a bunch of words that don't mean a lick a nothin'? You don't go killin' nobody over no words!

LEROY: They was dirty words he was talkin'! Soilin' your name. He had to pay the price!

BERTA: Crazy! Foolish! Just beside yourself.

LEROY: Sit down, baby.

BERTA: Crazy!

(Leroy looks away, recounting the moment.)

LEROY: I should a known that Shoe Shine Boy was gon' tell. He was watchin' from 'cross the road. Went and snitched to

Curtis's bossman. Thought he'd get himself an extra quarter for turnin' me in. That boy ran hollin' to the cracker, and I ran for the trees. Crackerman caught up close to me, trailin' on my heels. He say, "That's my best driver you just killed boy! You gon' pay for that!!!" So I kept runnin'. Fast as all the souls in me could run. Then, seemed like outta nowhere, I lost him. Wasn't nothin' 'round me but dark quiet. Then a rustlin' in the ground. That's when I saw 'em . . .

BERTA: Wait a minute now, so you sat your ass in the dark 'til you decided to bring the blood to my doorstep?? This ain't had nothin' to do with no love and affection and three-years-a-widow and what God say!! You just a killer on the run lookin' for a place to hide!!!

LEROY: They was comin' outta the ground every which-a-way. Swarms of 'em. More than you can count. They put they eyes on me. They knew I was in trouble.

BERTA: Now we BOTH in trouble! What if they come up in here lookin' for you?! Everybody in Nellieburg know Leroy Grant got a loud beatin' heart for Alberta Watkins. And they know Alberta Watkins live **in Meridian** up the road past the jacaranda tree!

LEROY: I thought they was there to bring judgment on me. Devour me for my sins. Then I realized, they was there to protect me.

BERTA: Of all nights Leroy! Course you would. You *would* pick tonight to do this!

BERTA: The night of the cicadas!	LEROY: I made an oath to the cicadas.
WHAT YOU SAY?!	WHAT YOU SAY?!

LEROY: What you know 'bout the cicadas?!

BERTA: What YOU know 'bout the cicadas?! You don't know like I know. You ain't been waitin' on 'em like I been. Only come once every—

BERTA: —seventeen years.	LEROY: Seventeen years.
	I know.

BERTA: What all you know?

LEROY: I told 'em, "I know what all you can do. I done heard the stories. If they true, grant me one wish: let me get to my Berta. Let me make peace with her. Then I'll turn myself in."

BERTA: Did it . . . did it work?

LEROY: I'm here, ain't I?

(Berta slowly sits down, trying to calm herself.)

The cicadas put a hedge around me Berta. I bought us some time. We ain't got long though; only got 'til—

BERTA: —Just hush. Hush up and eat the greens so I can think straight.

(Berta's mind races. She clutches her cup of coffee for stability. Leroy studies her face.)

LEROY: You mad?

BERTA: I don't know if mad is the word.

LEROY: What's the word then?

BERTA: Ain't nobody ever kill't nobody for me before. I don't know how to place the feelin' just yet.

LEROY: I ain't meant you no harm Berta, I swear.

BERTA: I know what you meant. I know.

LEROY: Don't seem like you know. Seem like you mad.

BERTA: Maybe I am, alright?! Maybe I am mad! What then? You can't take it back!

LEROY: Damned if I would! I'd kill him all over again if I had the chance. I'd kill the shoeshine boy, the crackerman, the sheriff, and all they mamas! If it's for you, it means blood!

BERTA: What you want, a "thank you"?!

LEROY: You ain't got to thank me; just look at me. Look at me like you done before. Like you know who I am.

(Berta looks deeply at Leroy for what feels like the first time in ages.
He reaches out his hand to her across the table.
She takes it.)

BERTA: You know I can't never stay mad at you. Not for long. You ain't the most of my problems, no way. I got my own dealin's with the cicadas.

LEROY: What about?

BERTA: Nothin' I wanna let come outta my lips yet. I got to know it's real first.

LEROY: Oh, it's real. Realer than real. They led me here. Surrounded me like a cloak. Covered my body from head to toe. The cicadas strong, Berta. Whatever it is you got goin' on with them, they can—

BERTA: —I don't wanna talk 'bout it no more. Now come on, I can hide ya in the barn out back. Keep ya under the floorboards 'til the sheriff give up lookin' 'round these parts and start for the next county.

LEROY: Ain't you heard me woman, I say they put a hedge around us! The cicadas coverin' us. We safe in here for now.

BERTA: I heard what you said!

LEROY: Then just be with me. Here. In the light where I can see your face. Say things I been needin' to say to ya all these years. Why you wanna go hidin' me away?

BERTA: *Just in case!*

(Leroy looks at Berta, absorbing the intensity of her fear.)

LEROY: Don't you know, I could be back in **Parchman** already?

BERTA: *Back* in **Parchman**?

LEROY: I been there Berta. Three years ago. Eighteen months they had me.

BERTA: Jesus . . . Is that why . . . ? *That's* where you disappeared to? **Parchman?**

(Leroy nods.)

What did you do? Did you—?

LEROY: —I was a Colored man breathin' in the wrong part a town, that's what I did.

BERTA: Oh. Oh no.

LEROY: I ain't never kill't nobody before tonight; I know that's what you thinkin'.

BERTA: Course that's what I'm thinkin'.

LEROY: I went to town one day to pick up some fabrics for my mama. I seen this white woman drop her pocketbook so I chased after her to give it back. I caught up to her, and she looked like she ain't know what to do. She holla'd and holla'd 'til she finally grabbed hold a the idea that I wasn't tryna to pop her upside the head. She calmed down. Actually thanked me. But that ain't mattered one bit to the sheriff when he came runnin' after me. I ain't even run. What for? I ain't did nothin' wrong. She even told him I ain't did nothin' wrong. The white woman! But he ain't cared. Sheriff carted me off to **Parchman** faster than you can slap a mosquito. Mama never did get them fabrics.

BERTA: That was stupid, Leroy! Go chasin' after a white woman? Don't care if you meant well by it. Good deed don't change the color of your skin. You know the world we livin' in.

LEROY: It's a hot-ass backwards world is what it is! I sat off in **Parchman** eighteen months waitin' trial. That's what they said, I was waitin' trial. Wasn't never no trial. Ain't never even been to court. They just let me go outta nowhere. Soon as they saw I was broke down, broke in. Had us chained together in there. Grown men chained up like cattle. Sweatin' like burnt offerin's. Couldn't even turn over while we sleepin' without callin' out a number. Number eight, turnin' over! Number eight pickin' cotton all day and bustin' rocks all night 'til my bones bled. 'Til I coughed up dust. **Parchman** dust. It rested in my chest; comin' out with ev'ry breath like a puff a smoke. Prison guards sittin' back laughin' at me. Callin' me every unholy name. Spittin' on me. Got so bad I started playin' with the idea of chokin' one of 'em to death. But all that would a did was earn me my stay for real. That's what they wanted. I ain't do it, bad as I wanted to. I just put my head down and took it. I let them make me they lil nigga. They good lil nigga. Did what I had to do to stay alive. Then they let me go free. Once they tamed the Colored beast. But what I didn't know, I wasn't never gon' be free like I was before. They put the mark on me. The prison mark. All that white-hot fire built up from turnin' the other cheek; it followed me home. Like a cell block candle lightin' my way. Callin' me back to the cage. That's what they do to us Berta. Colored men. Decide we ain't slaves no more, but find another way to own our time. Lock us away in prison for nothin' and let us go 'til we come back for somethin'. I'm a Parchman man now, Berta, and ain't nothin' left of my life but to go back. I'm glad I got Curtis's neck for it! I'm glad he's dead. Least some righteous justice came outta all this . . .

(During the above speech, the candle has gone out. Neither of them notices.

Leroy looks off, trying to drown out the sound of the chain gang threatening to swell in his mind.

Berta leans in, staring deeply at Leroy with imploring eyes.)

BERTA: You ain't got to go back to **Parchman**, Leroy. It ain't signed in blood.
LEROY: What's done is done. I can't go back on my word to the cicadas.
BERTA: This hedge you say they built . . . how long does it last?
LEROY: 'Til sunrise.

(Berta's eyes widen, absorbing the truth. Her gaze intensifies.)

BERTA *(Under her breath)*: Sunrise, huh?
LEROY: What you got goin' on with the cicadas, Berta?

(Berta looks over toward the box and candle. She finally notices that the flame has gone out.)

BERTA: Oh no! NO!

(Berta runs over to the candle. Striking a match, she lights it again.)

(As she lights) Forgive me . . . Here I am . . . Here I am . . .

LEROY: What all done happened to you?

(Berta kneels before the box and candle.)

I know Ernie's passin' had to a been hard on you. You too young to be a widow.

BERTA *(Still prostrate)*: It was all my fault Leroy.

(Leroy goes to Berta's side.)

LEROY *(Lifting her head up with both his hands)*: Don't you go talkin' like that. Wasn't your fault. God took him 'cause He say so.

BERTA *(Sharply)*: God don't take nobody! Not no young man like Ernie. That's just what the backwards folks say.

LEROY: It was *my* fault then! Blame it on *me*. Charge *me* with the fact that you sittin' up a house all by yourself. No husband. No babies.

LEROY: Blame it all on me.   BERTA: HUSH YOUR MOUTH!

(Berta gets up from the floor, making her way to the kitchen with labored steps.)

LEROY: If I'da been half the man I am now, if I'da been him back then, you wouldn't be no widow. We'd have everything we talked 'bout back when we was still young enough to dream. That's why I say it's my fault Berta. Life learned me to be a man too late to love you right.

BERTA: You think you can just come up in here with your big hands and your soft words and make it all go away?! You don't know what all I been through!!!

(Berta opens a cabinet and pulls out a large mason jar filled with liquor, half empty. She takes a long swig.)

LEROY: You right, I don't! That's why I come all this way: to get the truth out and clean between us. How can I know what you don't tell me? *(As Berta keeps drinking)* Hey! That's enough!

(Leroy takes the jar from Berta.)

BERTA: Give it back!   LEROY: What is this?!

LEROY *(Smelling it)*: 'Shine?! You puttin' it away like *that*?
BERTA: I say GIVE IT BACK!
LEROY: Not 'til I get me some answers! Get to talkin', Berta!
BERTA: I killed Ernie, Leroy!! Alright?? There you have it! You and me, we *both* killers!
LEROY: Whatchu talkin'??!!
BERTA: Ernie wanted a baby. He wanted a baby bad, like how the sun want the moon, but they don't never do more than wave goodbye to each other. Took a long while for me to get pregnant in the first place. He tried and tried, every night seemed like. Sometimes he'd even be prayin' while he was tryin'. Beggin' God. Must a worked, finally. I never saw a happier man. Ernie's whole face was sunshine. He watched that baby grow inside my stomach. Talked to it when he came in from tendin' the crops. Whispered to it in his sleep. Then the day came. Ms. Merlie told me it was gon' ache, but she ain't said nothin' 'bout this. Felt like I been gutted open like a watermelon. All matter of blood and watery depths just runnin' everywhere. Ms. Merlie changin' rags left and right. Ernie on his knees. Then the baby come out, but he ain't had no breath! Ms. Merlie did all she could. Put him on my chest, see if he could catch my heartbeat. Ain't nothin' worked. My baby born dead. Ernie ain't wanna believe it. He took the baby from me. Wrapped him up in rags and held on to him for three days. Prayin' him back to life. I had to pry the baby body from Ernie's cold hands. I killed Ernie, Leroy! He died squeezin' on to our son. They both dead 'cause of me!

LEROY: That ain't true! Ain't your fault, Berta. Ain't nobody to be blamed for why it happened. It's just one of those things that—

(*Leroy tries to comfort Berta; she turns away.*)

BERTA: —I was gettin' ready to bury 'em both out back, up under the jacaranda, but Ms. Merlie stopped me.

(*Berta sets the lit candle aside.*)

She say, wait for the cicadas. They can bring the baby back to life. She seen it happen the last time they came. The backwadda cicadas. First seen when Old Man Calhoun lost all his slaves. Say they hid underground 'til seventeen years later when he died. Then they all came up at once. They came up out the ground and grew wings. Flew to the trees where Old Man Calhoun done hung they other kinfolk. And they wept like Jesus. 'Til they eyes turned red. 'Til they turned into cicadas. Hosts and hosts of cicadas. Singin' their song of mournin'. Mournin' for all the blood that been shed on them trees. They promised to come back once every seventeen years to help those who got reason to mourn. They'll grant ya one wish on the night of their return. And it's s'posed to happen before sunrise.

(*Berta opens the box.*
    She lifts the body of her baby out, wrapped in bloody cloths, rocking it in her arms.
    Leroy is stunned silent.)

I been waitin' three years for this night, Leroy.

(*Berta places the baby back in the box and pulls up a floorboard to reveal a large shotgun.*)

LEROY: Berta, what—?!
BERTA: —Everythin' I had been taken away from me, Leroy! My husband, my baby, you! Even the farm I got don't belong to

me. Every crop gotta go somewhere. Only a little bit come to my table. The rest of it go to this grocer, that one, the woman with the four babies, the man and his wife. Everything that come from me, everything I grow, get taken away! I don't get to own the ground, I just get to be the mule that work it. What I got to live for anymore?

LEROY: Live for you. It's a whole lot more inside of you than all what died. Ain't that enough?! Live to see what gon' come on the other side a this!

BERTA: I got 'til sunrise, Leroy. Right when you gotta leave me again. I tell the cicadas, bring my baby boy back to life, or I'm leavin' to be with him and his daddy. If I don't hear cries comin' outta that box, I'm pullin' the trigger. *(Out)* You hear me?! You got 'til the sun open its eyes. Is you gon' make a fool outta me, or is you gon' do what you promised?

(Suddenly a loud rumbling encroaches. It rolls like thunder exploding from the ground. The rumbling shakes the house.)

LEROY: What in the world . . . ?

(The thunderous transitions into the sound of a swarm of cicadas making their way. Berta sets the shotgun down at the sound.)

BERTA *(Jubilant, relieved)*: Finally.

(The chickens outside erupt into a squawking frenzy as the cicadas move past them. Leroy runs to the window and sees.
Berta rushes to the box, removing the baby again. She lifts up the corpse, falling to her knees.)

(Tearfully) Please . . . Please . . . PLEASE!

(The cicadas surround the house, building to a frenzied pitch. After a crescendo, they back off the house and fly to the nearby jacaranda tree where they settle. Berta and Leroy both look to the baby for signs of life. They wait. And wait. And wait, until:)

LEROY: D'you think—?
BERTA: —*Shh!*

(*Leroy backs away, giving Berta her space. He retrieves the mason jar with moonshine.*
   After a moment, Berta slightly deflates.)

(*Perseverant*) I got 'til sunrise.
LEROY: That's right, baby.

(*Berta places the baby back into the box. Leroy hands Berta the jar of moonshine. Berta staggers to the couch and takes a sip. Leroy joins Berta on the couch. She passes the jar to him. He sips and winces.*)

Shit strong as hell.
BERTA: Just how I like it.
LEROY: Woman ain't s'posed to be able to drink like this.
BERTA: Woman ain't s'posed to be able to make it neither.
LEROY: You made this?
BERTA: From my sweet potatoes. Makes it and sells it.
LEROY: **Alberta, Berta** makin' sweet potato 'shine! You the type a woman a man'll kill for.

(*Leroy and Berta each take another sip, swimming in their thoughts.*)

I wonder if this what it felt like to be Ernest. Gettin' to sit next to ya ev'ry night. Sip on somethin'. Hear what be on your mind. Even if you's just fussin' at me. You know how you get that look in your eyes and your voice jump up and down. Ya hips be just a-switchin' while ya mouth be runnin'.
BERTA: Ernie never sat on the couch. Or at the table. Wouldn't be still 'til he lie down at night. Always in a hurry to do the next thing or the other.
LEROY: He was a fool.

(*Leroy takes his final sip. He offers to Berta, but her mind is elsewhere.*)

BERTA: Thank you. For tryin' to protect me. Ain't too many men who would a done what you did. Why you did it. 'Specially after all you been through. You risked it all for me. I know it ain't right, but somethin' 'bout your heart makes it feel . . . special I guess. Listen to me, I'm talkin' crazy.

LEROY: No, you ain't crazy. Ain't one bit crazy.

BERTA: Crazy as it all is, I'm still glad to see ya.

LEROY *(With a gentle smile)*: No foolin'?

BERTA: Don't get to goin' now.

LEROY: Course you is. Course you's glad to see me. You my **Berta gal**.

BERTA: This ain't how I wanted it to be. When I finally laid my eyes on Leroy Grant again, it was s'posed to be like the clouds openin' up. Like the rain's first kiss on a blade a grass. But you came in like a flash of lightnin'. Stormin'.

(Berta places a hand on Leroy's face.)

Leroy Grant. A storm in the middle of a dream.

(Leroy places his hand on top of Berta's.)

LEROY: We ain't gotta wake up just yet.

BERTA: The mornin' gon' come, Leroy. The rooster gon' crow and it's gon' be time for us to face all what we hidin' from in the dark. I done nearly forgot this kind a dreamin'. Forgot all about dreams and sweet nothin's and warm breath. If it don't come from the ground, I ain't felt it in a good long while.

(Berta gets up from the couch and hangs her apron on a hook in the wall.
The hook collapses and falls to the floor. Berta just stares at it.
Leroy gets up to investigate. He sees her blank expression and doesn't know what to make of it.)

LEROY: It ain't no big thing; I can fix it.

(Berta breaks out into hysterical laughter.)

BERTA: Least he could a done was leave me a house that worked!!! What about dyin' make everythin' livin' wanna fall to pieces?!! Hahahahaha!!!

LEROY: It's alright, baby, I'll fix everythin'. Anythin' you want.

BERTA: I done fixed it! Patched it up a hundred times already. Just leave it on the floor, right where it is!

(Leroy picks up the hook and finds something makeshift to help secure it in the wall.)

LEROY: It's alright, baby, look. Look a here.

(He tests it for good measure.)

See there. Good as new.

BERTA: What you do?

LEROY: I fixed it.

BERTA: How? Lemme see.

(Berta examines his work.)

LEROY: You always said I had the magic touch.

(Berta turns to Leroy, then kisses him impulsively, fiercely. She lets go without warning.)

BERTA: Sorry, I . . . I don't know what came over—

LEROY: —What if I married you, Berta?

BERTA: What you say?

LEROY: You heard me. I said, what if I married you?

BERTA: Marry you? Marry Leroy Grant?

LEROY: I done made it this far. The cicadas got the hedge up—

LEROY: —good and strong around us.	BERTA: Don't play with me, Leroy.

LEROY: Maybe it can stretch! Maybe they can watch over us 'til we make our way outta town. North! We can hop on a train and head up somewhere like Chicago. Where Colored folks ain't gotta drop they heads when a white man pass by on the sidewalk. You hear me? *Sidewalk!* I heard they got side-walks up there!

BERTA: I got a house, Leroy! A house and a farm and chick-ens!! I can't just leave it all behind. It's Ernie's! He gon' know I left him!

LEROY: Damn Ernest! Damn his dead body in the dirt! Ain't you tired of livin' with a ghost?!

BERTA: What about my baby?!

LEROY: Bring him with us. Baby gon' need a daddy, right? Why not me? I'll get me a new name. New life. Won't nobody ever know. 'Bout **Parchman** or none a this.

BERTA: You really? You really wanna marry me, Leroy?

LEROY: I do.

(Leroy gets down on one knee in front of Berta.)

BERTA *(Breathlessly)*: Oh my Lord . . .

LEROY: I know this ain't the proper way. I ain't got no ring in my pocket.

BERTA: I don't need no ring. Done had one before.

LEROY: Just go pack up a bag and we can figure out the rest when we get up north.

BERTA: I don't need no bag. Everythin' I got to pack is wid-owed. Widowed clothes and widowed shoes in a widowed suitcase. I don't wanna be widowed no more. I want new things. Married things.

LEROY: We'll get you married stockings and married shoes. Move into a married house. Buy a brand-new married bed! I know you got your own money, but I gots money too now, Berta. *(Pats his trouser leg)* **Railroad** pay good money. **Every day Sunday; got dollars in my hand.** From my hand to yours.

(Leroy takes Berta's hand.)

I'm ready now Berta. Been years and years of me waitin' to look you in the eyes and say, I can. I can be the kind a man you'd be proud of havin'.

BERTA: You done had it wrong. I always been proud of havin' you. You the only one that been doubtin'.

(Leroy lifts up Berta and pulls her into a passionate kiss. He lets go and grabs the mason jar.)

LEROY: Here we come: Mr. and Mrs. Leroy Grant!

(Leroy downs the rest of the moonshine. Berta winces as she watches.)

BERTA: Careful now!!

LEROY: Mr. And Mrs. Leroy Grant! We gon' be well-to-do Northern Negroes with money in the bank and "yessir," "no sir," from Colored folks and white folks. And we gon' have a house full a babies. They gon' grow up big and strong and knowin' how to read, write, and count on all they fingers and toes. They gon' have all diff'rent color friends: Black, White, Brown, Yellow, hell, Green! They gon' come over the house to play after school. And you gon' be cookin' up cabbage and dumplin's for supper. With some more of them greens! And I'm gon' come home after workin' long and hard on some **railroad** up there. Kick off my boots. Sit me down in one of them big ole chairs made a leather. With a cigar in my mouth. Pull all the kids up next to me. Tell 'em 'bout how life was down south. How I had to scrape and pray just to get somethin' to put between two slices of bread. Now we got whole chickens in the icebox! Warm covers on the bed. New shoes on our feet. Tell 'em how good we got it up here. But ooohhh Mississippi . . . Mississippi make God turn His head. 'Cause Mississippi take the wings off an angel. And smear the blood on your hands . . . One red night in Mississippi change everythin'. When the moon ain't hangin' right and you know all the Haints is watchin' ya, countin' every wrong step you make. You know the Haints: your mama's-mama's-mama somebody buried in the dirt after they hung her on a tree. And all the other kinfolk that was swingin' next to her. Them's the Haints. They lives was taken against they will. Now they spirits is troubled, unsettled. And they watchin'. Watchin' when ya slippin' and let the devil sneak thoughts in your mind. You take 'em. Swallow the worm that slidin' down into your chest. Somethin' change inside of ya. You feel it changin'. And you know what you gotta do. You WRING HIS NECK! He cough up blood. It get on your shirt. You try to wipe it off. But it don't come out all the way. It's still on your hands. The blood is on your hands! Don't look at me! Don't look at me, Berta! It's blood all over my hands!

(Leroy breaks down, sobbing.)

BERTA: Leroy!

LEROY: Everything I do, everything I touch got blood all over it!! It's all over my hands and in between my fingers!!

BERTA: Get a hold a yourself man!

LEROY: What am I thinkin'?! I can't marry you Berta. I can't go wipin' my mess on you. Washin' my hands with your skin. You too clean. You too clean for me!

BERTA: Ain't nothin' clean between the two of us, 'cept for the two of us! We gon' get through this together! That's shine talkin'! You just drunk!

LEROY: I better go before I do you any more harm than I done already. Comin' over here like this, stealin' time. I better g'on and hand myself over.

BERTA: You better not!!!

LEROY: I gotta take what's comin' to me. Leave you to the rest of the good life you promised. You s'posed to be **livin' at ease**. I'm a g'on and get out your way.

(Leroy heads out of the kitchen. Berta gets in his way.)

BERTA: You ain't goin' nowhere! You hear me?!

LEROY: Outta my way woman. I gotta pay my debt.

BERTA: We gettin' married! You said we was gettin' married!

LEROY: **Go 'head and marry**, Berta. **Don't wait on me.**

BERTA: Look at me, Leroy! Look at this house. We both fallin' apart! You said you can fix anythin' I want. Fix me, Leroy. I'm what need the fixin'.

LEROY: Woman, ain't nothin' wrong with you.

BERTA: Look at me!

LEROY: Look at me! I'm a guilty man. A red-handed man. Ain't safe.

BERTA: Your hands the only safe place I got.

LEROY: **Go 'head and marry. Don'tcha wait on me.** Just marry ya a **railroad man** this time. Don't marry no **farmin' man** again.

(Leroy gives Berta a long-lasting kiss.)

Well now.

(He gathers himself and heads for the door.)

BERTA *(A hungry declaration)*: Fill me up, Leroy.

LEROY: **Alberta—**

BERTA: You heard me. I said fill me up.

(She approaches him.)

(Anxiously) You ain't gon' come in here smellin' like sweat and sweet nothin's, danglin' your affection in my face and then take it away. I remembers every inch a you. Been achin' for you. Just couldn't work up the nerve to say nothin', not the kind a woman I am. But I ain't got nothin' left to lose now. All I got is this back-breakin' empty that done found its way inside a me. And you gon' fill it up.

(She removes her robe.)

(A hungry declaration) Fill me up, Leroy. You take whatever been burnin' on the inside of you and you let it go. I can take it all. Might a been too scared before 'cause what might a happened. But I say, g'on and let it happen. Ain't got

nothin' to be scared of no more. You don't be scared neither. Fill me up.

LEROY: You mean it?

BERTA: I do.

(Leroy picks Berta up and flings her over his shoulder. He carries her to the bed.
    Blackout.)

SCENE 3—AN HOUR LATER

Lights up on Berta's bedroom.

Leroy and Berta lie together in bed, half-naked. They are asleep. Moonlight shines on their skin through the window.

Leroy stirs in his sleep as the sound of a prison chain gang returns. It slowly swells in his mind. He hears the axes, chains, and feet stomping in sync. It all culminates in a loud strike of metal. He shoots out of his sleep.

LEROY *(Sitting up)*: JESUS!

BERTA: What?!! They here?! Somebody here?!

(Leroy catches his breath.)

LEROY: No, I . . . I thought I heard somethin'. Just thought I heard somethin'.

BERTA: What?

LEROY: Nothin'. It was nothin'.

BERTA: You sho'? Do I gotta go get Agnes?

LEROY: Agnes?

BERTA: My shotgun.

LEROY *(With a chuckle)*: No . . . No. It's alright.

BERTA: And you?

LEROY: I'm fine.

BERTA: You got sweat on your forehead.

LEROY: That's your fault.

(Leroy leans back, pulling Berta into his arms.)

BERTA: I got your fault.

LEROY: Yeah you got my fault alright. You got all my faults now. Every one of 'em.

BERTA: I ain't been so full in a long while.

LEROY: So sweet. So thick and so sweet.

BERTA: Sweeter than before?

LEROY: You still as tight as you always was. Maybe even tighter.

BERTA: It's been . . . a good long while.

LEROY: Ernest ain't made no mold.

BERTA: Don't say his name! We in his bed!

LEROY: I know where I am, woman.

LEROY: What that matter?   BERTA: Lord forgive us!

LEROY: Back bend just the same.

BERTA: You a heathen from the stem to the stern.

LEROY: Your two fav'rite parts.

BERTA *(Unraveling from his grasp)*: I oughta wash your filthy mouth off a me.

LEROY: You know you like trouble. Don't know what you playin' shy for.

BERTA: Like I said, it's been a good long while since . . . any man been in this house or this bed or . . . with me.

LEROY: I don't think he was givin' you all what you needed.

BERTA *(Offended)*: How you figure that?

LEROY: You ain't never been hungry like that before.

BERTA: It's been three years, Leroy!

LEROY: Naw, naw. That don't matter. I know you. Know your body. How it feel when it been gettin' what it need, even if it been a long while. You all but devoured me whole.

(Berta looks away, split between satisfaction and sorrow.)

I got lost inside a you and I didn't care. Would a never came up for air if I had my way. It felt good to be wanted like that again. Like I was the only thing in this world that could satisfy you. All I wanna do is satisfy you, Berta.

(Leroy pulls Berta back into his arms.)

How you get so fine? So juicy.

BERTA: Leroy . . .

LEROY: Ripe and juicy. Eden comin' down like rain over the face of the earth. I missed my Eden.

BERTA: I missed you too.

LEROY: Done finally got her back.

BERTA: Leroy do you think . . . it happened?

LEROY: What?

BERTA: They say it s'posed to feel like that when a woman gon' make a baby. Say she open up on the inside and swallow the man whole like it's a hunger deep down that ain't nothin' else in this world gon' satisfy. So you think it happened? You think we done made us a baby?

LEROY: Ernest said this to you?

BERTA: No.

LEROY: Then what other men you been talkin' to 'bout a thing like that?!

BERTA: Nobody!

LEROY: It came from somebody!

BERTA: Wasn't nobody I was with! It don't matter! Is it true or not?!

LEROY: I don't like the men friends you been keepin', woman.

BERTA: Never mind. Forget it.

(Berta turns away from Leroy. He considers.)

LEROY: I ain't never made a baby before, so I wouldn't know. But if any a that's true, then maybe we did. Maybe we did make us a baby. We'll see.

(Berta turns back to Leroy.)

BERTA: You right. We will. We'll see.

(Leroy and Berta gaze into each other's eyes, swimming in their dreams of each other.)

LEROY *(Singing)*: Oh Alberta, Berta. Oh Lord gal.
BERTA *(Flustered)*: Boooooooyyyyyyyyyyyy!!!

> *(Berta tries to hide her face under the pillows and bed sheets. Leroy fishes her out, holding her close.)*

LEROY: Oh Lord, Berta, Berta. Oh Lord, gal. Say now.
BERTA *(Giggling)*: Quit now! Quit now!

LEROY:

> Oh Alberta with your hips so wide, well now.
> Look at Alberta with her hips so wide.
> She feel so good she make a grown man cry, well now.
> She feel so good she make a grown man cry.
> Berta got heaven livin' 'tween her thighs, say now.
> Berta got heaven livin' 'tween her thighs.

BERTA: Leroy quit now! My face! You got my face hurtin'!

LEROY:

> Leroy gon' love her 'til the day he die, say now.
> Leroy love Berta 'til the day he die.

BERTA: That part's new.
LEROY: Ain't new to me.
BERTA: Always makin' up songs 'bout somebody.
LEROY: **Oh Lord, Lord, gal.**
BERTA: Thought I wasn't never gon' hear it again. My song.

> *(Their eyes connect, fusing to each other.)*

> I thought you forgot about me. Thought you done wandered off somewhere for good.

LEROY: I told you where I went.
BERTA: Not then; I mean before. When I met Ernie. Why I met Ernie. When you was off doin' Lord knows what.
LEROY: You ain't never gon' let that go.
BERTA: When a man say he got "a thing or two to settle," he really mean "a woman or two."

LEROY: You got all these rules in your head 'bout men and women that don't mean a cotton-pickin' thing in real life.

BERTA: Tell me it wasn't no woman.

LEROY: Wasn't no woman; it was me.

BERTA: You had a slew a women on your tail.

LEROY: Don't mean I ever did nothin' with them.

BERTA: Did you?

LEROY: Not all of 'em.

BERTA: See there!

LEROY: When you and me was together, no.

BERTA: And when we wasn't?

LEROY: Course I had me a somebody. You did too! We both had somebodies. But I ain't got married to mine!

BERTA: You told me to move on.

LEROY: What dream you dreamin'?!

BERTA: You said you couldn't give me what a man oughta give the woman he gon' make his wife.

LEROY: I said give me some time and I would!

BERTA: What this matter now?

| BERTA: Talkin' in circles ain't gon' get us nowhere. | LEROY: You the one brought it up! |

LEROY: I needed time, alright? Had to get myself together and stop fightin' bein' a man. I was scared a failin' at it, like my daddy. He ain't never got it right. Always had a lie or a bottle or a woman fallin' off his lips. Broke Mama's heart ten, twelve times over. I ain't wanna do that to you.

BERTA: You ain't your daddy.

LEROY: I kept slippin' up, just like him. Found a woman that said somethin' sweet to me, I hid all my demons inside a her.

BERTA: I don't wanna hear this no more.

LEROY: 'Til the demons in me stirred up some demons in her, and I couldn't stand to be 'round her no more, so I found me another one. Then I'd miss the old woman while I was with the new woman, so I'd go back to the old one. She missed me too, and then we got back in bed with our demons. Then the demons in the new woman got lonely, so I went to go check on 'em. Now her demons jealous of the other woman's demons. Then all the demons, mine, the old woman's, and the new woman's, was wrastlin' while I'm 'sleep. And the devil was sittin' up in the corner with his pitchfork laughin' at me. So I threw a bottle of whiskey at him. Then another bottle, and another bottle. Me and the devil got drunk together and he liked to kill me! Somethin' in me stood up, grabbed the devil by the horns, and said, "You get on outta here, fool! And you take my demons, my daddy's demons, Louise's demons, and Mabel's demons witcha!" The demons left with the women and the whiskey. I got right with God. Been a man ever since.

BERTA: So you lied!

LEROY: Lied?

BERTA: It's just like I said! It was *women* that was keepin' us from bein' together!

LEROY: Woman ain't you heard me? It wasn't women, it was the devil and all them demons!

BERTA: You a cotton-pickin' fool, you know that?

LEROY: What it matter now? We here and all the women is gone.

BERTA: Been knowin' you was full a the devil.

(Berta sits up with her arms folded. Slight scowl. Leroy studies her face.)

LEROY: You mad? Again?

(Nothing.)

(With a sigh) You mad.

(Leroy adjusts.)

How you get mad?

(Still nothing.)

How you get mad, woman, we just made love! Good love. Good, good love. And you gon' get mad?!

BERTA: I'm not mad . . . I love you.

LEROY *(Breathless)*: You say . . . ? You say . . . ?

BERTA: I love you, Leroy. Been in love with you the whole time, all these years; I just didn't know it. Couldn't admit it to myself. You was gone. I thought naw, that ain't love, that ain't how it s'posed to go. That's what ya tell yourself when the man you in love with ain't the man you married to. I been carryin' these stones in my heart all these years 'cause I love you Leroy.

(Berta takes Leroy's hands.)

And now . . . Now we can make it honest. Like we always should a done.

(Berta kisses Leroy's hands and gets out of bed. She reaches open her chest of drawers and riffles through, pulling out a man's shirt.)

Can you fit this? It was Ernie's but—

(The rising sun starts to pour in through the window like a warm bath. Leroy and Berta don't notice.)

LEROY: —Those are the words. Those are the words I been waitin' to hear. All these years I been waitin' to hear you say . . . that you loved me. You really love me, Berta?

BERTA: I thought you knew.

LEROY: It's somethin' 'bout the way it sounds comin' outta your heart.

(A rooster crows loudly. Berta and Leroy snap out of their trance. They look to the window, observing the sunrise together.)

BERTA: Sweet Jesus.

(Leroy's countenance falls.)

LEROY: Well now . . .

(Berta runs over to the box. She places her ear to it, listening for cries. Nothing. Berta pulls the baby out of the box. It's still dead. She rocks it vigorously.)

Berta . . .

(Leroy watches as Berta solemnly places the baby back in the box. She then reaches for the shotgun. Leroy tries to stop her.)

Berta, DON'T!!!

BERTA *(Brandishing the gun)*: We outta here, Leroy. We outta this coffin with windows. We gon' make our way up north and start livin' new. And I'll be damned if a sheriff or a crackerman or a cicada get in our way!

LEROY: Berta, you ain't thinkin' straight. You know we can't. It's over.

BERTA: The cicadas lied, Leroy! You see it for yourself. Ain't none of this even real. And if it ain't real, then we got us a chance. We ain't got to sit around waitin' on a wing and a prayer. We can make our dreams happen ourselves. Now do you believe in me or not?

LEROY: I do.

BERTA: Then get dressed.

(Leroy obeys. Berta follows right behind him, frantically dressing and stuffing things into a suitcase.)

I'll write my sister. Tell her to come look after things for a while. Or not! Why not just let it all die?! Let it all die and start over! Just me and you.

LEROY: Me and you and whoever might be growin' on the inside a you.

(Now fully dressed and packed, they join hands and prepare to exit into their new life. Leroy picks up the suitcase. Berta picks up the gun. They head for the front door. Leroy tries to open it, but it's fused shut.)

What's goin' on?

(Berta attacks the door with the full force of her might, but it won't budge. The sound of the cicadas, pouring in like a swarm, approaches the door.)

BERTA: Get back you LIARS!!

(The cicadas surround the house. Berta points the gun at them.)

LEROY: Berta!!!

BERTA *(Pointing the gun at the surrounding cicadas)*: If you wouldn't do all what you promised, least you gon' do is leave us to the good life we deserve! You heard me?? I said LEAVE US!!!

(Berta cocks the gun, preparing to pull the trigger.)

LEROY: Berta, DON'T!!!

(Berta pulls the trigger, but it doesn't fire. The cicadas have clogged the shotgun.
    The cicadas rumble in anger, causing a violent shake of the house.
    Lights shift.
    We see Berta fallen to the ground, lifeless.
    Leroy runs to her.)

No. NO! Berta!!!

(Leroy furiously searches for Berta's heartbeat.)

Berta, wake up! Wake up!!!!

(Leroy cradles Berta's body in his hands, weeping over her.)

(Out, to the cicadas) PLEASE! PLEASE!!! I'll keep my word! I'll go. Just please bring her back. Bring her back! I'll go in peace. You have my word.

(The sound of the cicadas softens. A light flickers as Berta sharply exhales. She sits up, like an ignited flame.)

BERTA: I saw her! Leroy, I saw her! A little girl! She had your eyes and nose. With my smile. She was such a precious little thing. Laughin' as I held her in my arms, and she—

LEROY *(Painfully resolved):* —Give our baby a good name Berta.

BERTA: Whatchu—? Whatchu talkin'??

LEROY: Tell her how much her daddy Leroy love her. How it break his heart that he can't look her in her big beautiful eyes and say he sorry. Daddy sorry for all this. But she got the best mama the world got to offer.

BERTA: No you, you gon' name her yourself Leroy! You gon' name her and hold her and tell her how much you love her. We got a whole new life already in the makin'. You and me together. We walkin' outta this house together!

LEROY: Nah Berta, don'tcha see? It wasn't never gon' be what we wanted it to be. That ain't what was fated. We was never meant to be each other's everythin'. Only, just what we needed, right when we needed it.

(Leroy grabs Berta's face and kisses her deeply. Tears cascade down both their faces. The sound of the cicadas violently pounds on the door.)

BERTA: We love you, Leroy. Me and Baby. We love you.

LEROY: I love you more than my own life, Berta. Don'tcha ever forget that.

(Leroy walks out toward the cicadas.
    He fades away, with the sound of buzzing.
    Berta listens as the cicadas and Leroy disappear into the distance.
    Feeling a beam of light in her belly, Berta places a hand on her stomach.)

BERTA *(To the cicadas, gently):* You kept your word.

(Berta laughs, cries, exhales all at once. She picks up the white rose and places it to her belly.)

Baby Girl, your daddy is a king. Shame is . . . we the only ones that know it.

(The song "Berta, Berta" pours in.
   Lights fade.)

END OF PLAY

ABOUT THE PLAY

Berta, Berta was produced at Everyman Theatre in spring 2020. It had its world premiere in 2018 at the Contemporary American Theater Festival and encored in 2019 at the National Black Theatre Festival (NBTF). Out of five hundred submissions, it was the only play chosen for the 2017 Bay Area Playwrights Festival at Playwrights Foundation's Rough Readings Series in May 2017.

Berta, Berta is copyright © 2021 by Angelica Chéri, and is published by TRW Plays, a division of Theatrical Rights Worldwide. For further information contact: Beth Blickers, APA Agency, bblickers@apa-agency.com, 212-621-3098. The song "Berta, Berta" was sung by prisoners at the Mississippi State Penitentiary, "Parchman Farm." Authorship is unknown.

ABOUT THE PLAYWRIGHT

Angelica Chéri is a playwright, musical theater book writer/lyricist, screenwriter, and poet. Her "Prophet's Cycle Trilogy" includes *The Seeds of Abraham* (mentored by Lynn Nottage; Signature Theatre, The Billie Holiday Theatre); *The Sting of White Roses* (North Carolina Black Repertory Company, NBTF); and *Crowndation; I Will Not Lie to David* (Center Theatre Group, NBTF—I AM SOUL Residency). Other plays include *The Wiring & the Switches* (developed at the Geffen Playhouse); *Learn to Speak Doll* (Peppercorn Theatre commission); *Slow Gin Fits* (Fire This Time Festival); and *The Yin & The Yang* (Columbia University). She and collaborator Ross Baum received the Richard Rodgers Award for their musical *Gun & Powder* (Signature Theatre, directed by Robert O'Hara). Angelica was one of six writers chosen for the inaugural Geffen Playhouse Writers Room and she was the Master Playwright in the Frank Silvera Writer's Workshop Inaugural 3in3 Playwright Festival. Angelica has also written for the Obie Award–winning 48 Hours in Harlem Festival.

Angelica is co-writer of the *Highway to Heaven* reboot on Lifetime and she is story producer for *Dear . . .* on Apple TV+. She is currently writing for the award-winning series *Godfather of Harlem*.

Angelica received a BA in Theatre from UCLA, a MFA in Playwriting from Columbia University, and a MFA in Musical Theatre Writing from NYU. www.angelicacheri.com.

LOOKING FOR LEROY

Larry Muhammad

2019

PRODUCTION HISTORY

Looking for Leroy was presented at the 2019 National Black Theatre Festival. It was produced by Woodie King, Jr. The director was Petronia Paley; the set design was by Chris Cumberbatch, the costume design was by Kathy Roberson, the lighting design was by Antoinette Tynes, the sound design was by Bill Toles; the stage manager was Bayo. The Producing Company was New Federal Theatre. The cast was:

BARAKA	Kim Sullivan
TAJ	Tyler Fauntleroy

CHARACTERS

TAJ, twenty-something theater intern, African American

BARAKA, sixty-something literary icon, African American

NOTE

The " / " notes when overlapping dialogue occurs.

SCENE 1

Study decorated with African art. A bookcase stuffed with volumes that seem to spill in stacks onto the floor and a nearby desk littered with papers where Baraka, sixty-ish Black male, wearing a dashiki, is typing furiously on a computer as Coltrane, Miles, or Monk plays on the stereo.

He bangs on the keyboard seemingly in cadence with the music, bouncing in his chair and sometimes popping to his feet to spin in place, dance a jig, and clap hands loudly, viscerally satisfied with a passage he's written, then sits, again attacking the keyboard.

Before long, Taj, twenty-something Black male dressed for a job interview, enters nervously and stands at a distance, not daring to interrupt.

For quite a while Baraka ignores him, continuing to write, until finally:

TAJ: Amina said I should come up? About the intern job?

(Beat.)

BARAKA *(Still typing)*: So which one are you?

TAJ: Taj Jeffries? Two o'clock interview?

(Beat. Baraka checks his wristwatch.)

BARAKA: At least you're on time.

(Baraka stares at Taj without speaking. Long pause, then Taj launches into a desperate spiel.)

TAJ: I can quote your poems like people quote Shakespeare.

> Fuck poems and they are useful, would they shoot
> come at you, love what you are,
> breathe like wrestlers, or shudder
> strangely after pissing. We want live
> words of the hip world live flesh &
> coursing blood. Hearts Brains
> Souls splintering fire. We want poems
> like fists beating niggers out of jocks . . .
> Black poems to
> smear on girdle-mamma mulatto bitches
> whose brains are red jelly stuck
> between Elizabeth Taylor's toes. Stinking
> Whores! We want poems that kill.

(Baraka, unimpressed, gets up and walks past Taj to a teapot and pours himself a cup.)

How about this check this out.

> The white man, at best, is corny
> But who is the how is the Black man to say.
> What? When he sits biting his ass in the sun
> Or laid cross a puddle, for snail titty to cross over
> How, with what logic and moral

Who is fed by the meanest of streams
Will we move or will we be merely proud?

(Beat. Baraka doesn't respond, Taj pleads.)

I went to the mosque because you said so, man. I was Clay
in a school production of *Dutchman*.

(Beat.)

BARAKA: Clay. The protagonist as victim. A respectable bourgeois Negro minding his own business on the subway is
seduced and murdered by Lula, a trashy Caucasian chick.
And why? Why is he so enticed by this crazy white bitch
and why'd it end in a vicious stabbing? *(Taj is about to
answer but Baraka stops him)* Think. Before you speak,
think. What's your name again?
TAJ: Taj.
BARAKA: Taj.

(He slowly paces a circle around Taj, sizing him up.)

Malcolm said to think five times before you speak. Let the
question gestate. Let it slowly develop in the mind. Think
like an artist for once in your life. Wittgenstein said ethics
and aesthetics are one. I believe this. The artist's role is to
raise the consciousness of the people. To make them understand life, the world, and themselves more completely.

(Baraka turns off the stereo and faces Taj.)

So. Is Clay weak for Lula's malicious advances because he's
culturally assimilated—as he calls himself—a "middle-class
fake white man"? He developed racial amnesia? Forgot
about all the Black men throughout American history bru-
tally killed for messing with white women?

(Beat.)

TAJ: It's absurd.

BARAKA: There are elements of absurdist theater. The other white subway passengers complicit in the ritual sacrifice of a Black man. And afterwards a Black conductor shuffling through the car tips his hat to Lula as she scribbles in a notebook. Keeping tally, another one bites the dust.

TAJ: What I meant . . . I should have said, ironic, but . . . whatever.

BARAKA: *Whatever?* That's the trouble with you millennials. Everything is everything. You think nonchalance is woke, but it ain't woke. Acuteness and passion for Black theater— that's woke. If you saw irony then express yourself. Make your point.

(Beat.)

TAJ: When you wrote the play you were living in Greenwich Village and married to a white woman, Hettie. Isn't that ironic?

(Beat.)

BARAKA: That's a load of crap that's what that is. Clay and Lula don't represent real people. They're symbols in a theater of racial conflict.

TAJ: But you switched it up. You turned hyper-Black. And I love it man. *Black Fire*, I wore that book out. But I've been following you since *Preface to a Twenty Volume Suicide Note* and your first play, *A Good Girl Is Hard to Find.* Then before I could fully grasp LeRoi Jones the phenomenon, Beat icon right up there with Jack Kerouac and Allen Ginsberg, you're Black-cultural-nationalist Amiri Baraka. You switched it up.

BARAKA: I was under the influence of a lot of writers in the Village. I said to myself, I'm not going to do that anymore. Why? Because when you imitate people's writings, you also imitate their point of view. Clay is the victim of white conspiracy to slaughter Black males. He lashes out at Lula's racial slurs and thus is condemned to die. He accuses and attacks because he looks at the world through the eyes of a victim. So that his brothers in the audience will understand that they are victims too. Protest is the foundation of Black literature. You see it in Richard Wright and Jimmy Baldwin. Even Langston Hughes. All the way back to Frederick Douglass you see it. And obviously in Amiri Baraka. When you stand on the shoulders of those who have gone before, those who have struggled and overcome, you are obliged to move from criticism to defiance. *(He stares at Taj)* You got that kind of attitude?

TAJ: I do.

BARAKA: And intend to express it how?

TAJ: I'm trying to write plays, be a playwright.

BARAKA: A Black playwright, or a playwright who happens to be Black?

TAJ: A Black playwright.

BARAKA: Ditch that outfit. Dress more Afrocentric. You look like a management trainee. Or a bean-pie-selling Black Muslim. Take off the necktie and suit jacket.

(Taj discards them.)

Aren't any "suits" in here. You're a journeyman, an intern. You're going to pay some dues.

(Baraka busies himself shutting down the computer, sorting papers at the desk, etc.)

You'll work flex hours. Part time, full time, or more than full time meaning overtime sometimes depending on my needs. Understand? You have any learning disabilities?

(Beat.)

TAJ: What? No I don't have a learning disability.

BARAKA: As my assistant you'll help with research. You'll photocopy scripts. You'll read aloud from my drafts so I hear how they sound. You'll perform any chores I deem necessary to moving from the page to the stage. Which is not co-authorship and does not entitle you to credit as drama-turg. Let me disabuse you right now of any cockamamie notions your contribution is other than marginal. We clear?

TAJ: Is there compensation?

BARAKA: You'll be unpaid. You're a theater artist doing it for the love. For the proximity to greatness, the chance to be mentored and learn. Maybe I'll look into a modest stipend for you but I am not responsible for your financial well-being.

TAJ: Understood.

BARAKA: And just so you know, I have enemies galore. I'm not just talking about other playwrights and theater owners and Tom-ass Black politicians and white professors blocking academic freedom. And the Jews—you can't say anything critical about the Jews or you're anti-Semitic. Plus the immense congregation of flag-waving Americans who revile and dismiss me simpatico with the most repressive forces in the nation. Not to mention the motherfucking critical establishment, which disparages my artistic achievements because they lack the courage the skill and intelligence to properly judge the work.

TAJ: Okay.

BARAKA: For quite a while now I've been writing a play about W. E. B. Du Bois. *(He opens a desk drawer and produces a thick file, places it on his desk with a thud)* Years in the making. Bill Cosby asked me to write a play about Du Bois a long time ago. He got the money but then decided to make a movie about himself as a superhero. So Woodie King is producing it at New Federal Theatre. Runtime's four hours now. It's done but not done. Needs correction. It'll go through drafts, one after another, until it's ready.

TAJ: How will you know when it's ready?

BARAKA: When I feel like it's ready.

TAJ: Umm.

BARAKA: Let's drink a toast.

(He gets a bottle of apple juice, gives it a vigorous shake.)

TAJ: To what?

(Baraka pours two glasses.)

BARAKA: *Most Dangerous Man in America (W. E. B. Du Bois).* That's the title. It's what the FBI called Du Bois. At eighty-three. And if you can be *that* bad at eighty-three . . .

(They click glasses then drain them. Baraka studies Taj.)

Tell me something. Straight up. Who's your favorite playwright?

(Beat.)

TAJ: Ed Bullins.

BARAKA *(Annoyed)*: Then maybe I'd prefer to work alone.

TAJ: Come on, man. You asked.

BARAKA: Fine, that's fine.

TAJ: Ask me again.

BARAKA: No, it's okay. I like Ed Bullins, terrific playwright. I know him very well.

TAJ: Let me try again.

BARAKA: I told you it's okay.

TAJ: Ask me again.

BARAKA: Who's your favorite playwright?

TAJ: August Wilson.

BARAKA *(Playful)*: You know he loved my work, said I influenced him greatly.

TAJ *(Playful right back)*: He still the one.

BARAKA: You're an overeager assistant, I was about to cut you some slack.

TAJ: August Wilson. Even you can't argue with that.

(They laugh, elaborate Afro handshake, hugs, slaps on the back.)

BARAKA: People compare August to Eugene O'Neill but he deliberately stayed unfamiliar with the Western theater canon.

TAJ: I knew that.

BARAKA: What about Artaud?

TAJ: Who?

BARAKA: Antonin Artaud. French dramatist from the early twentieth century. What are theater departments teaching nowadays?

TAJ: Not so many dead French playwrights.

BARAKA: Understanding Artaud is essential to understanding me. You'd know that if you read my essay "The Revolutionary Theatre." Actually what have you read? You read Harold Cruse?

TAJ: Yes /

BARAKA: / Carter Woodson?

TAJ: Some /

BARAKA: / Albert Murray?

TAJ: Not really . . .

BARAKA: Zora Neale Hurston—John Edgar Wideman—Toni Morrison? I'm assuming you've read Baldwin, Wright, Hughes, Ellison. Well with Ellison it's just the one novel.

TAJ: And the essays, *Shadow and Act*, I read the essays.

BARAKA: Du Bois? Don't fuck with me now. Tell me you've read Du Bois. Quote me some *Souls of Black Folk*. Right now.

TAJ: "The problem of the twentieth century is the problem of the color line."

BARAKA: That it?

TAJ: "One ever feels his twoness—an American, a Negro; two souls, two thoughts, two unreconciled strivings; two warring ideals in one dark body, whose strength alone keeps it from being torn asunder."

BARAKA: Impressive, young brother. Well done. Writing is fighting. And knowledge, especially knowledge of self, is a powerful weapon. Knowledge of the past rewards all research in the future. To be a creative intellectual from an oppressed group means articulating the grievances, needs, and desires of said group. You cannot articulate those grievances, needs, and desires until you are ethnically conscious. Know the history, literature, the religion, and music of your people. *(Indicates thick file on his desk)* Most Dan-

gerous Man in America (W. E. B. Du Bois)—it's history, it's biography, it's political philosophy.

TAJ: It's encyclopedic.

BARAKA: Call it Shakespearean. Two hundred and fifty pages. Ossie Davis lit into me at the table read: "Look, you can't give an actor no two-hundred-and-fifty-page play!" But white people do it all the time. *Long Day's Journey into Night* is four hours. *Angels in America* run-time six hours total. Run-time for *The Ferryman* is over three hours. Why can't Black dramatists do it? Because Black theater today has virtually no infrastructure and little if any financial resources to keep it sustainable. I'm not criticizing Woodie. I'm not criticizing Ossie. You know Ossie Davis, the great actor, director, and playwright?

TAJ: Not personally.

BARAKA: Now how would you know him personally? I meant figuratively. Don't be dense. Ossie Davis, in the first read, begins citing the page-per-minute rule. Remedy for which is jettisoning several characters including—I kid you not—Paul Robeson. Woodie complains he could never find an eighty-year-old actor to play Du Bois at the current page count. Ossie Davis and Woodie King, Jr., Black theater pioneers, legends really, together are pressuring me to dwindle down an admiring and affectionate portrait of Black America's greatest scholar. *(While Baraka picks up and thumbs through the file and puts it back down, and goes to stereo and cues some music)* It has to be panoramic. Layer on layer of cascading scenes. Political demonstrations, courtroom drama, supporters in Harlem barbershops, our hero visiting Moscow and other world capitals in video projection.

TAJ: Writing is rewriting.

BARAKA: Not for me it isn't. My rewrite is—bam—right in the trash. If it looks like it's not going to work, I throw it away. I'm not going to torture it. You've got to be free and open to write. You've got to trust yourself. You have to create.

TAJ: It's . . . two hundred and fifty pages.

(Impulsively Baraka goes to his desk, gets the Du Bois draft, and dumps it into the trash.)

BARAKA: I made it, I can kill it, and make another one better.

SCENE 2

Months later, Baraka at computer writing, jazz playing on stereo. Enter Taj, wearing a kente-cloth shirt and carrying a watermelon. They speak some Swahili.

TAJ: *Habari yako?* [How are you?]
BARAKA: *Njema.* [Good.]
TAJ: *Unaandik vizuri?* [Are you writing well?]
BARAKA: *Sijui.* [I don't know.]

> *(Taj slices big wedges of the melon for both of them as Baraka comes over to him.)*

You know the Swahili word for holocaust? *Maafa. Maafa.* When the African brothers ask us how it is in America, tell them, "It's a *Maafa!*"

> *(They crack up because Baraka pronounces "maafa" like "motherfucker," then sit side by side eating watermelon. Baraka smacks and sucks his fingers, enjoying it.)*

TAJ *(Pleased with himself)*: Sweet, huh.
BARAKA: I got busted for eating watermelon when I was going to Howard. I'm sitting on a bench on campus when the dean comes up and asks what I thought I was doing. I said, "What's it look like I'm doing? I'm eating watermelon." He pitched a fit: "Do you realize that you're sitting right in front of the highway where white people can see you? Do you realize that you are compromising the Negro?" I loathed Howard. It showed me how sick the Negro could be, that our top university was teaching students self-hate. We did

Baldwin's *Amen Corner* on campus, about poor Blacks in a storefront church, and an English professor said it set the department back ten years.

TAJ: I read *The Sidney Poet Heroical* last night.

BARAKA: And?

TAJ: Why a cruel satire ridiculing Sidney Poitier and Harry Belafonte? They marched with Dr. King.

BARAKA: Poitier and Belafonte were token integrationists of the movie business. Modern-day Fausts selling their souls to the devil.

TAJ: That's harsh.

BARAKA: But not untrue.

TAJ: I don't know . . .

BARAKA: You don't know much of anything. But what specific lack of knowledge are you referring to?

TAJ: How a race-mixing beatnik writer got taken seriously as the sole judge and arbiter of what it means to be Black.

BARAKA: Having been taught that "art" was something that white men do, I almost became one, to have a go at it. But it's a helluva thing to sit around writing extraneous little poems and stage plays with the Black liberation struggle going full blast. So I started the Black Arts Repertory Theatre and tried to destroy the assimilationist art form. Me and Bullins and Larry Neal and Jimmy Garrett, Sonia Sanchez, Ben Caldwell, and Barbara Ann Teer and Ron Milner and the others beat it into the ground. Publicly condemned any and all tendencies in Black theater opposed to the cultural-nationalist project.

TAJ: Charles Gordone /

BARAKA: / Not Black enough.

TAJ: Come on. *No Place to Be Somebody* won him the Pulitzer. He was the first Black playwright awarded it.

BARAKA: A Black nationalist–rejecting extension of white culture! Lonne Elder, Douglas Turner Ward—also insufficiently Black. I tried to murder the apolitical theater of pessimism and ambiguity. Do you understand why?

TAJ: Because Black people need theater describing our sociopolitical reality and methods of changing it.

BARAKA: The existentialist drama of Sartre, Beckett's theater of the void, the theater of games and masks in Genet and Ionesco, are what?

TAJ: Irrelevant.

BARAKA: Why.

TAJ: Because they are disassociated from objective reality and we need raw, epic drama that can grow the Black theater franchise.

BARAKA: Give me an example.

TAJ: *Experimental Death Unit #1*. From your collection *Four Black Revolutionary Plays*. Two heroin-addicted white bums are fighting over a Black prostitute when a paramilitary group of young brothers marches up. They kill the wretched trio, impale the two bums' severed heads on a spike, and march away.

BARAKA: Not necessarily the example I would have chosen.

TAJ: You're right. The narrative's simplistic, structurally it's undeveloped /

BARAKA *(Annoyed)*: / That's not what I meant.

(Beat.)

Some crazy nigger involved with the project hauled off and slapped the star, Barbara Ann Teer, and I had to step in and direct. I love theater, love the effect of words turning into action. But you have to deal with a lot of nuts.

TAJ: You sure you didn't encourage it? In your play *Madheart* the brother looks heroic pimp-slapping the sister in a courtship ritual.

BARAKA: That was your takeaway?

TAJ: It's stressing Black patriarchy. I get that.

BARAKA: August Wilson's first play, *Black Bart and the Sacred Hills*, was so sexist women got up and walked out. Based on the Greek comedy *Lysistrata*, so evidently he read one of the classics. Shit happens. Listen, I've written a lot of plays I don't even agree with anymore. Somebody will say, "I just saw such-and-such a play." Yeah but that was from

1970-something. That ain't me. I don't have a worshipful relationship to my work in that way.

TAJ: I was down with the bohemia aesthetic and miscegenation of LeRoi Jones. I had me a white girl, cute blond, legs that went all the way up to Heaven. We'd planned a trip to Madrid. Then you went on your hate-whitey rant and I had to cut her loose. I went through a whole bunch of changes trying to keep up with you, man. Now I'm down with the Blacks Arts thing, theater raising the consciousness of our people.

BARAKA: We took it to the streets. Every night in the summer we flooded Harlem parks and playgrounds with new plays, music, new poetry, new dance, new paintings. Four trucks, every night. The sweep of the Black Arts Movement had recycled itself back to the people. We had huge audiences, mass audiences at the time. You think your work is any good? Take it to the streets. To these brothers working construction and eating their sandwiches on half-hour break. Sisters pushing baby carriages pulling toddlers behind. See if your work interests them. Dare that. To interest people on the real side, out in them streets, you have to come up with the real deal.

*(Taj clears away watermelon rinds and tidies up.
   Beat as the mood settles.)*

TAJ: You ever write longhand?

BARAKA: You mean, without a keyboard?

TAJ: Yeah.

BARAKA: Not if I can help it. Makes my hand hurt.

(Taj laughs.)

Traveling all the time I don't have much choice. Laptop on an airplane tray table during long flights doesn't work for me. I resort to pen and paper. Then I'm disgusted I had to do it in the first place and it's more work typing the longhand into the computer. Worst of all I can hardly read my own handwriting. I don't know why I even bother. Du Bois wrote ten thousand magazine articles. Did you know that? Published. How did he do that? First you have to live to be ninety-five. Then you have to write maybe ten articles a month, one hundred and twenty a year, for seventy-five years and that still wouldn't be enough! You get the entire majestic scope of his intellectual journey. From Du Bois the isolated Democrat to Du Bois the Black capitalist to Du Bois the Pan-Africanist and Du Bois the socialist and Du Bois . . .

(Suddenly Baraka goes to the computer and types furiously.
Stunned, Taj watches for long pause, gradually ambles up behind, and isn't noticed peering over Baraka's shoulder.
Baraka stops typing as jazz ends on the stereo.)

(To himself, befuddled and frustrated) Umm . . . That ain't supposed to . . . What's it missing?

TAJ: Pacing?

BARAKA *(Startled)*: I wasn't talking to you!

(Spins up out of the chair into Taj's face, pushing him down almost, and stomps around the study enraged.)

And don't be sneaking up on me from behind. I've forgotten more about theater than you could ever hope to learn. I've won the Obie, the PEN/Faulkner, the Guggenheim. I taught at Stony Brook, at Rutgers. I started the Black Arts Movement, nigger. What have you done? What gives you the right to even think about opening your goddamn mouth to comment on my process? "Pacing"?! You want to write this play? Here!

(He takes freshly composed scenes of the draft lying in the printer tray and starts slinging them at Taj.)

Here's pacing! That's pacing! You want some more?! What the fuck does that even mean, "pacing"? You mean dramatic action? You mean plot? You mean character development-story-arc-spectacle-comic-relief? What is "pacing"?!

(Taj picks pages up off the floor as Baraka fumes, gathering himself.)

TAJ: I should have said structure, that's more what I meant.

BARAKA: Structure?

TAJ: I meant pacing in structure, the flow of the piece.

BARAKA *(Sarcasm)*: "Pacing in structure." What's that even mean?

TAJ: The speed at which the action progresses. The rhythm and tempo.

BARAKA: Pacing isn't structure.

TAJ: Yes it is.

BARAKA: I'm telling you it's not. Structure is the narrative framework that delivers your theme as characters and events interact.

TAJ: Isn't that what narrative framework is, the scenes? Action scenes fast, tender scenes slow.

BARAKA: And incomplete scenes that abruptly alter the speed. Stop partway through—cut straight to a different scene.

(Taj thinks about this, keeps cleaning up.)

TAJ: Okay but that's change of pace. That's mixing it up.

BARAKA: Texture's more important than structure.

TAJ: What's texture?

BARAKA: The mood and rhythm of the piece. The way tension and intrigue and suspense get introduced by a character. A character, say, who's got a secret.

TAJ: Citizen Barlow in *Gem of the Ocean*, who stole that bucket of nails.

BARAKA: The burglar playing God in *Prayer Meeting*.

TAJ: Camae, the angel playing hotel maid in *The Mountaintop*.

BARAKA: Troy in *Fences*, knocked up his woman on the side.

TAJ: Dad in *Stick Fly* knocked up his maid.

BARAKA: David in *Choir Boy*, headed to the seminary hiding he's gay.

TAJ: The widow Bronson airing her late husband's dirty laundry in *Who's Got His Own*.

BARAKA: Peterson, the killer in *A Soldier's Play*.

TAJ: Miss Leah made the poison pie in *Flyin' West*.

BARAKA: In *Blues for Mister Charlie*, Lyle, the acquitted serial killer of Black men.

TAJ: That motherfucker.

BARAKA: You want to talk villains, Zooman, the street thug in *Zooman and the Sign*.

TAJ: Him too.

(Baraka sits at his desk, takes off and cleans his glasses.)

BARAKA: Frank, the wife-beating swindler in *Flyin' West* who ate Miss Leah's poison pie.

TAJ: Booth killed his girlfriend and brother in *Topdog/Underdog*.

BARAKA: That's depravity.

TAJ: Art dropped a dime to the cops on his roadies in *Goin' a Buffalo*.

(Taj has cleared all pages from the floor and stacks them on Baraka's desk.)

BARAKA: Betrayal. Fantastic subject for drama.

(He puts his glasses back on, stares at his laptop.)

TAJ: The Mayor in *Day of Absence*, hilariously stupid.

BARAKA: Simple is adorable in Langston's musical *Simply Heavenly*. And you know what?

TAJ: What?

BARAKA: Music.

(Baraka abruptly begins writing.)

TAJ: Music?

BARAKA: Music's what it needs. I've always used music as a catalyst or paradigm for my writing . . . Got that from Langston. He used the form and content of jazz and blues and was the first person I saw reading poetry to music . . . Ron Karenga invalidated blues because he said it meant political resignation. But blues was my thing. The old talking blues, I loved that . . . Language is musical, rhythmic. Sometimes I feel like a saxophone player or a drummer or trumpet player . . . You get that music in you, the words fly on the rhythm and you're writing before the words even come to you. *(Beat; ordering Taj)* Music!

(Taj goes to stereo, cues another selection, and watches Baraka write from across the room.)

SCENE 3

Taj alone. He's at a side table transcribing some of Baraka's long-hand notes from a stack of legal pads.
   He pores over one of the pads, squints, and scratches his head trying to decipher the scribblings, then tentatively types on a laptop. On the floor nearby is a bookbag with an envelope holding a manuscript of his play.
   His cell phone rings. He answers.

TAJ: Sup . . . I've been forewarned. Never ask that he critique my plays . . .

(He pulls the envelope from the bookbag, glances at it, and puts it back.)

I drank the Kool-Aid, you don't have to remind me . . . Yeah I told him I'm a playwright . . . He's a difficult personality, I don't know why I brought it. Say something supportive, okay? . . . It's a crapshoot figuring where his head's at any given moment . . . He went to the Pan-African Congress in Dar es Salaam, Tanzania, and on the plane ride made notes on legal pads can't nobody read . . . Nah, it's unstructured how he writes, all experimentation and change.

(He hears Baraka approaching from outside.)

He's like a character in one of his plays, I gotta go he's here. *(Hangs up. To Baraka as he enters carrying a briefcase and books) Habari yako?*

BARAKA: *Njema.* How's it coming?

TAJ: It's indecipherable.

(Baraka laughs.)

BARAKA: Where are you?

TAJ: It's 1950, runup to the McCarthy era, and Du Bois is indicted for leading a nuclear disarmament group thought to be a Communist front. Government's taken his passport. Colleagues at the NAACP, which he helped found, abandon him. Act Two, Scene 2, he and wife Shirley sit silently in the courtroom as various antics swirl around them.

BARAKA: That's fine. Email me what you've transcribed.

(He goes to his desk.)

So when the play is set, Shirley is fifty-four years old and Du Bois is eighty-three. He'd gotten close to her after his first wife, Nina, died. But he'd known her since she was thirteen years old. Shirley's friend Ellie said, "Child got a lot of patience."

(He laughs.)

TAJ: Isn't this basically a courtroom drama? Why is that romantic backstory important?

BARAKA: The tender scenes help audiences to empathize and invest emotionally. And Shirley Graham is a significant literary figure. If you don't know her work, you should. She was lauded as a great writer until people started calling her Communist, which she was.

TAJ: You have these jump-cut scene changes. Action moving abruptly from the courtroom where Du Bois is being tried, to a beauty salon where regular folks monitor events on radio—for all of six, eight lines of dialogue—then abruptly back to the courtroom. Have you thought about how back-and-forth switching of the sets is going to be handled?

BARAKA: The way they always are. Stagehands hauling furniture on and offstage. Don't act retarded. It's not a good look.

(Baraka goes to the stereo, looks through CDs.
Taj emails transcribed notes with a few keystrokes, closes his laptop, and nervously takes the manuscript from his bookbag.
Baraka puts on some jazz, walks toward his desk, but is intercepted by Taj offering him the envelope containing his play.)

TAJ: Don't get mad.

BARAKA: Oh no, I already told you, don't bring me no plays.

(Baraka avoids touching the envelope like it's disease-infected, backpedals as Taj pursues him, leading with the envelope.)

TAJ *(Pursues)*: It's not a submission to *Spirit House*, per se /

BARAKA *(Backpedals)*: / I know damn well it ain't no submission, it's a distraction. Your role is to assist me with *Most Dangerous Man*, not bring in shit for me to dramaturg.

TAJ *(Pursues)*: Just a quick read, see if it has value.

BARAKA *(Backpedals)*: Get your professor to read it, some of your classmates.

TAJ *(Pursues)*: When I got access to Amiri Baraka, my literary hero? *(Drops to his knees)* I'm begging you, man. Don't break my heart.

(Baraka snatches the envelope from Taj.)

BARAKA: Get up off the floor.

(Taj stands as Baraka pulls out the manuscript.)

Murder the Devil.

TAJ: It's about homegrown terrorism.

BARAKA: Interesting title.

TAJ: Unlikely heroes—a backstreet gang—foil a terrorist plot and set a hostage free.

BARAKA: I'll look at it when I get some time.

(He puts the play back in the envelope and goes to his desk.)

TAJ: I read "The Revolutionary Theatre" like you advised.

BARAKA: Like I advised?

TAJ: You said that understanding Antonin Artaud was essential to understanding you.

BARAKA: Sounds like me but jog my memory.

TAJ: That I'd get the Artaud connection if I read your essay. Written in 1965.

BARAKA: What did you think?

TAJ: It's old, and still kickass, like you.

(Baraka is pleased.)

But contradictory. Also like you.

BARAKA: How so?

TAJ: How can revolutionary theater be a theater of victims? Victims are objects of a story, not the subjects. You said that Clay in *Dutchman*, Ray in *The Toilet*, and Walker in *The Slave* are all victims—as heroes. But that's protest theater appealing to the conscience of the oppressor. De facto it makes racists and despots likable for merely admitting their crimes.

BARAKA: Totally correct but for incorrect reasons. Artistic innovation in this sense was a call for social upheaval. I said revolutionary theater should force change and be change. A weaponized art, if I remember correctly. I said it should slaughter dimwitted fat-bellied white guys who think the rest of the world exists for them to slobber on.

TAJ: But why Artaud?

BARAKA: Because Artaud wanted to rupture the Western theater tradition.

(He opens laptop on his desk, keystrokes a few commands: opening email and searching the internet.)

TAJ: August Wilson intentionally didn't study the Western classics. Not Shaw, not Ibsen, not Shakespeare, not Tennessee Williams. *Death of a Salesman*? Never read it.

BARAKA: I'm one of August Wilson's "four Bs."

TAJ: His what?

BARAKA: His four major influences: The blues. Argentine writer Jorge Luis Borges. Black-American artist Romare Bearden. And me. Said I taught him that all art is political.

TAJ: Get the fuck outta here!

(Taj gathers the stack of legal pads at his side table.)

BARAKA: He came to Newark a couple of times. When we first met, he wanted to know why I wasn't a beatnik anymore.

TAJ: He was looking for Leroy, trying to follow your lead.

BARAKA: Next thing I hear he'd joined the Nation of Islam /

TAJ: / Wonder why? /

BARAKA: / Which he stayed with for a hot minute. But August was a poet back then. He wasn't writing plays yet, just a young poet talking to me about poetry. And his movement into theater was a Marvtastic development.

(Taj takes the stack of legal pads and places them on Baraka's desk.)

TAJ: He hated colorblind casting. That's what "The Ground on Which I Stand" is partly about. How an all-Black production of *Who's Afraid of Virginia Woolf*, or any white play for that matter, denies us cultural identity and turns Black actors into mimics. Some of our own Black theaters are the worst offenders. Instead of developing Black playwrights and producing work that tells our story, full of joy and wonderment that makes the whole world wanna go skinny-dipping, they're insinuating their Black selves into the white man's tired-ass boring aesthetic. Brothers bitching online because they can't do an all-Black *American Buffalo*, sheesh.

BARAKA: Our slave mentality, it never goes away. We've been perversely inclined to create for white folks ever since master had us skinning and grinning in the plantation big house. But Negro versions of the American canon ain't the only problem, believe you me. *The Mountaintop* had to be pulled from production after the outright abomination, something we never imagined we'd see, of a white actor playing Martin Luther King. Greedy white showmen out here stealing talent and patrons from struggling Black theaters, enabled by colorblind casting. Colorblind casting supposed to promote diversity but they're discriminating even within the diversity.

TAJ: People try to reverse-psyche implicate *Hamilton*. *Hamilton* ain't colorblind casting, it's color-conscious casting. But Shakespeare's my pet peeve. I'm all for Black actors getting work. But brothers and sisters in period garb playing sixteenth-century European royalty? It's a sham. I can't watch the shit. It's fake.

BARAKA: Blame it on Ira Aldridge, the African Roscius.

(Baraka's desktop printer begins spilling out pages of a document into the tray.)

TAJ: Actors mangle my dialogue but memorize verbatim Shakespeare's pompous, incomprehensible limericks, and half the time don't even know what they're saying. Fuck Shakespeare.

BARAKA: Fuck Shakespeare?

TAJ: August Wilson did just fine without him.

BARAKA: Shakespeare's revolutionary. Shakespeare showed us how to eviscerate the rulers and aristocrats. Five hundred years ago he examined sociopolitical topics still relevant today. *Julius Caesar* was about the relationship between government and people. *Taming of the Shrew* about the oppression of women, and *Hamlet* about the development of liberalism. The problem with Shakespeare right now is magical-realist, mumbo-jumbo presentation that puts people to sleep.

TAJ: His antique scripts monopolize so many resources that original works struggle getting produced. And I ain't just throwing shade on Shakespeare. You read *Outrageous For-tune: The Life and Times of the New American Play*?

BARAKA: Any fool can see that American theater today devalues art. Companies of resident actors disbanded long ago. Managers and administrators get the real money, creative artists get the crumbs. And last I checked, not one of the seventy-some League of Resident Theatres that book refers to is Black-owned and likely to produce your work. So how's it pertinent to you? Who are you writing for?

TAJ: For whoever. I'm constantly sending out synopses and dialogue samples. Entering contests with submission fees. The one or two theaters interested in my work want to do it for free.

BARAKA: Playwrights are the bottom of the theater food chain. You haven't figured that out?

TAJ: Nonprofit white theaters regularly mount a diversity token. One season it's a female-themed play. Next it's LGBT, then Latin, Asian, or whatever, like a rotation to display their equal-opportunity bona fides. Mostly open submission so by-and-by they schedule a Black-themed play and might be my chance to get lucky.

BARAKA: Those theaters aren't going to do your work. Stop emailing your scripts around like a thousand other unknowns hoping to get discovered. Open submitting's a waste of time. And whoever discovers you is going to turn you into something you wished you wasn't, I can guarantee you that.

TAJ: But going for the Black theater audience I'm up against church pageants. I'm up against morality plays. I'm up against Tyler Perry's *Madea*.

BARAKA: You into some deep doo-doo now. Our people love buffoonery.

(Baraka arranges pages from the printer tray and staples them into two copies of a short scene.)

Tyler Perry made the *Colored Girls* film, give him that. Tyler Perry got white-folks type of money.

TAJ: With that level of competition who is going to put on my plays?

BARAKA: Put them on yourself. I never believed in waiting for somebody to produce my plays. I never believed I was going to be discovered by nobody. You love plays, you write plays, you want people to see them, put them on yourself. Say what you want about Tyler Perry, but that's what he did. Print copies of your script and get a group of friends to read it. Maybe a church or neighborhood bar will let you stage it and charge a few dollars at the door. Playwrights hold on to work talking about one day the theater god is going to put them on Broadway. That's make-believe. Produce yourself. Build a reputation in the Black theater community and develop an audience of brothers and sisters who come see your work. We're all we've got. *(Hands Taj a stapled script)*

TAJ: What's this?

BARAKA: Scenes from *Most Dangerous Man in America*. We're going to read it aloud. Not a table read but a dramatic reading. Never relax, and mean what you say—that's good acting.

TAJ: Got it.

BARAKA: You sure?

TAJ: Sure I'm sure. Keep it simple. Speak clearly and be human.

BARAKA: Trust the playwright.

TAJ: Right, don't be a showoff.

BARAKA: I'll read Du Bois and the stage directions. You read Shirley Graham and her friend Ellie.

(Baraka hums a soft melody to set the mood, rearranging furniture as necessary, then he and Taj read lines and dramatize them to the max.)

Shirley Graham and her friend Ellie are seated close to each other, talking, a dinner table nearby.

TAJ: *Ellie: I think it's wonderful. You have to tell me.*
Shirley: Well, he got back to that killing schedule of his.

BARAKA: Montage of photo images: The U.S. Senate. Du Bois attorney Vito Marcantonio. U.S. Congress. Du Bois speaking at Madison Square Garden.

TAJ: *Ellie: That was a great campaign.*

> *Shirley: It sure was. You know he got sixty-four thousand votes. Well he came to dinner one night. I had gotten an award from the American Academy of Arts and Letters for my contribution to American literature.*

BARAKA: Du Bois comes and sits at the table. Shirley comes to the table, pretending to bring dessert after dinner.

> *Du Bois: I'm really proud of you winning the Academy of Arts award.*

He finishes the meal, raises a glass to toast.

> *Du Bois: Here's a woman who can write, speak, and cook. Unusual.*

He and Shirley laugh.

> *Du Bois: Shirley have you ever thought of marrying again? You'd make some man a wonderful wife.*

TAJ: *Shirley: Any candidates?*

BARAKA: Spot on Ellie's face.

TAJ: *Ellie: No, he didn't say that?*

BARAKA: *Du Bois: He'd have to be somebody who, who . . .*

TAJ: *Shirley: He'd have to be somebody I could look up to.*

BARAKA: *Du Bois: Poorly stated but probably correct.*

He looks away.

> *Du Bois: Don't you have anybody in mind?*

Shirley looks directly into his eyes.

TAJ: *Shirley: I've had only one man in my mind for a long time.*

BARAKA: A slight flush comes to his cheek.

> *Du Bois: So you've been keeping secrets from me?*

TAJ: *Voiceover Shirley: He would go for long walks and return to find me at my typewriter. He settles himself by a window with a paperback. The previous subject was not touched on again.*
> *Ellie: Oh.*
>
> *Shirley: He'd come out to St. Albans to rest. He'd rake leaves in the yard, build a bonfire; we drank cocoa, went to the movies. We saw Ingrid Bergman in* Arch of Triumph. *We even stopped at a corner drugstore and bought ice cream. But then when he was ready to leave . . .*

BARAKA: *Du Bois: Shirley, you really provided me with a haven of rest.*

He takes her hand, gravely.

Du Bois: I'm a selfish old man, Shirley. You have your father's generous goodness, I've monopolized your time and youth, it isn't fair and I'm going to stop.

TAJ: *Shirley murmurs: Please don't.*

Voiceover Shirley: He kissed me goodbye with a gentle finality, but being a woman I was sure I only had to wait.

BARAKA: Exit Du Bois. Ellie joins Shirley at the table.

TAJ: *Ellie: So . . .*

Shirley: I didn't see him again until an emergency meeting at the Peace Center. We heard there was some investigation, something coming. We didn't know what to expect.

Ellie: So what happened?

Shirley: He wanted to take me home from the meeting but I wouldn't hear it. The phone was ringing when I unlocked my door. There was some talk about the meeting, but then his voice took on a totally different tone. He asked me would I spend New Year's Eve with him. I said I'd love to.

Ellie: Okay, okay.

Shirley: So as the year 1951 rolled in, our future was settled. He kept telling me he was selfish and too old, but he didn't act old.

BARAKA: They laugh.

TAJ: *Shirley: I tried to hide the flow of happiness that filled my being. Undoubtedly I'd been in love with him for a long time. He'd dominated my life to an extent that no other man had come near. But my love made no demands. The fact that we shared work together was enough. But that was no longer true for either of us.*

BARAKA: Enter Du Bois to join Shirley and Ellie.

Du Bois: I've been watching the whole drama being acted over here by you two. You going to let me in on it?

TAJ: *Shirley: You know all about it.*

BARAKA: *Du Bois: What's that?*

TAJ: *Shirley: How I swept you off your feet.*

BARAKA: Du Bois laughs and hugs her.

Du Bois: The only sane person was her mother. Not only did she say that I was too old, but how did she put it, Shirley?

"He mighty high-hat." All our earlier plans got botched by this investigation, but I swore that wouldn't stop anything. Now that we're married we're going to get married again. Shirley hopes people will stop telling her she's married a dirty old man.

(They're finished. Pause.)

Well . . . Satisfactory . . . Probably work, a few tweaks here and there . . .

(Beat.)

What do you think?

TAJ: You want my opinion?

BARAKA: You just read it didn't you?

TAJ *(Placating)*: It's . . . I like the pacing, and the texture, I like the texture. There's a lyrical flow.

BARAKA: We'll see how it fits with the other.

TAJ: I can't believe you care what I think.

BARAKA: I don't.

(Taj thumbs through the script. He stares at it with an awkward expression.)

What? What's the matter?

TAJ: I'm flattered you even asked.

(Taj hands Baraka his script, gets up quickly, busying himself replacing chairs, table where they belong.)

BARAKA: No you aren't.

TAJ: You don't remember but I met you before.

BARAKA: When?

TAJ: More than once actually.

BARAKA: Really.

TAJ: The time I'm thinking about is a writers conference hosted by Third World Press, you were keynote speaker.

BARAKA: In Chicago.

TAJ: It was one of those formative experiences from years ago that came back on me suddenly just now. For a minute there I couldn't believe I'm really here. Right now. Working with you. On a play.

BARAKA: Why would that be?

TAJ: Chicago was the first time I'd seen you in the flesh. *(Beat)* This is embarrassing, I sound like a little bitch.

BARAKA: Fascinating. Do go on, continue, continue.

(Taj shakes his head. Beat, then he relives the incident.)

TAJ: Beautiful afternoon, perfect springtime Chicago weather, couple of years ago, I'm in undergrad . . . Along with a hundred or so others I'm staring at an empty lectern, so excited I'm about to piss my pants. Because any second the leading intellectual of our time will take the stage. Loud, rude, badass provocateur who uses his art for racial uplift. A mysterious and mythic figure with whom we are all obsessed . . . I catch my breath and distinctly remember thinking, maybe this is how Rastafarian pilgrims felt at the coronation of Haile Selassie fifty years ago, anxiously waiting for a glimpse of the King of Kings, Lion of Judah, the Elect of God. Then you come out. Our prophet of Black liberation. The room explodes with applause, whistles, and hoots . . . I'm blanking now on your remarks they were so far over my head, except, apropos of nothing, you open with a hilarious putdown of our Supreme Court Justice. That sometimes reversing a person's name reveals their true identity: Clarence Thomas, Tom-ass Clarence. Funny. Anyway afterwards you're taking questions from the audience. I'm carefully rehearsing one in my head so I don't sound like a fool. I'm gauging the opportune time to raise my hand. I'm standing kind of in the back and repeatedly don't get recognized. I keep raising my hand, afraid you're not going to notice me. Finally you do, I'm saying my name and where I go to school but you cut me off—"What's your question brother?"

(Beat.)

BARAKA: Well, what was it?

TAJ: Maybe it was the way it came out. Like I was bugged by your sleight-of-hand identity-swap from beatnik to nationalist, way after the fact, and that crept into my voice or something. But what I asked was . . . "What is your response to critics who say that propaganda had replaced artistry in your plays?" Then you asked me what I thought. That put me on defensive, I'm already a jumble of nerves, and I say, "You're the bigtime intellectual, I'm asking you." And you said literary criticism was class warfare, and did I understand that. But the Marxist ring to it threw me and I didn't know what to say. Then you said I had constipation-face and needed a brain enema, and everybody laughed.

(Beat.)

BARAKA: Then what happened?

TAJ: Nothing. You took a few more questions, wrapped things up . . .

BARAKA: Memory fails. Particular details I honestly don't recall.

(Baraka takes the two scripts to his desk.)

TAJ: Good.

BARAKA: There were cocktails after. Someplace in Hyde Park . . .

TAJ: Wall-to-wall literary elite talking intelligent. I'm sheepishly gliding around the periphery, trying to get your attention, when out of nowhere comes a disembodied hand giving you a double scotch. You say emphatically, "This here is a drink what am!" Everybody laughs and I fade into the background.

BARAKA: What more were you going to say at the cocktail reception?

TAJ: That you didn't answer my question.

BARAKA: I did so answer you, according to your own play-by-play.

TAJ: No you didn't.

BARAKA: I said criticism was class warfare.

TAJ: If you had remembered me from Chicago, would I have this job?

BARAKA: Probably not.

TAJ: Am I fired?

BARAKA: First you answer my question: Do you think my work has deteriorated? You think I've sacrificed craft and form for political content?

(Beat.)

TAJ: You'll get mad.

BARAKA: So?

TAJ: I think . . . *Arm Yourself or Harm Yourself.* It's typical. A morality play too simple for critical interpretation. One-dimensional stereotype characters—killer white cop, Black cop that's racially disloyal, Black family that's victimized. The predictable good-versus-evil narrative lacks dramatic interest.

BARAKA: That play is literal, exact, and direct. It sends a message that Black audiences understand.

TAJ: An audience you evidently underestimate.

BARAKA: That's bullshit.

TAJ: You write the propaganda plays because you think Black audiences can't understand drama that's thoughtful and aesthetically rich.

BARAKA: Aesthetically rich as defined by whom?

TAJ: By accepted standards and criteria.

BARAKA: Set by an evil cabal of bourgeois white males who think they have better taste.

TAJ: You're denying there are qualitative measures of art and beauty?

BARAKA: I'm questioning what are valid critiques of art intended for social impact.

TAJ: Because you value ideological content over craft.

BARAKA: What you are saying is more important than how you are saying it.

TAJ: And isn't that the dilemma of writers from oppressed communities? Whether to turn art into propaganda?

BARAKA: Ahh, so you've digested Harold Cruse. *Crisis of the Negro Intellectual*. Bravo. Unfortunately the crisis of the Negro community makes the disengaged Black intellectual pretty much useless.

TAJ: That's not the conclusion Cruse reached.

(Baraka moves from his desk to face Taj.)

BARAKA *(A mild rant)*: Let him tell it I shouldn't have helped Ken Gibson become first Black mayor of Newark. I shouldn't have convened the National Black Political Convention. It drew eight thousand activists and elected officials from across the political spectrum. Richard Hatcher, Jesse Jackson, Andrew Young, Vernon Jordan, Maynard Jackson, Roy Innis—they all were there. You think Black voters would have been better off without it?

TAJ: What's amazing is that during it all, you still wrote plays. That's incredible.

BARAKA: I helped organize the first African Liberation Day, don't forget that.

TAJ: I can't wait to read *The Motion of History, What Was the Relationship of the Lone Ranger to the Means of Production?* Blatantly political I'm sure.

BARAKA: *Dutchman* is a political play.

TAJ: It's a lot more than that.

BARAKA: Critics called me all kinds of names, stupid, crazy, evil.

TAJ: I'm talking about plays that make deliberate political statements.

BARAKA: So let's talk about them. Your hero August Wilson loved the Black Arts plays.

TAJ: He didn't write political plays himself.

BARAKA: But he staged mine repeatedly at Black Horizon Theater of Pittsburgh, him and Rob Penny, back in the day.

TAJ: *Dutchman* is the one people are still doing now. It's going up at the same theater where it premiered forty years ago.

BARAKA: Please. I wrote *Dutchman* on an all-nighter. Stayed up one night, wrote it, fell asleep at the desk, woke up next morning, looked at it and said, "What the fuck is this?"

TAJ: It's your masterpiece, that's what it is. And you followed it up with *A Black Mass*, a play dramatizing Nation of Islam mythology? *Home on the Range*, a baffling sendup of white people acting goofy?

BARAKA: For years I've had people telling me I was a better playwright before I got political. That has never influenced me. You know why? My parents. I came out of a little petit-bourgeois family.

My mother was a social worker and my father was a postman. They gave me piano lessons, trumpet lessons. I used to recite the Gettysburg Address every Lincoln's birthday in a Boy Scout uniform. But they also equipped me to go out and fight white people. Every night at dinner they'd be running it. You're sitting there eating biscuits and whatnot and they'd be telling you the history of the South. The history of Black people, the history of Black music. I didn't understand it at the time but they were preparing their boy to contend in this racist environment. I don't know if that's still done in Black families.

TAJ: It was sure done in mine.

BARAKA: But Black writers have to continue that tradition. That's one of our functions in the community. We cannot wait for others. We have to do for ourselves. We have to think and create and bond together and move forward.

TAJ: Little Everett Leroy Jones, in a Boy Scout uniform. I can't imagine.

BARAKA *(Taking offense)*: It's pronounced L*eroi*, not L*eroy*, and spelled r-o-i not r-o-y.

TAJ: I read in the *Autobiography of LeRoi Jones* you were born "Leroy" but started using "LeRoi" in college after the journalist Roi Ottley.

BARAKA: Did I write that?

TAJ: In black and white.

BARAKA: Must have been selective memory.

TAJ: Or you constantly remixing who it is that you are.

BARAKA: I was born LeRoi, French-ified because of my father's middle name, Leverette.

TAJ: How'd you become Amiri Baraka?

BARAKA: The man who buried Malcolm X, a Muslim imam, came to me after police had whipped me half to death in the Newark riots. "You don't need an American name," he said. And the meaning of the new name—"blessed prince"—seemed fitting to me.

TAJ: Wasn't an "American" name you were changing. It was your family name.

BARAKA: My father said, "What, 'Jones' ain't good enough for you boy?" But all these white-folks names we're wearing came from slavery. I was discarding a "slave name" and embracing Blackness.

TAJ: That was the 1960s. What's slavery have to do with it?

BARAKA. More ignorance from millennials. Black people were four hundred years in slavery and been one hundred and fifty years so-called free. Do the math. And that's including one hundred years of terror and lynching after emancipation in 1863. Right now today we are still living in the aftermath of slavery, yet to overcome the lasting tribulation centuries of servitude inflicted on our people. It was 1963 Klansmen dynamited the Birmingham church, killing four little Black girls, justice for the perpetrators delayed until 2001 and 2002. Welcome to post-racial America.

(Baraka returns to his desk and Most Dangerous Man *script.)*

TAJ: Change your name, change your identity. It's that simple?

BARAKA: What you want to be today you might not want to be tomorrow. What you called yourself a few minutes ago, you might not want to call yourself the next time I see you coming around the corner.

TAJ: Will the real Everett Leroy Jones slash LeRoi Jones slash Amiri Baraka please step forward?

BARAKA: People question how I got to wherever they think that I am. Ask why would I leave where they thought that I was before. But was I ever there, where they thought I was? And where were they?

(Taj looks at him, unconvinced.)

SCENE 4

Writing study. John Coltrane's unrelentingly dissonant "Jupiter Variation" blasts from the stereo at earsplitting volume.

The room is gloomy, nearly dark, barely lit by the glow of a laptop screen on the floor, surrounded by complete disarray. Many different versions of Most Dangerous Man *litter the floor, along with loose papers, several books opened to specific pages, magazines, and newspapers.*

The desk is covered with debris as well. Trash basket overflows. There's half-eaten pizza and empty coffee cups lying about. In the middle of this accumulated refuse on the floor sits Baraka, staring transfixed at the laptop but not writing. He's blocked.

Long pause, then enter Taj.

TAJ *(Shouting)*: CAN I LOWER THE VOLUME?

> *(No response from Baraka. Taj turns down the music, turns on some lights.*
> *He halts, stunned at the sight of his mentor incapacitated.)*

What the . . . ?

> *(He starts gathering scripts, books, and periodicals and stacking them in no particular order.)*

. . . Shit . . . You need anything? You been up all night?

BARAKA: I'm mutilating it.

TAJ *(Cleaning up)*: What?

BARAKA: It's my valedictory, probably my final play, and I'm butchering it to death.

TAJ: Uh-oh.

BARAKA: I cut it down to ninety pages.

TAJ: Damn.

BARAKA: Shooting for a fifty-page final draft.

> *(Beat. Taj is astonished, unsure how to respond.)*

Is it still going to be a play at all? Characters coming across as underwritten stereotypes. And with eighteen characters in fifty pages, casting's an issue.

(Baraka gets up with effort.)

I'm telling myself, be explicit as possible with stage directions. Next I'm thinking, don't be so explicit. Theater's a collaborative art so let the cast and crew bring the script to life. Allow it an existence beyond yourself.

(Taj reads some pages while gathering them up.)

And however enlightened or thrilled or sublimely inspired the audience, I can hear the critics now: *(With utter disgust)* "Baraka prefers to tell rather than show. Baraka's haphazard structure is so bewildering that nobody could find the drama. Baraka's forceful poetic voice isn't in evidence here. An unmusical grace note to Baraka's vibrant career. Du Bois deserves better. Baraka can do better."

(Beat.)

TAJ: You worried that it won't go up?
BARAKA: An Amiri Baraka play? Going unproduced? Get real. Woodie's doing it and he's done all my plays, damn near got arrested and had his theater shut down for doing *The Toilet*, years ago in Detroit. With *Most Dangerous Man* a lot of presumptuous, cockamamie production demands are making the project contingent on other people's approval.

(Baraka gets the laptop and takes it to his desk.)

TAJ: You said it had to be panoramic. Layer on layer of cascading scenes. Now it reads like a slipshod history lesson.
BARAKA: It's a draft.
TAJ: Second draft? Third draft?
BARAKA: Draft number five.

TAJ: Master of the theater idiom running into a little problem?

BARAKA: I ain't got no problem, American theater's got the problem. Artifice and deception and reliance on metaphor and ambiguous theatrical terminology. Abstract depictions of Black people's oppressive, suffocating quality of life—they're fine. But call the devil by his name and address directly how we've been fucked over for centuries and cheerlead some retaliation, then you're lecturing the audience.

TAJ: Which you never get tired of doing. You never get tired of telling people what to think, telling them what art is, what theater is.

BARAKA: And never will. Until people take art seriously in our struggle for liberation.

TAJ: This time looks like you're the one standing in judgment and found wanting.

(Baraka looks at Taj and snorts dismissively, but helps him straighten up.)

BARAKA: I am not in the mood, so piss off.

TAJ: Think about it. None of your Black revolutionary plays have seen the light of day in I can't remember when.

BARAKA: That's censorship. The powers that be hide theater that challenges their rule. Because when people see depicted onstage how they're being exploited and disenfranchised, it leads to activism.

TAJ: None of the plays by your Black Arts disciples, Garrett, Neal, Caldwell and others, none of them have held up either.

BARAKA: They weren't written for posterity. Those plays came at a special moment in time as part of a staggering creative explosion.

TAJ: "A fad that lacked artistic integrity." That's what Stanley Crouch called it.

BARAKA: Ignore that Negro nemesis Stanley Crouch. And how he got a Genius Award and Marvin X didn't lets me know that he's writing something somebody who hands out Genius Awards wants him to write.

TAJ: Marvin X is no Stanley Crouch.

BARAKA: Since Marvin X ain't writing the shit the MacArthur people want, then he ain't no genius.

TAJ: It must work your last nerve that Lonne Elder, who thumbed his nose at your revolutionary theater diktats, saw his play *Ceremonies in Dark Old Men* made into a TV movie and is still being produced after forty years.

BARAKA: And you think that's good.

TAJ: What's bad about it?

BARAKA: It's an embarrassment.

TAJ: You're jealous.

BARAKA: Why would negative depictions of Black men being broadcast on national TV make me jealous?

TAJ: That play's about a Black family's struggle to overcome racism. Critics compare it to *Raisin in the Sun*.

BARAKA: Here you go again with the ineffectual out-to-lunch theater critics. *Ceremonies* is a tragedy about Black social pathology. Involving a bunch of jobless barbershop lay-abouts who can't even trust each other. What it deserves is a critical beatdown.

TAJ: That's unfair.

BARAKA: It's theater of pessimism and ambiguity.

TAJ: Douglas Turner Ward didn't get the grand pooh-bah Imamu Baraka's seal of approval either. His play *Day of Absence* inspired *Key & Peele* to do a reverse satire, "Negrotown," about a utopia for Black people. You know Keegan–Michael Key and Jordan Peele, Black sketch-comedy team on television?

BARAKA: Not personally.

TAJ: How would you know them personally? You know what I meant. Don't be facetious.

BARAKA: I bet Jordan Peele read *Dutchman* a few times before he made the movie *Get Out*.

TAJ: Good you didn't try to tell him how to make it, like you tried to tell Spike Lee how to make *Malcolm X*.

BARAKA: What Spike Lee did to Malcolm's life is a betrayal of Black people.

TAJ: You're just mad because he didn't submit to you authorizing the script.

BARAKA: I'm mad at Hollywood Negroes making a lot of garbage.

TAJ: So says the revolutionary artist who played a raggedy-ass bum in the Warren Beatty movie *Bulworth*. You can't get more Hollywood than that.

BARAKA: I played Rastaman, a griot in the West African tradition. *(Proudly)* I float through the film dispensing incantations of sage advice. I wrote my own lines.

TAJ: I thought it was a straight up sellout for a writer of your stature. "A modern-day Faust selling his soul to the devil." That's what you said about Belafonte and Poitier. You're a gigantic narcissist, dude, always have to be the center of attention. Performance artist as political leader.

BARAKA: *Bulworth* is one of the most progressive films to come down the pike and I was glad to do it. At one point Warren even used the word "socialist," which in America is like saying "cocksucker."

TAJ: It's "The White Negro" all over again. Hip Caucasian appropriates Black authenticity by going native.

BARAKA: To look at race as the decisive factor is grossly superficial.

TAJ: What? Since when?

BARAKA: Since I changed my ideology.

(Beat.)

Black nationalism blinded me to class differences and conflicting political interests in the Black community.

TAJ: Say what?

BARAKA: The more I came in contact with dialectical materialism and Marxism, the more I gained a scientific understanding of how to continue the Black liberation struggle.

TAJ: I thought you were all about raising the consciousness of Black people. Now you're a Communist?!

BARAKA: However many roads I've had to travel, whatever sacrifices it takes, I've always been politically engaged. But never have I considered myself to be fixed in any ideology or intractable on any point of view.

(Beat.)

TAJ: What time is it?

(Baraka doesn't answer.)

In Newark we always ask the time. What time is it?

(Beat.)

You know the response. "It's nation time." Fucking hypocrite. Changed your views? When were you planning to tell me?

BARAKA: I don't need to tell you. Who are *you*?

TAJ: Who are *you*?! That's the question. Your life is littered with discarded identities. Beat bohemian then super Black. And now you embrace the most dogmatic of all ideologies, Marxist-Leninist-Stalinism. People talk about you and don't even know who they mean. And you don't give a damn how repeatedly switching philosophies impacts your followers and those who hold you in esteem. You don't give a shit about us. Months I've been working here and you know nothing about me.

BARAKA: I know you're a theater intern anxious about the future and desperate that I write you a glowing recommendation.

TAJ: Do you even know where I live? Newark? The City? Harlem? Brooklyn?

BARAKA: No I don't know where you live /

TAJ: / Day in and day out picking up behind you, listening to self-absorbed rants and you never once inquired about my studies, my personal life, my family. Never once asked me to stay for drinks or dinner.

BARAKA: You work for me, I don't have to be cordial.

TAJ: You weren't even curious where it was we met other than that time in Chicago.

BARAKA: I won't remember.

TAJ: It was the Million Man March! *(Very emotional, like he's about to cry)* With my dad . . . bunch of people congratulating you after a speech and Daddy said, "Taj, this is the great writer Amiri Baraka. Amiri, this is my son, Taj." You smiled and said to Daddy, "You didn't have to tell me he's your son. He looks like you spat him out."

BARAKA: I meet lots of people all the time.

(Beat. Taj, befuddled, roams aimlessly.)

TAJ: I read *Home*. I read *Blues People, System of Dante's Hell*, the poems and plays. I adore your work. Even when you were calling people faggots and niggy hos and saying "I got the extermination blues, jewboys"—the sheer outrageousness had me in awe.

BARAKA: So now you're attached to a backward, bourgeois, nationalist, skin-color ideology. Sliding around the walls pouting about being Black. Well don't blame me. I've moved on.

TAJ: I wanted to *be* LeRoi Jones/Amiri Baraka! I thought I *was* LeRoi Jones/Amiri Baraka!

BARAKA: I am that I am, not who you think that I am. And stop your sulking. It's starting to annoy me.

TAJ *(Explodes)*: My sulking?! *Annoys you?!* I'm trying to grasp your chameleon-like transformations and *you're* annoyed?! Hold on hold on, Black nationalist true believers, Leroy's taking a sharp left! You think it's your inalienable right to turn gospel one day into blasphemy the next. Now I gotta figure out what clothes to wear. What's the accepted greeting, the right political slogans, the quotation-of-the-day from our dear leader Comrade Change-A-Lot! *(Roaming the room like a caged predator)* You say freedom for Black people in North America is a lifelong commitment. You even KNOW any regular Black people? You can't STAND the so-called Black bourgeoisie. You identify your own family by social class. You think church folks are fools. All the Black masses mean to you is an audience to be instructed and indoctrinated. Black liberation struggle just a good place for a self-centered, pretentious nigga like you to get his swag on. Telling people what it is to be Black and you didn't come from the African American literary tradition. *(In Baraka's face)* YOU CAME FROM THE VILLAGE! YOU CAME FROM WHITE PEOPLE!

BARAKA *(Mocking, sardonic)*: And that makes you better than me! Because I lived in the Village wasting my life as a traitor to the Black race! Because I tried to ruck every halfway-decent-looking white woman crossed my path! That disqualifies me and I'm an inferior person!

TAJ: No, it's because after you left your white friends, you turned your back on and publicly vilified every last one of them . . . Why didn't I see the same thing coming? So tell me, at what point did Blackness become not enough? One minute Black playwrights don't kiss your ass, they're subject to scandalous denunciation—bam—the next you're preaching Communist utopia?

(Baraka unfazed, Taj backs up off him.)

Never mind that the main Communist countries, Russia and China, done turned capitalist already. But you know everything. You have all the answers. No doubt can see some mystical utility for Black people in a system of authoritarian government control.

(Beat.)

BARAKA: You have student loan debt?

TAJ: What?

BARAKA: How much? National average is twenty-two thousand dollars.

TAJ: What's that got to do with what we're talking about.

BARAKA: Universities are capitalist enterprises, making billions off financial aid and leaving students like you to pay the bill. That's how capitalism exploits us and also puts us in bondage. It's modern-day slavery; you have to suck up to dictatorial bosses on dehumanizing low-wage jobs and still can't make ends meet. /

TAJ *(A dig)*: / Ain't that the truth. /

BARAKA: / You're a slave to the market when you're paying high insurance premiums and routine medical procedures aren't covered. If we want tuition-free college and universal health care and income equality, we have to confront the money-grubbing capitalist system with a clear alternative doctrine.

TAJ: Amiri Baraka, the American Lenin, comes to the rescue.

BARAKA: The main reason the urban rebellions of the 1960s didn't develop into revolution was the absence of Marxist-Leninist leadership.

TAJ: Well that explains *What Was the Relationship of the Lone Ranger to the Means of Production?*, and your other play *The Motion of History*. Characters shouting, "Forward the Party! Long Live Socialist Revolution!" At first I thought it was satire. But they're shameless propaganda. *The Lone Ranger* romanticizes labor strikes like it's the mid-twentieth century. All the dialogue is Marxist rhetoric. *The Motion of History* does dramatize African slaves and white indentured servants taking up arms against British rulers in colonial Virginia. But character development is nonexistent. In *Lone Ranger* one of them recites the difference between "use value" and "exchange value"? What's that even mean? Another one explains exploitation in the capitalist production process.

BARAKA: If it's any consolation, Du Bois was the cause of it all.

TAJ: Or you're a sucker for radical ideology. You were just as fanatical about Ron Karenga and kawaida.

BARAKA: This is different. Du Bois's path from capitalist to socialist to communist guided me intellectually. Researching *Most Dangerous Man* made it clear to me as day.

TAJ: No, you're a master of reinvention. It's surreal, your identity crises.

(Baraka considers this.)

BARAKA: There is a sense of the prodigal about my life that begs to be resolved. The struggle, within myself, to understand where and who I am, and to move with that understanding. And given that context I do worry how *Most Dangerous Man* is going to be received . . . if it will be judged on the merits or construed as a vehicle for something I wanted to prove . . . *(He thumbs through a draft on his desk)* Plays used to be important. They used to inspire people. O'Neill, Langston, Zora, Tennessee Williams—we need to have a repertory company devoted solely to presenting their work. And why don't we have it? Because that stuff is dangerous. Look at *The Hairy Ape* or *Waiting for Lefty*. Tennessee Williams, his portrait of America is out to lunch. *Cat on a Hot Tin Roof*, *Orpheus Descending*, *Sweet Bird of Youth*. But you want to see something, see *Suddenly Last Summer*. Devastating portrait of American colonialism. Those are hell of plays. They operate with a precision that puts the nakedness of the human spirit on display. That's what we aspire to with *Most Dangerous Man*. To preach virtue and feeling . . . So audiences will find themselves cleansed at what their souls have been taught . . .

TAJ: It has to be epic.

BARAKA: Right.

TAJ: A theatrical Molotov cocktail.

BARAKA: No doubt.

TAJ: Putting on vivid display the crumbling demise of McCarthyism.

BARAKA: Absolutely.

TAJ: A great play, about Black America's preeminent scholar / activist.

BARAKA: Yes.

TAJ: One that conforms to no accepted standards of art and beauty.

(Beat.)

BARAKA: What? No, that's not /

TAJ: / Conveying a political message beyond mere literary critique. /

BARAKA: / You're putting words in my mouth.

TAJ: I'm using words that came *out* of your mouth. You admit to valuing content over craft. And I quote: "What you are saying is more important than how you are saying it."

BARAKA: That's missing the point.

TAJ: Spreading ideology, that's your point. Why you pretend otherwise? Might as well ask the audience at intermission, "What have you learned so far?" You said yourself the latest draft of *Most Dangerous Man* doesn't read like a play at all. And the play's the thing. Am I right or wrong?

BARAKA: You're right, but /

TAJ: / So acknowledge the contradiction. You tell yourself you're creating a beautiful theatrical work honoring an American secular saint, but in reality it's just a daring piece of propaganda.

BARAKA: You envy me, don't you.

TAJ: What? No I don't envy you.

BARAKA: This love-hate dynamic you got going on, you're obsessed. You covet your mentor's celebrity, which you like being associated with, but you hate being in my shadow. So you subject my work to merciless scrutiny. Examine my aesthetic in withering detail. Because secretly, you believe you can be a better writer, and you're using me to help you figure out how.

(Beat.)

TAJ *(Busted)*: I try to be crafty with it, try to not let that show, but sometimes I get excited.

BARAKA: I read your damn play, *Murder the Devil*. Al-Qaeda reject slips through Homeland Security on a bloodthirsty mission, recruits a treacherous street gang, but learns too late who is hustling who. Racial animosities surface and heated disputes over killing in the name of God, as the fate of a hostage hangs in the balance. I liked it.

TAJ *(Brightens)*: That mean you gonna do it?

BARAKA: Hell naw.

TAJ: A reading?

BARAKA: Negatory.

TAJ: Give me some notes at least.

BARAKA: That's on you, the playwright, the theater artist, to assemble a cast—direct it if you have to—so you can hear it aloud and determine where it needs improvement. Mao Tse-tung said that art has to be politically correct but also aesthetically powerful. That if the thing is not objectively beautiful, no matter how correct the ideological statement, it is going to fail.

TAJ: You're just spouting rhetoric.

BARAKA: No, I believe it.

TAJ: That's the standard you're applying to *Most Dangerous Man*?

BARAKA: It underscores my sense of mission. I told you Cosby came to me about this play, but above and beyond that, I feel compelled to write it, I feel obligated.

TAJ: Seriously.

BARAKA: I met Malcolm. Dr. King came to my house. But Du Bois's writing changed my life. Finding the man behind the mythic reputation was an impulse I couldn't resist. I kept wondering what a play about Du Bois might feel like. What's the narrative scope, the settings, historical figures who might people the cast. You wouldn't write a paean to your literary exemplar? *(A dare)* Sure you would. Du Bois is the epitome for me. Skip Gates and them talking about Du Bois and *The Talented Tenth*. It was 1890-something when he wrote that book. They harp on it because they don't want to deal with Du Bois the Pan-Africanist and Du Bois the Communist. *Most Dangerous Man* comes later in his life and shows the underlying dynamic of his intellectual journey. But I'm not fooling myself. Du Bois's life was majestic, a pageant, that I'm supposed to whittle down to a thumbnail sketch. And it'll be the best fifty pages I can write. *(As he pushes play drafts from his desk into the trash; Taj incredulous)* Can't settle for the fifth draft or the sixth or the tenth. However many drafts it takes. Won't never settle won't ever stop.

SCENE 5

Taj alone typing on laptop. Iconic poster of Lenin, fist clenched, now prominently displayed among the artwork. Kendrick Lamar's "Alright" plays on stereo at low, background volume.

Beat. Baraka enters in a lather, tossing his briefcase and jacket on the desk.

BARAKA: I AM SUING THE STATE OF NEW JERSEY FOR ATTACKS ON MY CHARACTER! Not to mention the fact THEY OWE ME ten thousand dollars that came with the title Poet Laureate! "Somebody Blew Up America"—it's just a poem. Now I'm being splashed across the cover of the *New York Times*! Featured on CNN! Because a poem asked whether Israelis knew of the 9/11 attacks beforehand, I am subjected to public slander and personal threats and attempts to remove me as New Jersey Poet Laureate! I WILL NOT APOLOGIZE AND I WILL NOT RESIGN! These master Klansmen, these enemies of people's democracy whose foul stench is like rotting Nazi corpses—they must not be allowed to prevail! I represent the most ancient and para-dig-mythic poetic traditions. If you practice poetry the way it needs to be done you're going to put yourself in jeopardy. All the major poets of New Jersey have suffered, whether it's Walt Whitman, who lost his job over *Leaves of Grass*. Or William Carlos Williams, who was called Communist, or Allen Ginsberg, whose poem "Howl" was prosecuted. But no poet laureate, anywhere, has ever made poetry this famous!

(He stops.)

What are you playing?

TAJ: Kendrick Lamar.

BARAKA: I can't hear myself talk.

TAJ: Rappers love you. You recorded with the Roots.

BARAKA: Hip-hop is important as anything we've done artistically but I'm not feeling it right now.

TAJ *(As he kills the music)*: I was wondering when this poem would come up.

(Baraka performs a few lines:)

BARAKA:
>Who got fat from plantations
>Who genocided Indians
>Who tried to waste the Black nation
>Who rob and steal and cheat a murder and make lies
>>the truth
>Who call you uncouth
>Who made Trump the president
>Who believe the Confederate flag need to be flying
>Who talk about democracy and be lying
>WHO/WHO/WHO WHO

TAJ: All anybody remembers is /

BARAKA:
>/ Who knew the World Trade Center was gonna get
>>bombed
>Who told four thousand Israeli workers at the Twin
>>Towers
>To stay home that day

The Jews are trying to destroy me.

TAJ: That surprises you?

BARAKA: For the Anti-Defamation League to accuse me of anti-Semitism is like Negroes playing the race card. Israel warned the U.S. about the attacks. Why wouldn't it warn its own citizens? Look at the nationalities of the Word Trade Center casualties and you do the math.

TAJ: Well, there was bad blood already from the sixties.

>... dagger poems in the slimy bellies of owner-Jews ...
>... another bad poem cracking steel knuckles in a
>>jewlady's mouth ...

Remember that?

BARAKA: I repudiated those years ago in the *Village Voice*. I wrote "Confessions of a Former Anti-Semite," stating unequivocally that anti-Semitism was deadly as white racism.

TAJ: You don't think the Jewish reference in "Somebody Blew Up America" was . . . gratuitous.

BARAKA: That poem had been around the world on the internet but it wasn't until I became New Jersey Poet Laureate that I started getting attacked. But I have to carry that with me. Years from now some fool will say, "Baraka the anti-Semite."

TAJ: What's the latest with *Most Dangerous Man*?

BARAKA: Going into rehearsals as we speak.

TAJ: A compact fifty pages.

BARAKA: It is what it is. I've got other fish to fry. I've got two books coming out. One is called *Digging: The Afro-American Soul of American Classical Music*. The other one is called *Razor: Revolutionary Art for Cultural Revolution*. It's twenty years of essays about writing, painting, and the need for revolutionary art in the United States. About winning the minds of the American people away from FOX and Mickey Mouse. Then in February I'll be in Paris for the jazz opera I wrote with David Murray the saxophone player /

TAJ: / I quit.

(Beat.)

BARAKA: You can't quit, you're fired. Let the doorknob hit you where the good Lord split you.

TAJ: Like you give a fuck either way. /

BARAKA: / I don't.

TAJ: Then why am I fired?

BARAKA: You say the wrong thing at the wrong time and say it real loud. /

TAJ: / So do you.

BARAKA: So why are you quitting?

TAJ: The Du Bois play is done, you don't need me around here anymore. /

BARAKA: / That's bullshit, that's not the reason. /

TAJ: / Because I'm sick of trying to figure out who it is you are! Okay! I'm tired of the shape-shifting and dramaturgical flights /

BARAKA: / Can't keep up, that it? Teacher's pet need a tutorial? /

TAJ: / Beatnik one day, Black nationalist the next, Marxist by the weekend—if it ain't one artistic metamorphosis it's another!

BARAKA: You need a hero to worship? Ain't nothing for you here, my man. You so busy looking for Leroy, you need to be trying to find your own damn self. Do your own thing, find your own voice, you had it right from the git-go: You quit. Whatever unfinished business there was between you and me, over and done with now. I ain't mad at you. Matter of fact write down your address and I'll send you a stipend.

(Beat. Baraka grabs Taj by the shoulders and looks him square in the eyes.)

You listen to me now: You are the future of Black theater. You hear what I'm saying?

(Taj nods his understanding.)

The United States of America's in a bad place right now. White-supremacist nutjob Donald Trump the president now, and I hope that lying sack of shit goes to jail. But it's on you now, blood. Your job as an artist is to reflect the dismal state of our society and make war, unrelenting war, on the bullshit that's going down in this country. Is you with me?

TAJ: I think I can handle that.

BARAKA: You go out there and you pay these ofay motherfuckers back. For all the wicked detestable shit they doing to our people.

TAJ *(As Baraka moves away)*: I'm on it, you already know.

BARAKA: That's what I did. Pay these motherfuckers back. I could tell from the first reviews of *Dutchman* that they were going to make me famous. You're going to make LeRoi Jones Amiri Baraka a household name? Well I got something for your ass!

Who live on Wall Street, the first plantation
Who cut your nuts off
Who rape you ma
Who lynched your pa
Who got the tar, who got the feathers
Who had the match, who set the fires
Who killed and hired
Who say they God & still be the Devil

(Taj joins in.)

TAJ:
Who / Who / Who

BARAKA:
Who made the bombs /

TAJ:
/ Who /

BARAKA: / Who made the guns /

TAJ:
/ Who /

BARAKA:
/ Who killed the most people /

TAJ:
/ Who /

BARAKA:
/ Who do the most evil /

TAJ AND BARAKA:
Who! Who! Who!

END OF PLAY

ABOUT THE PLAY

Looking for Leroy has received two Equity productions: New Federal Theatre at Castillo Theatre in New York, on February 28, 2019; and New Federal Theatre at the National Black Theatre Festival, in Winston-Salem, NC, on July 29, 2019. It has received two staged readings by Elevator Artist Resource in association with 1619 Flux in Louisville, KY, directed by Isaac Conn, and starring Robert Thompson and Tyler Tate, on May 16, 2019; and by Robey Theatre in Los Angeles, CA, starring Ben Guillory and Benjamin White, directed by Ben Guillory, on February 16, 2020. The play also swept the forty-eighth Annual AUDELCO Awards, winning for Best Playwright (Larry Muhammad), Best Director (Petronia Paley), Best Set Design (Chris Cumberbatch), Best Lighting Design (Antoinette Tynes), Best Acting Ensemble (Kim Sullivan and Tyler Fauntleroy), and tying for Best Play.

Looking for Leroy is copyright © 2019 by Larry Muhammad. For further information contact: NC Black Rep, info@ncblackrep.org, www.ncblackrep.org. Excerpts from "Black Art" (*Liberator* magazine, 1966); "Black & Beautiful, Soul & Madness" (Jihad Productions, vinyl LP, 1968); "Somebody Blew Up America" (first performed in 2002; published by Amazon Books, 2003); "Most Dangerous Man in America: W. E. B. Du Bois" (play premiered in 2015, produced by Woodie King, Jr.'s New Federal Theatre). All printed by permission of Chris Calhoun Agency, The Estate of Amiri Baraka.

ABOUT THE PLAYWRIGHT

Larry Muhammad is a playwright and producing director at Kentucky Black Repertory Theatre, a Louisville, KY–based 501c3 arts organization that puts African American Bluegrass history onstage. His plays have been performed in Louisville at Actors Theatre, Kentucky Center for the Arts, Henry Clay Theater, The Alley Theatre, and Muhammad Ali Center; at Stage on Spring in New Albany, IN; at the Aronoff Center in Cincinnati; and at Robey Theatre Company in Los Angeles, CA. His plays include: *Henry Bain's New Albany, Jockey Jim, The Magnificent Stephen, Double V, Derby Mine 4, Sweet Evening Breeze, Buster! Boomerang*, and *Murder the Devil*.

THE NATIONAL BLACK THEATRE FESTIVAL CO-CHAIRS 1989-2022

1989
Dr. Maya Angelou

1991
Ossie Davis and Ruby Dee

1993
Della Reese, Harry Belafonte and Sidney Poitier

1995
Billy Dee Williams

1997
Debbie Allen

1999
Leslie Uggams

2001
Hattie Winston and André De Shields

2003
Malcolm-Jamal Warner and Melba Moore

2005
Janet Hubert and Joseph Marcell

2007

Vanessa Bell Calloway and Hal Williams

2009

Wendy Raquel Robinson and Ted Lange

2011

T'Keyah Crystal Keymáh and Lamman Rucker

2013

Tonya Pinkins and Dorien Wilson

2015

Debbi Morgan and Darnell Williams

2017

Obba Babatundé and Anna Maria Horsford

2019

Margaret Avery and Chester Gregory

2022

Lisa Arrindell Anderson and Petri Hawkins-Byrd

JACKIE ALEXANDER is an award-winning actor, writer, producer, and director; former Artistic Director of The Billie Holiday Theatre in New York; and current Artistic Director of the North Carolina Black Repertory Company, producers of the National Black Theatre Festival. His debut novel *Our Daily Bread* was published by Turner Publishing in September 2012. His debut feature film *Joy* was awarded Best Feature Film by the Black Filmmakers Hall of Fame, and also earned Jackie best actor and best screenplay honors on the festival circuit. Stage directing credits include the world premieres of his critically acclaimed plays *Brothers from the Bottom*, *The High Priestess of Dark Alley*, *The Legend of Buster Neal*, *The Desire*, *The Right Reverend Dupree in Exile*, and *Birthright*. A short list of additional directing credits includes *Jelly's Last Jam* by George C. Wolfe; *The Waiting Room* by Tony-nominee Samm-Art Williams; *Lemon Meringue Façade*, written by and starring Ted Lange; and the world premieres of *The Sting of White Roses*, *Plenty of Time*, *Fati's Last Dance*, *Finding Home*, and *Matisse's Self-Portrait*, by two-time Obie Award–winner Charles L. Mee; and *Maid's Door* by Cheryl L. Davis (winner of seven AUDELCO awards).

DR. MAYA ANGELOU was an acclaimed poet, storyteller, children's book author, screenwriter, playwright, autobiographer, and activist. She also worked as an actress, singer, dancer, and composer. As a civil rights activist, Angelou worked for Dr. Martin Luther King, Jr., and Malcolm X. She served on two presidential committees, for Gerald Ford in 1975 and Jimmy Carter in 1977. In 1993, President Bill Clinton invited Angelou to write and read a poem at his inauguration. She riveted audiences around the world as she read "On the Pulse of Morning," which challenged the new administration and all Americans to work together for progress. In 2000, Angelou was awarded the National Medal of Arts by President Bill Clinton. In 2010, she was awarded the Presidential Medal of Freedom, the highest civilian honor in the U.S., by President Barack Obama. Angelou's most famous work is the autobiographical *I Know Why the Caged Bird Sings* (1969). In 2013, she became the recipient of the prestigious Literarian Award for Outstanding Service to the American Literary Community, a National Book Foundation Award given for lifetime achievement "in expanding the audience for books and reading." Dr. Angelou died in 2014 at the age of 86.

MICHAEL D. DINWIDDIE is an award-winning playwright, theater historian, composer, and journalist. He is a contributing editor of *Black Masks* magazine and an associate professor at the Gallatin School of Individualized Study, New York University, where he teaches courses in dramatic writing, popular culture, African American theater, and migration studies. His plays have been produced in New York, and by educational and regional theaters. A past president of the Black Theatre Network, he currently serves on the executive boards of the College of Fellows of the American Theatre and NewFest LGBTQ+ Film and Media. Member of the Dramatist Guild, Writers Guild of America, and ASCAP.

DR. TOMMIE (TONEA) STEWART is an acclaimed actress, educator, director; and retired Dean of the College of Visual Art, Music and Theatre at Alabama State University. She was the first African American woman to receive a doctorate from the FSU School of the Theatre and the first McKnight Doctoral Fellow in Theatre Arts. Dr. Stewart earned an NAACP Image Award for her role in the film adaptation of John Grisham's *A Time to Kill* and a New York World Festival Gold Medal Award for the narration of Public Radio International's series "Remembering Slavery." She has performed in Canada, Mexico, South Korea, Scotland, Turkey, and throughout the United States, including Carnegie Hall and the Kennedy Center. She has directed major museum exhibitions at the Rosa Parks Museum, the African American Museum in Philadelphia, and the International Civil Rights Center Museum in Greensboro, NC.

THEATRE COMMUNICATIONS GROUP
would like to offer our special thanks to the
THOMAS S. KENAN INSTITUTE FOR THE ARTS,
ESTABLISHED AT THE UNIVERSITY OF NORTH CAROLINA
SCHOOL OF THE ARTS,
for their generous support of the publication of
Holy Ground: The National Black Theatre Festival Anthology

The Thomas S. Kenan Institute for the Arts at the University of North Carolina School of the Arts encourages and supports the exploration and development of new knowledge to transform the way artists, organizations, and communities approach their creative challenges. Through its programs, the Kenan Institute for the Arts is empowering the next generation of artist leaders, entrepreneurs, and innovators, and engaging the creative community across the region to increase access, equity, and inclusion across the sector. www.uncsa.edu/kenan

Brian Cole, Chancellor, UNCSA

Patrick Sims, Executive Vice Chancellor
and Provost, UNCSA

Kevin Bitterman, Executive Director,
Thomas S. Kenan Institute for the Arts

THOMAS S.
KENAN
INSTITUTE
FOR THE
ARTS

UNIVERSITY OF NORTH CAROLINA
SCHOOL
OF THE
ARTS

tcg